THE DEATH MIST

ALAN G. FISCHER

*A FAITH-CENTERED MEMOIR OF A NAVY COMBAT
PILOT IN VIETNAM*

With respect to historical details that are scattered throughout this book, they were drawn from a variety of published sources. All of the political opinions or moral judgments portrayed in this book reflect my views alone. In addition, some names have been changed to protect the privacy of the individual.

Credits: American Patriot by Robert Coram, copyright © 2007. Reprinted by permission of Little, Brown and Company, an imprint of Hachette Book Group, Inc. Poems by Gayla Wiedenheft. Captain Red McDaniel - Scars and Stripes. Leo Buscaglia - Things You Didn't Do. Doctor Tom Dooley - The Edge of Tomorrow. George Hoar - Book of Patriotism. Murray Weiss -The New York Post. Ernie Pyle - Ernie's War. Winston Churchill - Gandhi and Churchill. Sarah Downey - Psalms of Life. The Bible. Mary Louise Haskins - God Knows. Squadronmate of Duane "Duffy" Dively - Warrior. James Durney - Vietnam: The Irish Experience. Fr. Daniel L. Mode - The Grunt Padre.

Cover Art - Mary Kathleen Fischer / Ron Jones

Editor - Russ Womack

ISBN 978-1-7322984-0-8

Dedicated to those who *"kept the faith"* in serving their country and especially to those who waited for a return that never happened

PREFACE

The low level night missions flown by the A-6 over Hanoi and Haiphong were the most demanding missions we have ever asked our aircrews to fly. Fortunately, there is an abundance of talent, courage and aggressive leadership in the Squadrons.
Admiral Chris Cagle, Commander Task Force 77

The Navy's Grumman A-6 Intruder was classified as an all-weather attack aircraft. That was both good news and bad news. The good news was that you could attack an enemy target at night in all kinds of horrendous weather when other aircraft couldn't even fly. That was the bad news too–you *had* to fly alone at night, very fast and only a few hundred feet about the ground in heavy rain and strong winds of the monsoons. The mission was unique to the A-6 since we hand-flew these night low-level missions relying on keeping correct heading, airspeed, and low altitude to complete the attacks. With its large, potent payload, the only plane that could carry more bombs than the A-6 was a B-52. However, we had no defensive weapons such as guns or missiles to fight off any MiGs (enemy fighters) that might attack us. The name *Intruder* perfectly fit the plane since it was an unwanted visitor who arrives when least expected in the middle of the night to deliver a devastating blow. Sounds a lot easier than it actually is! It also lived up to the "Grumman Ironworks" reputation, getting shot full of holes and staying airborne; or as in one case, flying through trees and bouncing off a hill, and still making it back to the ship. If the A-6 had a human quality, it would be "grit."

I was a Navy pilot flying the A-6 with Attack Squadron 75, the Sunday Punchers, off the USS Saratoga (CV-60). In the cockpit with me was a Bombardier/Navigator, referred to as a B/N, who worked the computer and radar systems that were the heart of the A-6 attack capabilities. We were in the Western Pacific (WESTPAC) theater of operations fighting for the small country of South Vietnam, which was trying to hold off a communist takeover. As always, America was there to help, not conquer. As Mark Twain said: "It is a worthy thing to fight for one's freedom; it is another sight finer to fight for another man's."

We flew in combat from May of 1972 until January of 1973, which, in and of itself, seemed like a lifetime. The product of war is that it rearranged our lives and left permanent scars on our hearts. As it turned out, it was a pivotal point in the war culminating with the Paris Peace Accords, which was an agreement that in the long run actually meant nothing to the communists.

I kept a daily journal, but after a while many entries consisted of only one line, although the subject could have been extended to a few pages. However, I became too worn out to write anymore. No one else knew my complete story except me. In most cases, I found that there were many underlying stories that formed the foundation of what took place for me. There existed a long series of interwoven events, some within the maxim of six degrees of separation. So many of these were interrelated, some my doing, some from others. In any case, a strong pattern or fabric emerged, thereby supporting what had happened before, and beyond what was merely taking place. This book is a place where I can give my memories a location and a season in which to remain alive.

Although it's been some 46 years, I am still reverent of my time in the Navy and for those I served with. If you understand someone, then you appreciate him–if you appreciate him, then you revere him. I am fortunate to look back and understand, appreciate and revere the men who were my squadronmates. They amazed me with their courage. Their friendships became a great treasure, and if ever there was sanctity in relationships, this was it. They did in fact "keep the faith" in their country, their own personal faith, and most of all their faith in each other. This kind of loyalty stood out in direct contrast to what was taking place in some segments of American society. During that time, many young Americans thought themselves to be self-righteous and indulged in their favorite pastime of avoiding the draft and protesting the war in Vietnam. The total rejection of established laws and institutions became the new mantra. Many young people were sleepwalking through life while living up to the counter-culture slogan, "turn on,

tune in and drop out." Not so for the men who made up Attack
Squadron 75. Our loyalty and sense of duty was in direct
contradiction to many of our contemporaries. We stood up and
proudly answered when our country called; we were a new
generation who served and sacrificed. And yet, we were
completely unaware of the realities of war.

These were my true feelings at the time. Some passages or
stories I learned from others. I regret that I am unable to trace the
source of some of them, and thus unable to ask permission to quote
them. Rather than leave it out, I acknowledge my gratitude in these
terms and trust that the presumption may be pardoned. Also,
having relied upon my memory, the exact wording may be
incorrect.

I am most proud to have been a Naval Aviator and to have
served alongside such wonderful and loyal men. We in the aviation
community were all volunteers. Former POW Admiral Stockdale
correctly stated that military people rarely volunteer for anything
unless it involves sacrifice. A recurring theme in American history
is the sacrifice of a few. As we know, freedom is never won
without sacrifice. All people of faith share the belief that
something is made sacred by sacrifice which means to make holy
and dedicated to God. These men showed that even in the bleakest
of times, honorable virtues such as courage and fortitude were not
mere sentiments. The spiritual realm of life became evident in

concrete actions. This doesn't happen very often; but then again, not everyone could have been a Sunday Puncher in 1972.

In the end, of course, a true war story is never just about war. It's about doing things you are afraid to do, like flying alone, low-level at night, in the pouring rain deep into enemy territory of North Vietnam. It's about love and memories, some sweet, some sad, and some actually tender. These were majestic activities of heroic virtues. It's about sorrow and anguish, and coming home to people who never listened, didn't even care, and who didn't understand that there are evil people in the world.

"Past events, when they are recounted, enlighten the mind and strengthen hope for good things in the future." St. Augustine.

Because of these men, a mixture of affection and awe profoundly and permanently impacted my life. Their actions and friendships are not bound by time or space. My greatest admiration and respect are for all the men in our squadron–officers and enlisted alike. I was blessed to have served with them, and anytime I think of these guys I am happy as well. The joy I derived from them is very powerful and has deep, lasting roots. In Bangali, the word for love is baluvashi, meaning," I live in your good." It was a wonderful feeling to live for the good of others and experience it in return. I treasure their memory, and feel that if I don't tell their stories, they and their memories will vanish. For me, it was an uplifting experience from a shattering one. The takeaway was that I found how very precious life actually is, and that if you receive blessings you must pass them along. There is a Saxon saying: "Adversity introduces a man to himself." By knowing yourself, you know others. We certainly learned about others and ourselves. In most cases, although a little part of us died in that war, I believe that the experiences went on to define our place in the world by adding a certain forcefulness in our attitude toward life. It turned out to be a full-time endeavor. Someone correctly wrote:

> *The ocean never sleeps*
> *The sea never sleeps*
> *The sky never sleeps*
> *Naval aviators operate here*

To this day, we have a warm sincere regard for each other. When I said goodbye and left the squadron, their handshakes left fingerprints on my heart. I always take time with squadronmates who are being forgotten by others all too soon. Chaplain Will Terry, speaking at the memorial service for former Vietnam POW Porter Halyburton, summed it up best when he said, "Our memories end not in grimness, but in the quiet joy of genuine gratitude.

CHAPTER ONE

DON'T WORRY THEY WON'T HIT US!

The whole world opened up on us with massive anti-aircraft fire the second we crossed the beach into North Vietnam at 200 feet and 420 knots in our A-6. Our plane was totally engulfed by gunfire; we were getting hammered, being shot at on all sides! We launched off the Saratoga some 45 minutes earlier and, just as we had been doing for the past four months, we were winding our way through the valleys and over the hills deep in enemy territory at barely 200 feet above the ground. The murky night was extremely treacherous, but the rain made it downright sinister. *This must be what mortality looks like.* My Bombardier/Navigator (B/N), LT Paul "Boot" Wagner, had his head in the hood searching for the target with his radarscope sending accurate steering information to my instruments. I was trying my best to avoid flying into the ground while following his commands steering me to the target. A deluge of 23 mm cannon shells headed toward us. It seemed we were hiding in plain sight. The tracers and the exploding shells were so bright that they completely blanked out my lighted instruments. I could easily see the gunfire; there was so much of it. The furiously dark night was split open by violent gunfire.

"OK, Boot, they're shooting over here."

"Don't worry–they won't hit us," replied Boot casually over the ICS in his oxygen mask, without removing his head from the scope. The gunfire raged on.

"OK, Boot, now they're shooting over there."

"Don't worry–they won't hit us," Boot still intently locked up on the target, sounded more like a math professor.

"OK, Boot, now they're shooting in front of us."

"Don't worry–they won't hit us." He was concentrated in the scope without a hint of movement, as if we're playing a simple game of dodge ball!

KABOOM! BLAM! AHAA!

Taking his head out of the scope, Boot looked at me and calmly said, "Don't worry–they won't hit us again."

"Oh good Boot, what! Have you been lying to me?"

How did I get here? And how do I get out?

*

Although I had studied pre-med in college with the idea of going to medical school, there was always a nagging voice in the back of my mind; ever since I was a little boy, I had thought about flying. Perhaps it was because my father was a pilot. In fact, it probably was just that. Although he never mentioned to me anything about flying, he did, in his own way, influence me. Looking back over the years, I now understand that all I ever wanted to do was to fly.

Later in my career, a dear friend, GaylaWiedenheft, wrote:

Boys had boats
their favored toy-
Not I
when I
was just a boy
I dreamt of wings
for soaring high
and cutting wakes
in yonder sky
And where my father's
footsteps went
I'd follow
in the firmament

My earliest recollections of anything "flying" were wooden bookends that Dad, affectionately known as "Pop", gave me when I was a little boy. They had a carving of a DC-3 in front of a hangar that looked like the one at Newark Airport. My "bookshelves" were made by Pop using old, wooden orange crates, which Mom covered with a piece of material. Years later, I saw the bookends at my kid brother's house.

Pop had been the Skipper of a B-24 Liberator in WWII, flying missions out of England and over Germany. The Brits, who flew at night, thought the Americans were crazy to do daylight attacks because of the powerful German air defenses. At age 22, he was the second youngest man in the crew. Together with its design and unboosted controls, the B-24 was considered the hardest airplane to fly. Pop told me that after a 12-hour mission he practically had to be pulled out of his seat–he was too weak to

3

move. It had taken not only his physical strength, but also his spiritual and mental acuity to fly the mission. As a member of the Eighth Air Force in England, he had a one-in-three chance of making it back. Crews averaged 8 to 12 missions before being shot down or disabled. Even though he was shot down three times, he somehow always managed to return with his complete crew. On one occasion, the local mailman who knew the families on his route, came running down my mother's street waving an opened telegram from the war department shouting; "He's alive, they found him, he's OK, he's OK!" It got to the point that after the briefing, other pilots would give his crew money, asking them to buy perfume for their wives if they made it to liberated Paris. "People thought we had died so many times that no one wanted to go up with us whenever we needed a replacement if someone took sick," Pop's crew member remarked. One time when they assigned a different crewmember to his crew, the guy turned white. Pop was only twenty-three when the war ended. The first thing he told my mother when he returned was that the only reason we won was because we had more men than they did, and that we should have stayed and fought the Russians. He always used to say, "People forget too fast." He also asked my mother not to run the sewing machine because it sounded like machine gun fire. Fifty years later, I reunited Pop with his tail gunner, Joe Homscher. The first thing out of Joe's mouth when he saw Pop was, "There's the only man I know who can fly a four engine plane on one engine."

4

When Pop passed away, I called his Radio Operator, Jerry Weiss.

"Jerry, I'm sorry to tell you that my father died yesterday."

He was devastated. "I'm sorry Alan; I always thought I'd go before your Dad. Your father's my hero and he'll be my hero until the day I die."

"That's nice, Jerry."

"It's not nice, it's the truth–I have to go now, I have to be sad alone."

Jerry's son, Murray, was a writer for the *New York Post*. He wrote a front-page tribute on Veteran's Day in 2005, honoring his father and uncle (who had been lost in the South Pacific as a crewmember of a B-24).Referring to our fathers, Murray wrote, *"The younger Weiss (Jerry) managed to survive crash landings thanks to his remarkable pilot, Al Fischer, who constantly found a way to bring their wounded, fiery bomber to safety."*

A photo of 2 Piper Cubs in front of the hangars at Murchio Airport, from a January 1946 magazine article (courtesy of Dan MacPherson).

The field was described as consisting of 92 acres, with 3 metal hangars & a combination flight office & restaurant.

An aerial view of the hangars at Murchio Airport from a January 1946 magazine article (courtesy of Dan MacPherson).

The actual Piper Cubs that I flew in with Pop

After the war, Pop did some flight instructing at Murchio Airport in northern New Jersey. It was a grass field, surrounded by a row of trees with a church steeple jutting up behind them. Many times, Pop would take out his pay in flying time. I would go up with him in a Piper Cub or a Stinson even though I was no more than five years old. I always felt so proud sitting in the front seat of the Cub, while Pop spun the prop before hopping in. I wished someone had taken a picture of us, but looking back, I'm sure we didn't own a camera.

About this time my father got a job driving a truck for the Little Falls Laundry. I loved jumping around on the cloth bags of laundry in the back of his truck. One day the truck was gone! Pop told me he was now an airline pilot.

"But where's the truck?"

It turns out that one of his customers was a Captain for American Airlines, named–of all things–Buck Rogers. He told Pop that American was hiring. He was hired and flew his first month with Buck (who unfortunately was killed in an automobile accident a month later on the way home from work). He went from making $500 a month driving a truck to $250 flying for American. Pop would come home from flying and work as a gardener for a neighbor for a dollar an hour. At one point he had to sell his pistol from the war to make ends meet. I learned early on the necessity and effort of hard work.

During my junior year at Villanova University, I was walking through Doherty Hall, our student center. A couple of brand new young Navy pilots were standing behind a table with a huge "Fly Navy" banner hanging down the front of it. Although it was the height of the Vietnam War, Villanova was considered a very conservative "Hawk" school. On Tuesday mornings, the Navy ROTC would march through the campus with their band leading the way. No one was doing any protesting.

"So what's going on?"

"Basically, we're doing some recruiting for Naval Air," the Navy Lieutenant Junior Grade (LTJG) told me. "To fly in the Navy you have to become an officer."

"How does that happen?" I asked.

"First you have to graduate from the Aviation Officer Candidate School known as AOCS in Pensacola, Florida. After you're commissioned an officer, you begin flight training. You can take the test for AOCS now and if you pass, it's good for four years yet it doesn't obligate you. If you fail you have to wait a whole year before you can retake it. You still have to graduate college first to get into the program." There was also a poster that said, "*If you're going to be something, why not be something special –A Naval Aviator.*" I figured that if I waited until my senior year to take the test and failed, I wouldn't be able to take it until after I graduated. By that time I would be eligible for the draft. Thinking *oh well, what's another test?* I said, "OK, I'll take it," and then thought nothing of it. A few months later, I received a letter from the Navy saying that I had qualified for the flight program. If I accepted, I was to report after graduation to Naval Air Station Pensacola for Aviation Officer Candidate School.

*

That summer I was working at the Bradford Bath and Tennis Club in my hometown of Cedar Grove, New Jersey, where the first order of business was redoing the clay tennis courts. This involved two of us chopping up the old court with picks. After that, an elderly Italian gentleman, Sal Marchetti, would smooth it out and level it just by eyeballing it. His talent amazed me. His sons, Tommy and Bobby, were friends of mine. At a High School party, someone asked Bobby if he was going to work like his Dad. "Are you crazy?" he answered. "My Dad can't even stand up straight from digging ditches. I'm going to college to get a good education so I don't have to do that." It was an excellent lesson to learn about the value of education at a young age, especially from a peer.

One day at the club, a cute girl with strawberry blonde hair and soft freckles walked in with a young man about her age. When she was standing alone I asked her if she "dated anyone else besides him?"

"Only if I want to date someone other than my brother," she replied. "I'm Corinne."

Corinne decided to take a summer course at the University of San Diego. She was the only girl in the school, and you'd notice her even if it was an all girls' school. With a family airline pass from Pop, I flew out to visit Corinne. She was staying with her sister who was married to a Navy pilot who flew the Grumman

8

HU-16 *Albatross,* a large, twin-engine, amphibious flying boat. He was currently assigned to ship's company on the USS Currituck (AV-7), a seaplane tender. Some evenings, we would eat dinner on the ship in the Officers' wardroom, and between visits to Sea World and Disneyland, hang around the squadron families at parties and picnics. Around that time, I just about had it with organic chemistry and the like, and was ready to finish college and get on with life. I noticed how happy these young couples were. All were college grads and seemed to honestly like what they were doing. Always having a smile on their faces, they were upbeat, positive, and fun to be around. I decided then and there to go Naval Air.

When I arrived back home, I called the Navy and asked them to process my papers. After a few more physicals and additional tests, I was accepted. During one physical, the previous candidate came out from the lab after a blood test. His eyes rolled back, he spun around and fell to the floor on his back with a "thunk"–out cold. The corpsman came out, looked at me and said, "Next." *Oh man, what have I gotten myself into?* A few weeks later, I took the formal acceptance phone call from the Navy in my parents' bedroom. Looking over, I saw my mother sitting on the edge of the bed crying.

I was sworn into the Navy on 7 September 1967 at NAS Lakehurst, N.J. This was right after the infamous "Summer of Love" when 100,000 hippies with their counter-culture behavior of sex, drugs, and psychedelic music descended on the Haight-

Ashbury neighborhood of San Francisco. There couldn't have been two more conflicting beliefs. My very first thought upon entering the Base was, *now I definitely can't become a priest.* I actually had these thoughts ever since the time I went on a field trip to St. Joseph's Franciscan Seminary in the sixth grade. I always had a great love for my faith and enjoyed attending Mass. However, I was more fond of dating and had discerned not to become a priest. I figured there were other ways to serve God.

The oath I took to "protect and serve" our country ended with "*So help me God.*" No act can be more sincere than this calling on God to be a witness to the heart of this solemn oath. There was a certain sacredness in the oath that we were expected to keep, and for me it was as genuine and fervent as any religious vow. Also, since I was blessed to love my country, I figured the best way to serve her was by being a Naval Aviator. Besides, there was a war going on and felt I wanted to do my part. For me I knew what mattered most in life. After being sworn in, the commander-in-charge took me up in a T-34 trainer and proceeded to get me so sick that I didn't feel right for four days. Pop told me that a lot of guys would like to be a pilot, but very few would want to go through what I would have to in order to achieve it.

*

I still had to complete my senior year and graduate before starting the program. And thanks to my roommates, it was my best year ever. During the second semester, I moved into a house off campus with Rich Core, Jim Fagan, Rich Merklinger and John

Gaw. Part-time roommates Burke Ward and Dominic Pisano completed the fun group. Every one of us was from North Jersey. Our house was just a few miles from Valley Forge; consequently, the winter was very cold. Even the squirrels that lived in the walls were cold. On top of that, our third floor room had no central heat. Roomie Rich Core and I had a small electric heater running 24 hours a day. When spring arrived, we couldn't unplug the heater because the plastic plug had melted into the socket. We were also convinced that a ghost named Gus haunted the house.

One weekend when we were all back home sitting around the kitchen table at Rich Merklinger's house in West Orange, N.J., Mr. Merklinger came in with his ubiquitous cigar in his mouth.

"OK, boys, here's the facts of life."

"Come on, Mr. Merk—we're college seniors. We know all about it."

Without pausing Mr. Merk said, "OK, if you think two can live as cheap as one, that's bullshit. And if you think that you can live on love alone, that's bullshit too. Now go out and get a good job!"

"Thanks Mr. Merk."

All my roommates were sincere, hard working guys, and those who were physically able eventually went into the service. To this day we keep in touch and watch out for each other. They are a wonderful group. According to Scripture, "A faithful friend is a sturdy shelter; he who finds one finds a treasure."

When I graduated college, I had five dollars in my pocket. No one else had any money either. The income I had earned in the summers was my spending money for the whole year. Any extra went toward a statue of the Blessed Mother as she had appeared at Lourdes. I always had a great devotion to Our Lady. Father Rongeoni, the librarian, helped me by having it hand carved in Italy. After I graduated, it was placed in the Villanova library with the inscription *"Dedicated to Mr. and Mrs. A.K. Fischer on the occasion of their twenty-fifth wedding anniversary –For those I love so much in a place I love so much. Alan '68".* To this day, it is the only statue in the library. When I started college, I signed a contract with Pop agreeing that I would pay him back after I

graduated and got a job. His graduation card read: *Congratulations Alan–paid in full–I appreciate the fact you didn't goof off. Love, a proud Dad.*

CHAPTER TWO

PENSACOLA

My orders read for me to report to the Naval Air Station in Pensacola, Florida on 16 July 1968, at 0800 to begin Aviation Officer Candidate School. I didn't even know where Pensacola was. I went into a Holiday Inn in East Orange, New Jersey to scan their location map on the wall. I looked all over Florida–mostly around Miami, Orlando and Tampa–but no Pensacola. I finally found it south of Alabama. As they say, it is located in LA (Lower Alabama).

Two months after graduation from Villanova, I was at Newark airport for the first of many good-byes. The last two weeks at home had seemed the longest of my life–just waiting to get started. With tears in his eyes, Pop hugged me and said, "I wish I could go instead of you." I told him he had already done his part and now it was my turn. I really wanted to serve my country. When I looked back from the airplane it was like seeing a puppy dog standing there, sad and lonely. I knew that in his heart he understood why I had to do this. I had inherited my love of country and loyal devotion to duty from him–a moral inheritance. We were both proud of this fact.

Following the orders to a T, I arrived at Naval Air Station Pensacola at exactly 0800, after spending the night at the local Holiday Inn. I didn't have a clue as to what was going to happen. The smart guys who had gotten the word didn't show up until midnight. I walked up the stairs and entered the Indoctrination Battalion, also known as INDOC. These were old wooden barracks left over from WWII and correctly referred to as "Splinterville." Seated behind a small desk in front of a big open room was a Candidate Officer who was in charge of checking people in.

"Hi, can I help you?"

"Yes, I'm here to learn to fly."

"What kind of planes?"

"Jets!"

"What kind?

"What kind do you have?"

"Oh A-4s, F-4s. Sign right here and we'll get you going."

I bent half-over and as soon as I signed my name, all hell broke loose! Out of nowhere three Marine Drill Instructors (DI) who were Vietnam combat veteran Gunnery Sergeants came running, hollering, and screaming at me. I couldn't understand a word they were saying. I grew up listening to songs on the radio by Dion and the Belmonts, Ricky Nelson and other Rock and Roll stars. You could comprehend every word they sang. Now I was totally confused by this raspy gibberish being shrieked. It was complete pandemonium.

"Brace me, brace me mister!" With their faces just inches from mine, they screamed at me ruthlessly. Their coarse words were so loud that my ears began to hurt. "Don't eyeball me, look straight ahead, why don't you drop out now? Just D-O-R, (meaning drop on request), D-O-R mister!" *He can't even spell. Besides, what do I want with a door?* The violent chaos continued with unbelievable screeching. "You're nothing but a maggot! You're kray-zee mister, did I ever call you kray-zee?–Well you're kray-zee!" *I didn't think I was crazy, at least not until then.*

"Yes, sir. Yes, sir," I answered, trying to salute at the same time. "But sir *you* said."

A high-pitched bellow of *"Youuu! Uuuuuu"* erupted. "Do you know what a 'you' is?" He was crazy with rage.

"Personal pronoun second person singular, sir?"

"A ewe is a female sheep–and we know what happens to them." It wasn't to be "you" or "me", but rather "us"–an early form of crew concept. But I didn't have any indication about such things.

We were run ragged all day long out on the parking lot, commonly referred to as the grinder. Later in the day, fellow officer candidate Dick Childers checked in. Some six feet tall he was standing up against the wall next to me in a relaxed, slouched over manner. Gunnery Sergeant Grealish who was the embodiment of tough and mean was in his face, and was yelling at the top of his lungs in a garbled, gruff voice. "Brace me mister, brace me!" (Meaning come to attention up against the wall). I already knew

15

the drill so I was in the proper position. Dick had this confused look on his face and remained in his effortless posture. The more relaxed he got the louder and harder the DI yelled.

Finally, Dick turned his head, looked at me, shrugged his shoulders and with a look of hopeless resignation lifted his left knee, took a step forward and embraced the DI in a big clutch. He

thought he was saying, "embrace me." "Oh, we got one of those, one of those!" the DI bellowed as he jumped back. For some of the guys, the flight to Pensacola was the first time they were ever on an airplane. One candidate from

First night in the Navy - my mother cried for three days when she saw this picture

southern California pulled up in front of the barracks in a bright red 1966 Chevy convertible. Sticking out of the back seat were his surfboard and golf clubs. He lasted just as long as it took a drill instructor to realize he was being called "dude!" We finally got to bed around 0400 in a spartan room with a thin mattress on a spring and not even a pillow, sheet or blanket. We were jolted awake by reveille a whole hour later at 0500 with the blasting sound of a

16

bugle over the loud speaker. By 0800, a few had already dropped out of the program–some on the payphone literally crying to their wives. They were reassigned to Battalion X (Batt X) for a few months doing manual labor on the base, after which they would either get thrown out of the Navy thus becoming eligible for the draft, or be assigned to the fleet as an enlisted man.

One night around 0200, our regimental commanding officer, Marine Major Stephen W. Pless, gave us a lecture. He went on and on about how the Wings of Gold, in Marine terms, were "golden girl getters." As a helicopter pilot, he received the Medal of Honor for rescuing, against orders, a group of wounded Marines in Vietnam. Unfortunately, a few years later he died while trying to jump an open drawbridge with his motorcycle.

*

The days were filled with calisthenics, cross-country races, classes, and briefings. "You don't get any time off–even to get married–if the Navy wanted you to have a wife they would have issued you one!" As time went on, more guys dropped out. The grueling cross-country course ran along side of the refreshing looking Officer's Club pool replete with young bikini clad officers' wives. The heat was oppressive and, as they say, if it wasn't for the heat the humidity would kill you! Running through the deep sand of the obstacle course in one hundred degree temperature felt like I was a lost prospector in the Mojave Desert. I kept wondering, *what am I doing here and why didn't I go to Med School? You've made a grave mistake Alan!*

The regimen was pretty grueling, especially with the DIs on your case all the time. I remember my Dad telling me I'd be so tired that I would fall asleep with my eyes open. He was right. I was standing in ranks sound asleep with my eyes wide open.

Of course, you never ever addressed a Drill Instructor as "DI". One cadet who innocently did was told by the Drill Instructor to "Meet me in the playpen (an area behind the barracks) at 1900, and when I'm done with you there will be nothing left but a poopy suit (our heavy coverall uniform) and a puddle of sweat."

We may have been college graduates, but we were naïve. During one physical exam, we were lined up naked and told to face the wall, bend over and spread our cheeks. Guys were using their index fingers to pull apart their lips while others were grinning as wide as possible, showing all their teeth. The biggest laughs came from the Corpsmen, and then later, ourselves.

The pressure cooker went on day and night as we moved from INDOC to a large brick barrack to join Battalion Three. We were officially members of Class 23-68. Each room had a little fan since the old barracks had no air conditioning. If there was a draft, you would put your towel over your shoulders because you didn't want to "break" the sheets so that you wouldn't have to make the bed in the morning. The second your head hit the pillow you were out cold. Every morning at 0500, you could hear the scratches on the record just a second or two before the bugle blasted reveille over the loud speaker. Some nights around 0300, a DI would start the record and just play the scratches to mess with your mind. The bugle was followed by "Reveille, reveille, reveille, all hands hit the deck, this is the three minute warning for falling out in front of building 626 for morning PT (physical training)." I realized then that AOCS was just a fancy name for Boot Camp and being a Seaman Apprentice was the second lowest rate in the Navy. Towering pure white cumulus clouds absorbed and reflected the first morning light as we ran outside. As early as it was it was already hot and humid.

There was no letting up or even a little break, and it didn't take long to realize that we all had to pull together if we were going to make it through this program. No matter what part of the country you were from, you had one mind set. Everything we did was to help the other guy. The competition was with the other two battalions to be the best. More so, it was between failure and success for us. On the obstacle course, I watched classmate Jack Keegan fall off a log beam, split his head open and get back up–not only finishing, but winning the race. We learned to think and care for others more than ourselves. We dragged, pulled, pushed and encouraged each other so everyone could finish, all while running in deep sand and terribly hot weather. This set the stage early on. Later, it would take the form of trying to rescue a downed pilot or quietly praying for a damaged aircraft to return safely.

*

Clear values emerged. We discovered that in life there is something bigger and more important than the individual. We had taken upon ourselves obligated duties and a dedication to a code of honor and a loyalty that was fortified with patriotism and discipline. The Navy definitely reinforced the love we had for our country. We had learned clear values as youngsters and knew what we should be as Americans. In a country where individuality is prized and independence valued, we were being asked to do more than our civilian counterparts even to the point of giving up our freedoms as individuals–including the freedom of speech. It took a firm backbone to stand up and be counted. For us, this was not just an empty theme, but also a lifelong way of living. To this day I could call classmate Jack Keegan at two in the morning and ask him to drive 65 miles to put a cup of coffee on my front porch. He'd do it without asking why. Who else would do that?

Learning to march with a rifle was an example of a classic Chinese fire drill. No one understood the DI as he sang out a lyrical cadence. As we bumped into each other, fell down or marched ourselves into the side of a Dempsey dumpster filled with garbage, the DI would yell, "Hold it, hold it, hold it! There's no way in hell that 'beff, boufh, beff' sounds like 'beff, boufh, beff!' Get it together, girls!" Man it all sounded exactly the same to me! I'm still trying to figure out what "boufh" meant! Later on we would march singing the same songs Pop did when he was an Air Corps Cadet. We were fortunate in having as our class DI Gunnery Sergeant Dunning who was an inspirational leader and mentor. He actually received a battlefield commission two weeks after we were commissioned. Some of the other DIs were harsh, tough and on the nasty side.

C.L. Overman from Knoxville, Tennessee helped translate for us Yankees what the Southern boys were saying. He said a real southern gentleman was going to teach us to speak English the way God intended it to be spoken. C.L. said that government was spelled (and pronounced) *gummint* and that the plural of "ya'all" was "all ya'all." Instead of "hello" they say "hey." He filled me in on grits (Southern caviar), chitlins and hog jowls, and how catfish eyes brought out the flavor in possum bellies. Seems in the South they have initials instead of names. Besides C.L. there was J.Q. Trimm, T.L. Anderson, etc. They also referenced their birthday in regards to confederate personalities who fought in the "late unpleasantness." For example, one cadet would explain that his birthday was the day Stonewall Jackson died, not wounded (that was eight days earlier). The Texas boys said they used a rock for a pillow out on the prairie. I told C.L. just to declare that he was from *Joisey* and if there was a problem that he should say, "I know a guy" and just "fuhgeddaboudit."

Of course, we all had to learn "Navalese." This included saying "niner" for the number nine. All day long guys were going around saying "fiver," "sixer," etc. just for emphasis. There were tons of acronyms such as "Comnavairpac", "Pacrim", and "Westpac". Years later, they tried replacing them with the full words but no one could understand what they meant. At this point we were just trying to figure out the 24 hour military clock as well as what was port and starboard.

One night, just after taps, our DI got on the loudspeaker and started reading a letter he had confiscated. We weren't supposed to be up after lights-out and a classmate was caught with a flashlight under his pillow, writing to his wife. In a rough, hoarse voice the DI intoned, "Dear Twinkles, I'm not supposed to be writing now and if I get caught I'm in big trouble…." All the intimate details for their next meeting were readout loud by the DI who ended with; "Well twinkles you *are* in a big load of trouble!"

*

We had mandatory Room, Locker and Personnel (RLP) inspections where everything was scrutinized, even down to the same correct size our underwear was folded or which way our toothbrush faced. It was part and parcel of "attention to detail." Helping each other get things right emerged into a sense of camaraderie and also produced a strong attentiveness to duty.

Marine Gunnery Sergeant Rufus Jackson Washington, a small, tight, tough black DI from Macon, Georgia began the inspection.

"Who's this Dunkerhead?!" Sergeant Washington bellowed in a gravelly voice as he surveyed the one "allowable" picture on my bureau in our barrack's room. The four of us were at rigid attention, terrified that he might find something out of place.

The girl in the picture was Cindy, a cute little blond from Seattle. My mind went back to when I had met her while on a trip to Hawaii with my parents only a few months earlier. We enjoyed listening to the soft, pleasant, exotic music of Martin Denny at the

22

Paradise lounge of the Hilton Hawaiian Village. His rendition of "Quiet Village" was a perfect melody for enchantment in the dimly lit lounge. We sat in a booth only a few steps from the beach, caressed by gentle breezes and the sounds of the ocean. Mai Tais and tropical music made for a very romantic evening.

"So who's this Dunkerhead?!" jolted me back to reality.

Sergeant Washington's muscled 150-pound body tensioned as the taunt deep black skin of his forehead glistened with sweat in the 95-degree heat of the barracks. His eyes blazed above a grinning mouth full of bright white teeth.

"Sir, it's this Candidate's girlfriend."

"Why tell her she's sweeter than the nectar of a goddess."

"Yes, sir!"

"Did you ever kiss her?"

"Yes, sir"

"Did you ever kiss her tenderly?"

"Yes, sir!"

"Did you ever kiss her passionately?'

"Yes, sir!"

"Where did you kiss her tenderly and passionately?"

"Sir, I believe it was New Jersey."

Laughter erupted over the low walls separating other rooms. Sergeant Washington rushed out of the room, bent over. The inspection was complete. I wasn't trying to be funny I was serious!

I began to see that some psychologist must have planned the program-it really worked. Basically, we were being broken down from our civilian life and remade into what the Navy expected us to be. There was wisdom in simple acts where little things meant a lot. Of course it was one of those situations where nothing you did was right. You were even told to "mill around smartly." However if you did do something to impress the DIs they would bellow "outstanding candidate!" The whole course was a great equalizer where a lifetime of future challenges was packed in each day.

Squared away a few months later

After three grueling months, it was time for graduation. Every Friday all summer long we had marched in the graduation parades, passed in review and went through the manual of arms with our rifles out on the parade ground in competition with the other two regiments. We won most times. Unfortunately, when it came our turn to graduate, it rained, and so the ceremony was moved indoors. Out of the 95 that began the program, 73 were commissioned as Naval Officers, which left me wondering how many will get their wings.

My folks arrived a week before graduation so they were able to go to all of the functions and meet a lot of the officer candidates and their wives. Out of the blue, Pop said, "A lot of these guys aren't going to make it."

"Why's that, Pop?"

"Many of these wives aren't going to put up with what you guys are going to have to go through to get your wings." Having gone through Aviation Cadets in World War II, he knew what he was talking about. After their marriage, he and Mom had a two-day honeymoon in Manhattan. When they went out for dinner, Pop didn't order the *filet* mignon because he didn't want fish. He was only a farm boy.

"Oh, come on Pop."

And he was right. Each man he mentioned ended up divorced.

A few guys got married the day we were commissioned. I got a room at the Holiday Inn on Pensacola Beach, and all I wanted to do was sleep. I no sooner got into bed when the door opened. Standing there was classmate Bob DiRomauldo, carrying his brand new bride, Jan, over the threshold. They had been given the wrong room. When Bob graduated from High School in Philadelphia, he went to work on the grueling Distant Early Warning System (DEW) line in Greenland for three years in order to get money for college. After his Navy service, he put himself through Harvard Business School and became very successful in business. Later on in life, he always shared his success with those less fortunate, especially helping our wounded boys from Iraq and Afghanistan.

Classmate Larry Kilpatrick was a genial guy with a heart of gold. His wife, Jane, joined him after we were commissioned. She was one of those wives who would help Larry get his wings. We became great friends as our careers became intertwined. All in all it was a very fine group of men. We weren't patriotic because we were in the service; we were in the service because we were patriotic. We had made it–at least up to this point. It really felt good. According to our commissioning certificates we were now "Officers and Gentlemen" and had the papers to prove it!

'Flight Jacket', the yearbook for AOCS stated: *Dedicated to Naval Aviators, past, present and future–who devote a portion of their lives in the service of their country for the preservation of our democratic way of living.* We were to find out that some sacrificed their very lives in this devotion.

Returning my first salute with my mother and brother looking on

CHAPTER THREE

AT LAST – FLYING!

After a few weeks of ground school, we finally started to fly. Flying at Pensacola, the cradle of Naval Aviation was like walking into the Notre Dame Football locker room or the great cathedrals of Europe. Pensacola embodied the great values and traditions of Naval Aviation. The tremendous legacy was filled with all the sights, sounds and smells of aviation. The present introduced me to the past, which I wanted to preserve and be a part of. There were planes flying day and night–jets, props, and of course the Blue Angels who were based there. I was always looking up in awe. Then there were the pilots who had gone before us which included combat pilots and astronauts as well. The first American in space was Navy pilot Alan Shepherd and eventually Naval Aviators commanded five of the six lunar landings. I was very proud to wear the same uniform of those who had gone before, and now I really wanted to add those Wings of Gold to it. There was great pride in this continuity of tradition and service. The big question was, *can I get to that goal?*

Our grades from AOCS, ground school and flying the T-34 trainer in Primary flight training would determine whether we went jets or props. I had always taken the harder route, whether it was in sports or subjects in school so it seemed only natural and much more challenging to fly a jet on and off a carrier that was moving than landing on a seven thousand foot runway that was standing still. The pressure continued. There were no second chances for mistakes. Stories abounded. Classmate Mike Gillease had a particularly bad instructional hop, not even close to getting it right. After landing and taxiing in, he asked the instructor where he should park the plane. His disgruntled instructor had his head down in the backseat, writing on his kneeboard. "Oh, just follow the plane ahead of you." Mike taxied into the hangar. The plane ahead was being towed!

The night before the selection of those who got jets or props, I called home from a payphone on the side of the hangar and talked to Pop. I told him I didn't know what I'd do if I got props and that I would consider dropping out of the flight program. I didn't want to fly prop planes or helicopters. Pop told me to hang in there. While I drove back to the Bachelor Officer Quarters (BOQ) that night, a new song by Glen Campbell came on the air– *Wichita Lineman*. Now when I hear that song on an "Oldies" station, it reminds me of that phone call. Fortunately, my grades were good enough to get jets.

*

Basic Jet Training took place at NAS Meridian, Mississippi where we to fly the T-2A Buckeye. It was a long way from New Jersey, both in distance and dimension. Not much had changed since the antebellum years. It was still the old 'Deep South' in

28

attitude and feelings. When the wife of a student-pilot applied for a job as a teacher, she was turned down. The principal explained that, because she was from California, her views on racial issues would be deemed too liberal and "a lot of the parents belonged to the Klan and they wouldn't go for it." I wrote my parents telling them that we had to sell raffle tickets to raise funds so that our base Little League team could travel. The local town Little League team wouldn't play our team because there were "coloreds" on it! However, the majority of the townspeople extended southern hospitality to us whenever we encountered them.

I was shocked to see men plow behind a mule, but I was horrified to see a man dragging a wooden plow. One weekend we visited a poor white, farm family. The sharecropper's shack was not much more than a lean-to. The bed for their baby was a box with newspapers in it. On Sunday nights a "Traveling Salvation Preacher" would set up a huge tent in the middle of a field and hold a revival meeting. The congregation would do "Gospel Sings" filling the night air with spirituals starting at 2000 and lasting until three or four in the morning. They were very dedicated, faith-filled people.

There wasn't much to do in Meridian. If you were able to find a date, her little brother would invariably ask if you were going out to Shoneys restaurant for RC Cola and moonpies. At a local Italian restaurant, the waitress would scrape off the cheese from the underside of the cardboard that covered the aluminum container the lasagna was in after she set it on the table. If you wanted a glass of wine, you ordered it from the menu that read: 1. Red wine 2. White wine! My clock radio woke me up with the sound of cowbells while the announcer was asking Lulubelle if she had gotten the cows out yet. And here I am driving a car with plates from New Jersey!

We found out early that even though we were flying jets, we couldn't out climb a cumulous cloud that was building skyward. However on our solo flights we did enjoy "flat-hatting" i.e. screaming just a few feet above the Tombigbee River. On our time off, we had to provide our own entertainment, so we made small rockets by filling straws with gunpowder and firing them out of a copper tube. Some went as high as a thousand feet. We were soon advised to stop by Marine Sentries since the tower had called up to the Main Gate saying the rockets were interfering with the landing pattern at the airfield. Another sidelight was driving up to Tuscaloosa and spending the weekend at the University of Alabama partying with the college kids. Our visits to the college were put to an abrupt end after we attended a fraternity party with a Hell's Angels theme. Seems that the son of our Base Commanding Officer was a student there. It was deemed that dressing as bikers in old WWII uniforms, German helmets, and worn-out leather jackets was not befitting a Naval Officer.

*

Reality hit hard and fast as we started losing friends. One morning, while I was driving the two miles from the BOQ to the airfield, the local news said that an Instructor and student had been killed earlier that morning. Their plane had iced up while shooting a practice ground controlled approach (GCA) to one of the runways. Two hours later it was 75 degrees. They were the first we lost, but not the last. When Pop was in flight training in World War II, one base put out a weekly schedule of events. There were so many tragic accidents that they scheduled a "Memorial Service" at 11 a.m. each Friday! Approximately 15,000 pilots and air crewmen were killed in flight training in WWII. Of the 324,647 who entered training during the war, almost 40% were either washed-out or killed in training.

For the first few months, I would really get airsick each flight. It got me thinking that maybe I was in the wrong line of work. It isn't easy to get your oxygen mask off, throw up in a bag and get it on again and fly. If the instructor briefed, "today we are going to do spins and stalls" I would dread even going out to the aircraft. I was part way through training on a flight when my instructor said, "You'll never make a pilot; you don't want to fly." I recalled that these were almost the same words Pop once told me were said to him during his WWII flight training.

CHAPTER FOUR

POP AND GREENVILLE

After a few months, I was given a weekend pass and went home for a visit and some home cooked meals. One morning, Pop and I were sitting around the kitchen table talking flying. The fact that we were father and son as well as pilots added more interest and concern. Our relationship was strengthened and deepened by the fact that we were sharing the same profession in life, thus allowing us to recount our experiences as equals. There was that unique unspoken respect of one pilot toward another. Following in Pop's footsteps was a matter of great pride for both of us. I could tell that Pop was concerned about how I was doing in the flight program at Meridian. I wanted to learn from him as well as gain his approval. I needed to know that what I had done was the correct thing. More than anything I wanted Pop to be proud–and he always was. We were swapping flying stories commonly referred to as "hangar flying." It seemed like only yesterday when the talk had been about how things were going in school. Grammar school, high school and college were a distant thought–just a means to make it to this time and place.

Looking into Pop's eyes, I once again saw the eyes of a Santa Claus. As a young boy in grammar school, I sat on Santa's lap and told him what I wanted for Christmas. I didn't know until high school that those very same eyes were my Dad's. He had played the part of Santa each year at Holy Angels grammar school in Singac, New Jersey. The school was in a large two-story brick building built in the 20s. The second floor was a huge auditorium with a stage. The bottom floor had four classrooms with two grades of 40 children per room, which meant that one nun had 80 students in her room.

Now as a young man, I was more than just a son who had always worked hard–I was a fellow aviator. This was that very special pilot bond felt by flyers exclusively. He told me how fellow American pilot, author and friend Ernie Gann, told him that after 300 hours of flying, a pilot thinks he knows everything, and then at 1,000 hours he realizes how little he knows. I was to find out that aviation entailed a lifetime of learning.

I told Pop about one particular solo flight which will always stay in my mind. At that stage of our flying we knew practically nothing of instrument radio navigation–we relied totally on landmarks to get back to the Base. We could not navigate using our instruments–that was to come later. Basically, it was "look out the window" flying. Using a roadmap we flew over little towns with names such as DeKalb, Moscow, Tupelo and the like. I was totally lost. On top of that, a radio call went out for all solos to return to base because the weather was closing in fast. If the weather was inclement, Instrument Flight Rules (IFR) dictate that you were required to fly relying only on your instruments, which we hadn't learned how to do yet. Our instruments were no use. I hadn't a clue where I was–all the small towns began to look the same, intersected by small rivers, bridges and roads. I couldn't call for help and, even if I could, I wouldn't anyway in order to save face–*better to die than to look bad.* In order to remain VFR (Visual flight rules i.e. see and be seen), I kept getting lower and lower as the cloud base descended with the oncoming Cold Front. I remembered Pop telling me to keep my head on a swivel to look out for other traffic. All I could see were birds and pine trees and cotton fields when all of a sudden I had to pull up for a water tower. Just as I did, I saw the name on the side of the tower "Greenwood." My map was folded over and just where it ended was the town of Greenwood on the Yazoo River.

Finding Greenwood was a stroke of good-luck. Now all I had to do was follow the Yazoo River south to the Mississippi river. There was a bridge that crossed the river downstream. This was highway 20. I turned east and followed the highway right into Meridian and back to the base. As I touched down, the tower advised, "The airfield is now closed." We used to say that when the weather got really bad, not wanting to jeopardize an instructor, they'd announce over the PA "launch all solos and foreign students!"

Pop just sat there looking at me with a wonder in his eyes. "Gee, Pop, it wasn't that bad," I said, belying how scared I really had been.

"It's not that, Alan. I was flying Stearmans from Columbus, Mississippi and, like you, was completely lost. I was thinking maybe the instructor was right since the day before he had told me, "You'll never make a pilot!" Not only was I lost, but it started to rain, as the sky got darker and darker, and the clouds lower and lower. Running low on fuel, I dropped down and flew along a railroad station. There was a man standing on the platform and I yelled, "Greenwood?!" He jumped up and excitedly shot out his arm, pointing in a southeasterly course. I turned and looked down at my map. Greenwood was right on the edge of my area. After I passed over the water tower at Greenwood, I turned northeast and flew until I hit the Tombigbee River. Flying south along the river I picked up Columbus and landed just as they fired a red flare signaling the closure of the base due to the upcoming storm." Thank God that Greenwood, a town of Southern charm, had saved two Yankee flyers.

*

Growing up on a farm in Northern New Jersey during the Depression, Pop's days were spent working before and after school to help the family survive. I remember him telling me that his mother would put heated potatoes in his pocket to keep him warm on the way to school in the winter. They then became his lunch. The engineer on the freight train that went near their house would slow down so Pop and his brothers could catch a ride to school. Their mother would bake a pie for the crew. His father worked long hours in the silk mills in Paterson. In fact, the 1910 census taker wrote that it was hard to count the Germans because they were always at work. Unfortunately, because of the Depression, he lost his job working in the mills and went back to farming. His Dad would travel to Paterson walking up and down the stairs in apartments trying, many times unsuccessfully, to sell a dozen eggs for 25 cents while his mother would bake as many as 300 pies on a weekend and sell them at a roadside stand for 15 cents each. Unfortunately, they eventually lost the farm. Right after that his father used his last bit of money to buy a slicker and boots so the Civilian Conservation Corps (CCC) could hire him. After only working a short time, the CCC was closed down by Congress causing him to lose yet another job. Like so many of his contemporaries, Pop learned firsthand about hard work and sacrifice and passed it along to me. For Pop, times might have been simpler then, but they weren't easier. First you see your family lose the farm, then you spend four years in a war. A few years later your younger brother and friends go to fight in Korea, and then your son in Vietnam. But they never complained. One of his earliest recollections was listening to his crystal set, which was basically a very rudimentary homemade radio that he had made, while in bed one night and hearing that Charles Lindbergh had landed in Paris.

At the beginning of World War II, together with his brothers George and Eugene, he worked on airplane engines at the Wright Patterson factory in Caldwell, New Jersey. At one point, the union shop steward came in and told them to slow up. Being from hard working German stock, they had been completing their work on nine engines a day. "The union wants you to do only six instead of nine!" Pop never had a fondness for unions after that; besides there was a war on. Because of his job description, he was "draft exempt." He didn't have to go to war; he could have stayed home, yet he volunteered. Like so many patriotic young men, he sacrificed his personal life and decided to serve his country hopefully by flying, not walking. Pop went to the Post Office in Newark to take the required battery of tests for the Army Air Corps. After the tests were over, they herded Pop and a fellow farm boy into a small waiting room. All they could think about was the fact that they probably had failed since all of the other applicants were college graduates from the likes of Brown and Princeton. As it turned out, Pop and his friend were the only two who passed. They were able to use a common sense approach when answering questions.

Pop's first flight ever was in an Army C-46, taking him to begin training as an Aviation Cadet. For many of the men like Pop, it was their first time away from home as well; some had never even driven a car. As a Buck Private, pay was low and treatment not much better. In those days you were a Cadet during the year and a half of flight training earning $50 a month base pay plus $25 flight pay. Training was 16-18 hours a day. They also jammed four years of college into one year at the University of Vermont. During a visit with him, my Mom would have to eat ketchup sandwiches since that was all they could afford. If you failed in any way, you ended up an enlisted man with a rifle, someplace out in the war.

*

Just as in WWI, Souther Field in Americus, Georgia was used as an Army Air Corps training base. That was where, in 1923, Charles Lindbergh bought a plane in a crate, built it, learned to fly and soloed. When my parents arrived, they were pleasantly surprised to find that the base Chaplain was Father Godfrey Weiterkemp, the Franciscan priest who had married them two years earlier. Since Pop was a non-Catholic, they had to be married at the side altar at St. Bonaventure's in Paterson, New Jersey. While based there, Pop surprised Mom by converting to Catholicism after secretly taking instructions from Father Godfrey at night. His parents had actually been Catholic, but when the priest baptized their first-born son he scratched him on the forehead and the child died of a staph infection two days later. They never went back to the Catholic Church, although his mother always kept a pair of rosary beads under her pillow.

A huge American flag that took six months of hand sewing by my mother and the other wives flew on a tall flagpole on the base. A plaque at the foot of the pole read:

Presented by
THE CADET WIVES
of
CLASSES 44-D & 44-E
NOVEMBER 25, 1943

After 18 months of rugged flight training, Pop received his wings and commission as a Second Lieutenant on the same day and pay went up to $125 a month. A graduation poem written by one of the wives read:

Why are you up in a silver ship?
And you must learn to fly?
What is it calls your heart from me
What do you find in the sky?

The wind might say if the wind could speak,
Of the Folks who have the mountain peak:
The winds could tell for all they know
Of the arrow flung from the hunter's bow.

But they are mute and I cannot
Tell you of the things my plane has taught
Except that I want until I die
Weather that's fair and a ship to fly.

By then, the Army Air Corps was now called the Army Air Force, which is why years later I think my mother used to tell people, "Alan is in the Navy Air Force."

I always wanted to visit the places Pop had been during his flight training as an Air Corps cadet. During part of 1943, he was in basic flight training at Columbus, Mississippi some 80 miles northeast of Meridian, flying the Boeing PT-17 Stearman, a wood and fabric creation. It was nicknamed the "Yellow Peril" because it was painted yellow and was hard to handle on the ground. It had open tandem cockpits, was rugged and handled easily in the air. Pilots who trained in it really enjoyed it. The first time the instructor rolled the plane upside down, Pop said he grabbed on to everything in sight to keep from falling out. Later on, the Cadets thought it was great fun to fly over the cotton fields and drop small paper bags of flour on the farm workers. On one such "mission," just as Pop was pulling up, his engine quit, forcing him to land in the very same field he had just "bombed." The farm workers thought it was neat that a pilot would land to say hello! Going before the Commanding Officer, he figured his days were numbered in flight training. Instead he was given a pat on the back for being able to land a plane in such a small space. They had to remove the wings in order to truck the plane out since the field was too short to take off from. Many years later, I flew the exact same Stearman from a grass field in Hanover, New Jersey.

Columbus was now a Strategic Air Command (SAC) base, housing B-52s, which were always on alert. Wanting to see where Pop had been based, I drove up from Meridian one weekend and went on the Base. Near a fence with a gate sat a B-52 guarded by a young enlisted man with an M16 rifle. As I approached, he issued, "Halt–this area is off limits." Almost in the same breath he asked, "Coach Alan?" It was a young kid who had been on the swimming team I coached at the Cedar Grove pool in New Jersey. He let me climb all through the B-52. I sat in the cockpit and couldn't believe all the switches and dials. I worked my way through the whole plane and ended up in the tailgunner's seat.

CHAPTER FIVE

...AND LEFT HIM HIS WINGS

As the grind continued, each week we saw the posted list of those who had dropped out of the flight program at other bases. They were the ones who had the necessary grades to go jets but chose to go props instead. If you went the "prop pipeline" route, you flew either helos or P-3 Patrol Planes–none of which interested me in the least. I wanted to fly something fast and hot. Later we found that the reasons the guys left were basically the same. Seems the wives would get together and discuss jets vs. props. They rationalized that if their husbands went props, they'd be shore based and be home more. The "gung ho gonna fly jets" guys became disenchanted with flying props and dropped out. When asked why, one mentioned, "I went along with the wishes of my first wife." They ended up making two or three cruises as ship's company. Their marriages went down the tubes just like their dreams of flying jets.

*

One training flight is memorable but not because of the flying. It was Easter weekend and a Marine captain instructor wanted someone to go on a cross-country flight to Dallas to visit his girlfriend. I volunteered in order to get more flight time and additional experience. The instructor turned out to be a real

41

screamer–yelling, ranting and raving the whole flight. When we got to Dallas, I decided to call Marian, my high school sweetheart, who was living in Los Angeles while flying for United Airlines as a stewardess. I wondered why I hadn't heard from her. Going into freshman year of High School, I met this cute little sophomore from East Orange Catholic High School. We hit it off and dated all through high school. We were inseparable. She was the main reason I got through Freshman Latin and stuck it out at St. Benedict's Prep. We became a fixture at both her school and mine. After high school, we went our separate ways. While I went off to college, she became a stewardess. Although we dated a few times after I graduated, I only received one letter from her after going in the Navy.

Marian answered the phone and half-jokingly I said, "Hey, I haven't heard from you. What are you married or something?"

"Almost. I'm getting married in July."

I was devastated. The flight back to Meridian with the screamer didn't help at all; it was a total blur.

I just happened to be home that July on weekend liberty and completely by chance drove by the Church as Marian came out as a new bride. I kept driving.

*

After six months in Meridian, it was great to transfer back to Pensacola for air-to-air gunnery and Carquals (to become Carrier Qualified–first time landing on a ship). Beautiful white sand beaches, the warm, clear water of the Gulf of Mexico and a magnificent Navy Officers' Club were just a few of the draws. In addition, great history abounded with stately homes of Admirals' row built in the 1880s. Spanish moss hanging from huge magnolia trees added to the graceful ambience. Twelve-foot high brick walls had been built around the hospital with the idea that a malaria-carrying mosquito could not fly that high. Nearby Fort Pickens was used from 1834 to 1947, and during the 1886 Apache war, Chief Geronimo was imprisoned there. My roommate in the BOQ, Bob Riera, was newly graduated from the Naval Academy. He was dating a real sweetheart named Cindy Hauser. As it turned out both their fathers were Admirals and had been roommates at the Naval Academy when they were Midshipmen. Bob and Cindy had a wonderful wedding at the Naval Academy.

We would practice our carrier approaches and landings, referred to as Field Carrier Landing Practice (FCLP) at outlying Barren field. It was known as 'Bloody Barren' from the number of pilots lost there during training in WWII. A popular hangout was "Dirty Joe's." The bar was owned by two Ensigns also in flight training; they were the only Ensigns I ever knew who were passed over for Lieutenant Junior Grade (LTJG), which normally was an automatic next promotion. Their days in the Navy were numbered. They proved that if you can't be good, be colorful.

The night before going out to the ship for the very first time, the instructors showed us three hours of movies of carrier mishaps that had taken place. We sat there transfixed as we watched planes hitting the back of the ship and disintegrating in a

43

ball of fire or flying into the water in front of the ship and being run over. That night, we learned the true implications of the phrase "hitting the boat," Navy parlance for landing on the carrier. The only real thing I knew about carrier ops was just from what I had seen on TV documentaries from WWII. The fear of God and carrier aviation was put into us that night. We were filled with terror, excitement and anxiety. We were excited over the prospect of becoming carrier qualified and apprehensive over, not only danger, but also knowing that if we failed we would get washed out of the flight program. In the end, fear of failure outweighed fear of death.

We flew out to the Gulf of Mexico to qualify on the very small carrier, USS Wasp (CV-18) from World War II. It had been hit by kamikazes in the war and survived (which was what I wanted to do now–survive). We went solo because the Navy didn't want to lose a student and an instructor at the same time. Approaching the ship, I looked down and saw blue-green waves hitting the side of it, breaking up into heavy white foam as it crashed up and over the ship's elevators lowered by the hangar bay. *I gotta land on that?–and it's moving!*

After a few touch and goes, I trapped aboard (which is what landing on a carrier is called) by catching a wire with the hook that I lowered beneath my plane–my first carrier landing! We then taxied up to the CAT (Catapult–basically a big slingshot) to be launched again for more landings. The Wasp had old hydraulic catapults, which gave us the full shot all at once. It was so violent and powerful that on my first launch, my knees went back and up over my shoulders. It would have been nice if just one of the instructors had clued us in on this. I was trying to figure out how I was going to fly the thing? Most of us qualified but a few more dropped out of the flight program.

Flight accidents were not limited to training hops. Some flew their plane into the ground while "flathatting." Every so often a student aviator would tell his girlfriend or wife to come down to the beach and he'd put on an air show, only to end abruptly as he crashed halfway through a loop into the water, right in front of her.

*

A few months later, I was transferred to NAS Chase Field in Beeville, Texas for Advanced Jet Training. I had to drive north up through Alabama and Louisiana before heading west since the coast highway was still not repaired from hurricane Camille, which had come through a month earlier. In fact, we had to "hurrivac" planes out of Pensacola, going first to Meridian, and then because the storm followed us had to fly to on to Dallas. A couple of student aviators who decided to remain near the beach held a hurricane party–and perished. The landscape looked like a huge hand had snapped off trees about six feet above the ground as far as you could see. When I ordered a cup of coffee at a diner in Louisiana, the waitress said, "You don't look like you're from here." It was my first taste of coffee with chicory in it. The menu on the wall showed the list of vegetable "sides" which included french fries that you could order with the BBQ ribs. I mentioned to the bulky-aproned stern lady behind the counter that french fries weren't vegetables. "They are here, Sonny!" At one point I stopped in Texas and asked for directions to Beeville but because it was so small no one knew where it was. However later on, at a Friday night high school football game, there would be 30,000 people in the stands.

Advanced Jet Training entailed flying the Korean War vintage F-9 Cougar. Known as the Lead Sled, it was totally underpowered and in some respects, due to its age, a flying emergency–which actually made it a valuable learning aircraft. Each flight something would go wrong. One night I was in the back seat "under the hood." This was cloth hood up over the cockpit so I couldn't see outside the plane for visual references simulating flying in the bad weather, so I had to rely only on my instruments. As usual, a small 'peanut light' illuminating an instrument went out. When I told the instructor he said, "I'll fly and you just take a bulb out from a non-essential instrument and replace it." I never realized there was such a thing as a "non-essential instrument?" All of a sudden he said, "OK you got it (i.e. control of the airplane) back." By now I had about ten tiny bulbs in my gloved hand and a completely darkened instrument panel, since none of them had worked. If I didn't complete the hop, it would result in a "below average" in the headwork column. I quickly put my flashlight between my knees and shined it on the instrument panel for the rest of the hop. I just hoped I didn't drop my pencil when it came time to copy a flight clearance from the FAA controller! Being so primitive and basic, the F-9 amazed and scared me at the same time. In case of a flameout, the air start consisted of two shotgun shells to provide the spark to ignite the fuel. Pulling a handle attached to a cable fired the shells.

*

Our practice field for FCLPs was at an outlying field at Goliad. The first Declaration of Independence of the Republic of Texas was signed there in 1835. However, in 1836, the garrison was defeated and Mexican General Santa Anna ordered all 400 prisoners who had surrendered executed. It was later the referred to as the Goliad Massacre. During one hop to Goliad as evening approached, fog rolled in and it got socked in real fast. A radio call went out to return to NAS Chase. Again, our navigation skills were still in the novice phase. I was flying all over the place, trying to find the field visually. The low fog became thicker. Just as I finished saying a real serious prayer, I looked down and saw that I was right over the field!

It was during this time that Bobby Wair had his fatal accident. We just couldn't believe it. He was such a good friend and an all around nice guy. Navy LT Bobby Wair was a tall, congenial, good-looking guy from Wisconsin. This easygoing student aviator was on his second solo hop in the F-9. The weather had changed so fast that no one realized it was too hot for the F-9 to fly on that August day. The weather was so crazy that there was a story that a farmer was plowing with two oxen—one died from heat exhaustion and the other froze to death the same day. He was three-quarters of the way down the runway when he knew he wasn't going to get airborne. Bob started to abort the takeoff by retarding the throttle and braking. He became aware that he couldn't stop before the end of the runway so he put the power back on in hopes of getting airborne. This procedure didn't work for the underpowered jet. The plane careened violently off the runway into the desert sagebrush at which point Bob ejected. His chute barely opened. He never had a chance. The heavy seat landed on him, cutting off his foot. In the helicopter on the way to Corpus Christi, he looked up at the corpsman and asked, "Why is this happening to me?" and died. At his memorial service, the Chaplain read a poem written by a friend of Bob's. It ended with "God took his engine and left him his wings."

CHAPTER SIX

... NOT JUST ANYTHING

One weekend we were requested to act as Escorts for the local Miss America contestants in Quihi, Texas, which sounded great to us. We did just that, wearing our dress whites. Afterward, the girls said that there was a "kicker" (as in shit kicker, aka cowboy) dance later that night and we should come. Jim McMurray and I drove to the location of the dance in the middle of nowhere. There was nothing there in the dim, black night–not even a building or a tree. "Boy, they led us down the path on this one!" Jim mentioned. All of a sudden, in the distance a small vertical sliver of light appeared. It was coming from a partially opened barn door. We pulled up and got out of the car. I had on tan slacks, a striped shirt and wingtip shoes. Jim, a dyed-in-the-wool New Yorker, had penny loafers on, a blue shirt and gray corduroy trousers. A big cowboy came out, looked us up and down and said, "I see you don't have cowboy boots on!"

Oh boy here comes a fight!

"No, sorry." I said.

"Well I have extra ones in the truck. I'll loan 'em to ya."

That night Jimmy Martin and the Texas cowboys entertained us royally. Even though we were "Randy Rexall Kickers" i.e. drug store cowboys, the girls taught us all the dances.

In addition to the square dance, there was the Cotton Eyed Joe, the Shoddish and the Paul Jones.

A sign on the wall read, *"Them as don't like a good hoss just ain't folks."* One of the girls mentioned that she was "fixin" to move. I said, "If the house is OK, why are you fixing it?" This went back and forth until I realized that she meant, "planning" to move. Also, it was the first time I heard the phrase "waitin' on ya." All in all, it was a great night. On the way back to Beeville, I stopped at a local diner for a cup of coffee. Sitting next to me at the counter was John Parry whom I swam with on the same relay team for three years at St. Benedict's! He got out of the Navy in Long Beach and was driving back home to Jersey. Over coffee we realized that we both dated the same Corinne back in New Jersey! Small, small world!

*

Another weekend, my roommate Drew and I went up to San Antonio to see Johnny Cash in concert. When we got to the front of the line we were told they were out of tickets. A gracious Texas lady asked us who we were. When we told her we were in Navy flight training, she gave us two free tickets showing how much Texans like the military. I was convinced that if the United States got invaded and no one else fought, the Texans would.

Grading for students was very interesting and precise. There were columns for below average, average, and above average. One that was a real motivator was the column labeled "headwork." It looked at how you approached a problem or a maneuver in a common sense sort of way. The very worst observation was if an instructor wrote NAFOD–No Apparent Fear of Death–that was a kiss of death for the student. When Pop was in flight training, the Army Air Corps still had grading sheets left over from cavalry days. There was a spot for *"Horsemanship."* Next to it the instructor would write, *"Unmounted."*

To this day, I can recall driving over the railroad tracks in Beeville and hearing for the first time *Leavin' on a Jet Plane* by Peter, Paul and Mary, which epitomized the range of emotions magnified by the intense learning curve of flight training. Part of it could have become our theme song during our combat cruise when the line "don't know *when* I'll come back again," could be changed to "don't know *if* I'll come back again."

*

On one formation hop, I was trying to join up or rendezvous with the lead plane. In the back seat was instructor pilot Denny Gillease, the brother of Mike, my classmate from AOCS. Instead of his helmet, he was wearing a huge rubber gorilla mask, laughing and pointing at my plane as I desperately struggled to join up. During this time I was able to take a weekend "cross-country" hop with my Instructor, LT Jim Mast. This allowed me to spend the weekend with the folks and an evening in New York City with dates. We flew into Floyd Bennett Naval Air Station in New York. On our return portion, we started up and were waiting for our Air Traffic Control (ATC) clearance, but none was forthcoming. It turns out that we were in a "blind spot" on the field where we couldn't hear any radio transmissions. Finally, the tower contacted us by ALDIS lamp (a big hand held flashlight) giving us the green light to move. Unfortunately, by the time we were airborne, we had already burned valuable fuel. We were 120 miles out from our refueling stop at Dobbins Air Force base in Atlanta when we saw the red *low fuel* warning light. In the F-9 you're supposed to be in the landing pattern when that light comes on! Jim and I both had our kneeboards off, anticipating a controlled ejection. *So much for graduating from this program! Or even surviving*! Jim was able to milk the power and do power off glides to stretch our meager fuel. We landed and taxied clear of the runway before the engine quit.

*

From the very beginning, I found flight training very demanding, it didn't come easy to me at all. I really had to work hard at it. The syllabus at Beeville also included firing rockets, dropping practice bombs and strafing. More formation hops came into play. You were expected to "stay-ahead" of the aircraft, which basically means you have to be thinking of what is going to happen next. On some hops, we students would say we were so "far-behind" the plane that when we landed we were still in the hangar getting ready to go! Ground school classes, getting airsick and losing friends added to the pressure. I put a sign over my desk which read "Don't just sit there, gnaw!" I had to keep working at it in order to make it through. We were so busy that many times after getting home late I would sleep in my flight suit too tired to change, and knowing that I had another early morning "go."

Our final test was to fly out to the USS Intrepid (CV-11) in order to carrier qualify again. It was another small carrier from World War II that also had been hit by kamikazes. At one point during the war the ship's rudder was so badly damaged that all they could do was go straight–in this case, right toward Japan! They rigged a sail made from canvas used to bury those killed at sea to help steer the ship to Hawaii for repairs.

Rolling into the groove on approach to the ship, I thought to myself *this is a piece of cake,* after which everything went to hell in a hand basket real fast! I had full power on and the correct flight angle for the best rate of climb and I was still descending! I barely trapped aboard when a voice in my headset announced "401 you hit the round down." I replied, "Ah roger" not having any idea as to what a "round down" even was. Turns out my hook had hit the back of the ship, known as the round down. Another inch or two lower and my hook would have caught the ship and torn my plane in half. I was almost the latest kamikaze! After that I never think of anything as being *a piece of cake!*

The jet fuel they put in the plane ashore was JP4, but at the ship they used JP5, a different grade of fuel. This caused the fuel control unit to try and adjust to the different fuel consistency. The procedure on the catapult was to give it full power and watch as the needle on the RPM power gauge wildly fluctuated up and down between 92 and 98 percent. If it averaged 95 percent–you went! We were "running the deck" to get the required landings and catapults shots. We would trap and taxi up for another launch. After getting airborne, we had two choices to get the hook back out and down: either cycle the landing gear (making sure to put it back down) or turn off all electrical power (hoping it would come back on). I was envious of my friends who were stationed at NAS Kingsville, Texas, because they got to fly the brand new TA-4 Skyhawk, which had plenty of power and all the latest gadgets. They were sent to Kingsville because it had better housing for the married guys. It seemed that married guys always got the good deals. Later on when we went on cruise, we bachelors had to give up the $180 per month Basic Allowance for Quarters (BAQ) while the married guys got to keep it. During our combat cruise, we even wrote the Secretary of the Navy, asking him what we were being paid to do in the Navy–fly missions or being married? We never received an answer.

*

The amount of time, effort and study we put into the flight program convinced me that we could have earned our Masters or PhD in the civilian world. Finally after a year and a half of grueling work and averaging a date every three months, I didn't know whether I was going to get my wings or get ordained? I got the former. Later on, living on the ship was like being in a monastery without the tranquility. So maybe I did get ordained? I was now a Naval *Aviator* as opposed to being just a pilot. *Pilots* land on runways; Naval *Aviators* land on ships! Out of the 73 who were commissioned with me in AOCS, only about 20 received the coveted wings of gold–Navy Wings. The Commanding Officer of the Base pinned on my wings. I told my parents not to come since I was leaving the next day for my temporary duty in Atlanta, but Pop always wished he had come. A few of us got flying jobs, while the rest got desk jobs. I was proud and relieved to have made it this far.

The Association of Naval Aviation said it best: *Winning the Wings of a Naval Aviator is a milestone in any individual's life. The wings are symbolic of distinguished achievement, hard-earned skill, unrelenting determination and service to country.*

There's no better feeling than to be a part of a legendary group, and I was very proud to be in that exclusive club. I thought it was neat to wear wings that also included a fouled anchor – the sky and sea.

*

Linda or "Lonnie" was a lovely devoted friend and cute, too. We dated occasionally back in New Jersey. She was teaching high school in a rough area of Paterson, N.J. When she went into the classroom on her birthday, there was a gift from the boys sitting on her desk with a note. "Happy Boithday Miss Linda." It was attached to the fire hydrant that had been in front of the school! It was their way of saying that they really liked her. After getting my wings, I received a nice homemade card from her congratulating me.

It read:

> *I've been reading and thinking*
> *And learning for years now*
> *And now I want to do something*
> *Not just anything but something.*
> *To get involved, to design and build*
> *Snoop around the sea and space*
> *Try to find out what makes our cities tick*
> *And help repair the years of standing still*
> *Then I'll be doing something not just anything*

*

I was offered "Plowback" duty (i.e. return as an instructor, which would guarantee me a few years of stateside duty as well as a lot of flight time). There was no way I wanted to go through all of this again as well as having some student trying to kill me; and besides, I wanted to be a fleet pilot. Other classmates were given orders to a shore facility with the promise of any flying slot they wanted after their tour was up. Unfortunately, when that time came there were no flying billets available. They were disgruntled, to say the least. When I told Pop I was awarded an A-6 slot he said, "They fly dangerous missions" having learned that from a former Navy pilot who was his co-pilot at the time.

"I don't know, Pop." All I knew was that it was a jet that flew in the fleet.

*

After getting our wings, Jim McMurray and I were rewarded with two months of "Feedback" duty in Atlanta to recruit for Naval Air. We were based with a small Navy detachment at Dobbins Air Force Base and were given a T-34 to fly around and a white Dodge convertible that said "Fly Navy" on the side. The people in the South just love military men and were very respectful. We visited Auburn, Alabama, Georgia Tech, Georgia and the Citadel. At Auburn, we went to The Southern Folk Festival in a small auditorium. These Minstrel shows went back to the 1840s. Rev. Pearly Brown was a black, blind street singer from Americus, Georgia. He danced and sang songs and spirituals learned from his grandmother. These included a "freedom now" song, while over on the wall hung a plaque dedicated to the school graduates who had fought for the Confederacy in the Civil War. He was very well received, proving that many had become more open minded. There was also a very real "Mr. Bojangles" who lightly danced his way across the stage.

One night, Jim and I were at a downtown discothèque in Atlanta where two Go-Go dancers were on small platforms in cages high up against the wall. Both had short hair and matching bare midriff outfits as they gyrated to Norman Greenbaum's "Spirit in the Sky." They looked like twins. The Disc Jockey proudly announced, "High atop their place of honor–Gary and Rhonda–Gary's the one on the left."

Another evening, after hours, we visited my college roommate, Rich Merklinger, at Ft. Benning where he was undergoing arduous Army Officer Candidate School. His class officer was Second Lieutenant Milner. We managed to convince him that a Navy LTJG outranked him, which permitted us to visit Merk even though it was considered off limits. For the next five months he was called "Navy Boy" and was harassed even more.

Atlanta was a great break after the rigors of flight training. We really had a good time while barely managing to stay out of trouble. Jim got called in on the rug for flying in between the girls' dormitory at Oglethorpe College. He already made five very low passes over the dorm. It may have had something to do with the fact that the girls would sunbathe on the roof–topless. The Master Chief in the outfit got him off.

CHAPTER SEVEN

A SINCERE SALUTE

After the short stint in Atlanta, I was able to take some leave before reporting to NAS Oceana in Virginia Beach for training in the A-6 Intruder. It was always good to go home and on this particular Sunday in February of 1970 it was cold and clear, perfect for proudly wearing my warm Navy Blues to Mass at Blessed Sacrament Church. My shiny new Wings of Gold stood out on my chest, reflecting the winter sun. After Mass, I was standing in front of the church when Mary Beth McDonough came up to me. I would see her at Mass on Sundays and at the town pool during the summer. She was a friendly, loving, warm little girl who always had a big smile on her face. If you asked her how old she was, she would hold up four fingers; although, at the time she was twelve years old. Mary Beth had been born with Down's syndrome. Her cognitive development and physical growth ended early, but although her mind was stuck in time, her heart grew. "Mary Beth, I finally got my wings!" I blurted out while proudly pointing to my brand new pair of wings. She quickly stepped back, stood straight up and saluted. "Alan I'm so proud!" I promptly returned her salute and gave her a big hug. Nothing could ever mean more to me than that. Perhaps people saw Mary Beth as missing something, but for me she had an incredible understanding in her heart. It was the purest form of love and respect for both of us. Years later I received a Christmas gift from Mrs. Anne Jones. She was a dear friend and neighbor of the McDonoughs. It was a hand-made ornament. Simply made, it was a clear plastic ball glued together and filled with little pieces of colored paper–a potpourri of sorts. Holding it up and shaking the paper around, I noticed one different color among the greens, reds and blues. One piece was bright yellow. Looking closer, I could see that this golden piece of paper was roughly cut into the shape of a small pair of wings, much like my Navy wings of gold. When I called Mrs. Jones to thank her, she said that she had ordered it from the institution in Pennsylvania where Mary Beth McDonough was living.

*

I reported to VA-42, the A-6 Replacement Air Group (RAG) at NAS Oceana in Virginia Beach, Virginia to begin a nine-month training curriculum for the Grumman A-6 Intruder. The very first day, LT Ron "Ronny Dean" Lankford came up to LTJG Ken "Knapper" Knapp and me and mentioned that he had an apartment for us to see. He asked if we wanted to room together. Ron had done his homework finding out who the bachelors were in the squadron. I had just picked up Ken at the airport after returning from leave and the first thing he said was, "I just met the girl I'm going to marry."

"Sure Ken."

We lived at 560 North Birdneck for the next year or so. There was always something going on there with different people coming and going. One night we decided to invite our flight surgeon, affectionately known as "Quack," over for dinner. Ken's girlfriend, Stephanie, was visiting from Chicago and was going to cook us a homemade meal. She worked very hard putting together lasagna—so much in fact that the kitchen had a red and orange glow to it from the sauce. The Quack took one bite and said, "You couldn't get a German Shepherd person to eat this!" So much for bedside manners. As we used to say, "A flight surgeon is someone who holds your hand until the real doctor gets there." In 2002, the apartment was hit by an F-18 that crashed on takeoff. No one was hurt.

The A-6 was one of the newer and the most sophisticated aircraft in the fleet. It had an attack-radar system with unique low-altitude terrain-following capabilities. Since its primary mission was to attack and bomb targets, mainly by flying low-level missions at night, it was considered an *attack* aircraft as opposed to a *fighter*. There was a *loving* rivalry, a friendly animosity of sorts, between the Attack and Fighter communities. There was a story about an attack pilot who said that one of his brothers was a fighter pilot, his other brother was doing time for armed robbery, and his sister was living in a house of ill-repute in Texas. His question was, "How do I tell my parents that they have a son who is a fighter pilot?"

One night I talked to Pop on the phone where we compared the capabilities of the A-6 with his B-24. Whereas we could carry a 15,000-pound payload, Pop would go all the way to Berlin with only one 2,000-pound bomb.

*

The A-6 training syllabus consisted of low-level flying (referred to as bush bashing in WWI), bombing, air-to-air refueling, and carrier quals. We started to feel like we had been students for years, first as officer candidates, then flight students, and now students in the RAG.

The instructors were legends to us. Most had one or two combat cruises in Vietnam. You weren't really accepted in the Navy until you got your wings. This didn't count for much until you made at least one cruise. The real recognition came only if you made a combat cruise to Westpac, Vietnam–the Mecca for Naval Aviators. Some of our instructors had been awarded the Navy Cross for the daring night low-level missions into North Vietnam that had been flown for the very first time. By the time we got there, these missions were so commonplace that they warranted only an Air Medal or perhaps a Distinguished Flying Cross. Instructor pilot Bill Westerman had been wounded while flying a night low-level mission. His B/N, Brian Westin, reached over and steered the aircraft out over the water since Bill kept passing out. Brian stretched his hand over and ejected Bill and then himself. In the water he swam over and kept Bill afloat until the helo rescued them. He was awarded the Navy Cross. The rows of ribbons on their uniforms told the stories. Just as importantly, they were allowed to wear an "I've been there" belt and buckle made in the Philippines. Instead of the standard issue plain brass buckle and web belt, they had a cloth belt and a buckle with their name and a pair of Navy wings engraved.

Classmate Dick "Gomer" Havaner was an authentic true-to-life character. He was from Hickory, North Carolina and went to Appalachian State teacher's college in Boone, North Carolina. He was a dead ringer for the actor Jim Nabors who played Gomer Pyle on TV. He looked like him, talked like him and thought like him— genuinely. He was just as good-natured, too. Gomer could make a clown laugh. Later on, we found out he could sing like Jim Nabors as well! In the RAG we had an Exchange Instructor from the Royal Air Force, Leftenant Peter Libby (a Leftenant is a British Lieutenant). He would ask a question, point, and say, "Go Maah" in the most sophisticated way. We all wondered, who is this 'Go Maah?' Of course it was Gomer, or just plain Goom to us. One time he was flying a low level training hop over the hills of Virginia with the Leftenant. Calmly and quietly, Peter said, "Go Maah, there's something radically wrong with this aircraft." Gomer quickly and nervously looked all around as he contemplated punching out. The fuel needles had erroneously run to zero.

"It's a bit wonkey Go Maah."

*

The stories of Westpac were amazing, but we were scheduled to do two Mediterranean cruises after we joined our operational squadron. Along with the majority of our class, I went to VA-75, The Sunday Punchers. The squadron origin dated back to 1943 when the squadron was commissioned as Bombing Squadron Eighteen and flew from the deck of the USS Intrepid. During the Korean War, the Admiral was asked when he was going to put VA-75 into the fight. He said he was saving them for his "Sunday Punch." This was in reference to the Friday night boxing matches. Some guys would punch so hard that his opponent was knocked out until Sunday. Before the A-6, the squadron was flying the A-1 Spad. In 1965, VA-75 introduced the A-6 Intruder to combat operations in Vietnam. It was the first, and later on, the final A-6 Squadron to fly in Vietnam.

We knew of the sacrifices constantly being made by members of the Squadron who had been shot down and captured in North Vietnam. CDR Jeremiah Denton was Commanding Officer of VA-75 flying with LT Bill Tschudy, his B/N. They were shot down on 18 July 1965 and ended up being held as prisoners and tortured for almost eight years, four of them spent in solitary confinement while in irons. Their treatment was savage-beyond cruel. CDR Denton was best known for a 1966 televised press conference that he was forced to partake in. He used Morse code to blink "T-o-r-t-u-r-e" and stated that he fully supported his country, a statement for which he paid dearly with bestial brutality. Our fellow A-6 squadrons at Oceana also had POWs.

We had to attend a "Dining In" which was the Navy's version of a frat parties-just for the guys. We had to don our dress whites and attend a four-course dinner at the O'Club. I felt that if we were going to wear our fancy uniforms, there should at least be women present. Drinks started with cocktail hour and continued with wine for the meal, followed by port. By the time the guest speaker got up, rolls were being thrown. When Admiral Leonard Alexander "Swoose" Snead was introduced, LT Greg "Tweedy' Honour (at 6'2" he was the original 200 pound canary) kept saying very loudly, "Who? Whooo?" The last time I saw one of the guys that evening; he was riding the huge floor buffer. He'd stand on it and switch it on, causing him to spin round and round until he was thrown off. When we got back to our apartment early in the morning Ken Knapp's uniform had one LTJG bar and one Admiral's bar on his shoulders.

*

One day while we were at the squadron we heard that there had been a mid-air collision between two TA-4 training aircraft assigned to Oceana. One pilot ejected safely while the other was lost at sea. Turns out it was a classmate from AOCS, George Gaunt, who was truly a nice guy. Unfortunately, he was not to be the last from our class to be lost in the service of our country.

The low-level training hops all over Virginia afforded us some great flying. We had to learn to interpret how our instruments translated and presented the low flying we were seeing outside our plane. We'd fly canned routes through the valleys and over the hills of the Shenandoah Valley at 100 feet. We got to know what houses were on the top of the hills in order to pull up over them in time. When we took a plane on a weekend cross-country, we were expected to fly at low level so we'd be prepared to do it at night. I had taken my 8mm camera on one such flight. When I showed the flick, someone asked what road I was driving on. At one point we were chasing a herd of elk in Montana on the way to NAS Whidbey Island in the Seattle area.

*

LTJG Roger Lerseth was assigned as my first B/N. We were born a day apart and both our fathers had been B-24 pilots in WWII. We prepared to go to the ship for our first night landings ever by practicing at Outlying Field (OLF) Fentress. It was located in the very bleak Dismal Swamp Area of Virginia. The name was incredibly relevant. It was dark, dangerous, foreboding and as the name says, dismal! On a corner of a runway were the markings of a carrier landing area with very little lighting. We were scheduled to "hit" the USS Lexington (CV-16). For some reason, I kept getting very small WWII carriers! The Japanese called the Lexington the "Ghost" ship because it had been reported sunk so many times yet it kept showing up.

On my first pass at the ship, the speed brakes retracted on their own in the groove, causing me to do a fast fly-by alongside the right side (and the wrong side) of the ship. The Skipper of the USS Lexington wasn't too amused and said so over the radio. We came around for my first night landing on a ship, but certainly not the last. The ship was so small that we had to fold our wings after trapping aboard to taxi up to the CAT for another launch. If we didn't, our wings would hit the island-bridge area of the ship. After about nine months of training, I received my designation as an A-6 Pilot–a real Attack pilot. Later on, bumper stickers would read, *"Fighter pilots make movies (i.e. Topgun) Attack Pilots make history."* That worked until the movie *Flight of the Intruder* came out.

To the "Combat Fish".
     A good friend and trusted 'stick'.
Keep the faith, but remember the lessons —
and most importantly, keep 'em flying!
                    G.B.U.
        —Roger Lersett.

CHAPTER EIGHT

AIR WING THREE AND USS SARATOGA

Our squadron was part of Air Wing Three assigned to the USS
Saratoga (CV-60), home-ported at the Mayport Naval Base in
Jacksonville, Florida. Our first cruise had taken us to the North
Atlantic and Mediterranean in 1971 as part of the Cold War forces.
In 1972 we were scheduled for another cruise to the same areas.
Before long, it was time to head back out to sea for workups prior
to this upcoming second cruise requiring us to fly our planes to
NAS Jacksonville. We had a day off, so I found myself hanging
around with some of the Senior Chiefs at a local oyster and crab
place called The Oyster Bar. It was in an old Quonset hut that had
been painted red with the décor inside being early garage sale. The
Chiefs were leftovers from WWII with plenty of stories and still
full of piss and vinegar. These guys forgot more than I could ever
know about the Navy. They ran the Navy. Senior Chief Radioman
Len Gray had been a radio operator on the USS Carter Hall (LSD-
3) in the South Pacific in WWII. He said he became a radio
operator because both his father and grandfather had been
telegraph operators at the train stations on the Louisville and
Nashville (L&N) train line. When it came time for the background
check for his Top Secret Clearance, he almost didn't get it because
they both had been arrested for selling moonshine. He told me

about being on the bridge as two torpedoes went along either side of the ship. Sitting across from me was retired Master Chief Bill Steelman who was just hanging around with his old buddies. A kindly man he said that he retired from the Navy in 1946 after 24 years. He went on to tell me that his very first job was planting tobacco plants for the RJ Reynolds Company in North Carolina from sunrise to sunset for 50 cents a day! When I asked him why he joined the Navy, he said that his older brother came home as a doughboy in WWI. At that time when you joined the army you got $21 a month and a horse blanket, while the Navy gave you $21 a month and a hammock—he said he wanted the hammock. I was enthralled listening how he had been on a gunboat on the Yangtze River in 1939 when the Japs attacked them. Later on, he was a skipper of a coal burning Navy Ferry boat in Manila Harbor. One time during a typhoon, it took him three days to go from Manila to Cavite, a distance of ten miles. On his way back to the states the CO of the transport ship said, "Bill, why don't you just stay on the ship instead of spending a few days at Pearl Harbor?" He did just that—the date was December 6, 1941!

We ate family-style and had to share menus that were hand written in pencil on a piece of paper. The waitress asked us to double up on them because there weren't enough to go around. The ashtrays were deep dents in the metal tabletop and food was served on paper plates. I figured I'd better eat fast as I half-expected the waitress to come along at any minute and ask me to return the fork because it was needed elsewhere. The jukebox played two tunes for 25 cents, and if you recognized any of them you got the third one free. For a while I thought there was a food-eating contest going on as plate after plate of oysters, shrimp and crab were being consumed. Turns out this was S.O.P. with the meal lasting upwards of four hours.

Every phone booth on the base was filled. There were banks of ten booths with lines of twenty or more sailors waiting to call home. They were just kids. The young enlisted men would count their small change to see if they had enough money to go into town. Many times they didn't.

*

We returned from our first North Atlantic and Mediterranean cruise the previous October, so when we put out to sea on 23 Feb 1972 to get ready for our next cruise, it felt like I had never left the ship. We were scheduled to leave on our next 'big' cruise in May. This meant that when we returned from this one in November, we would have been at sea on and off for 18 months! This began a two-month "workup cruise" and Operational Readiness Inspection (ORI). It was basically a shakedown cruise to get us ready for another North Atlantic/ Mediterranean cruise with the Second and Sixth fleets. It was one of those 24/7 types of Ops –pushing everyone to their limits–one big continuous test to see how well the Air Wing and Ship worked together. It just wrung the heck out of you. Max effort–flying around the clock with little sleep. It was around this time that LT Paul "Boot" Wagner became my B/N as well as roommate. Since we had been shore-based for a few months, we had to "CQ" (Carrier Qualify) all over again by landing on the ship; this involved doing a few "touch and goes" and making a few "traps." You'd trap aboard, taxi up, get launched and do it again–"running the deck".

It's a real hassle manning aircraft during CQ, which included unbelievable heat from the exhaust of other aircraft. You'd also get gassed with "stack gases" from the ship's funnels that would pour into the cockpit. I had four day traps and one night trap. At night or in very bad weather, an approach controller would talk a pilot down to three-quarters of a mile behind the ship helping with lineup and glide slope. I couldn't hear him very well, and when I got to two hundred feet above the water and three-quarters of a mile I could barely make out the 'drop lights' that hung down behind the ship that helped for lineup. Seems the ship had steamed into a thick fog bank. I went around and had to 'bingo' to NAS Cecil Field to refuel and do it again successfully, this time in the rain. This landing made me a Centurion (100 landings on the same ship) on USS Saratoga.

*

Back in our Ready Room, our Squadron commanding officer, said, "This is where it's at." We Junior Officers decided we would form a search party at 2100 to find exactly what it "was" that's "here" and then where it was "at!" Sort of like forgetting to remember to forget. Then the executive officer said "we're home" and LTJG Doug "DWA" Ahrens responded, "That's not true 'cause I wouldn't let this many idiots in my house." Doug was the

Supply Officer for the squadron. He felt that the supplies actually belonged to him instead of the Navy. In fact, the CO had to order him to issue the mandatory extra flight suits to the crews. It was said that he was so frugal that he put a nickel in the Navy Federal Credit Union five years earlier and had lived off the interest ever since.

There was always a big industrial-sized coffee pot in the back of the Ready Room. It was classified as "fresh," "still fresh," "mostly fresh" and "need a new pot." Of course, the older Chiefs said it wasn't any good unless a spoon could stand up in it, a horseshoe float in it or could be used for battery acid. It was ruthless.

One evening the Commander of the Air Group (in command of all the squadrons on the ship) known as CAG, CDR Deke "Guinea One" Bordone, presented Centurion certificates to

100 Carrier Landings ceremony with CAG Bordone, Terry "TLA" Anderson, and Jerry "Moon" Mullins on far right.

TLA (Terry L. Anderson), Jerry Mullins and me. The Captain of the ship made a nice announcement over the 1MC (ship's public address circuit) concerning the achievement of making 100 landings on the same ship. But I was still wishing I were in Vietnam doing something *real*. I even wrote my folks saying, "I still can't believe I'm at sea and that there's a war on and I'm not in it." Little did I know!

*

Operating off the Florida coast we would practice bombing at a military target area in Pinecastle in the southern part of Florida. One of our Lieutenant Commanders mistakenly put his armament switch to arm instead of safe causing his bombs to drop prematurely. They missed the target and set the Ocala National Forest on fire. A group of boy scouts had to hunker down to keep from getting hit by shrapnel. When he got back to the ship he laughingly said, "I don't do anything half-assed." He was right.

On the way back to the ship from the bombing range some 30 planes from the air wing would fly over, around and through the area where they were building Disney World in Orlando. We just wanted to see how things were coming along. Finally, Disney's Construction Manager sent a message to the ship asking that we stop because the planes were scaring his workers.

After a few days back ashore, we flew out to the ship on 1 Mar 1972 for more CQ. I had four foul deck wave offs (aircraft in the landing area) and then got four traps even though there was an unbelievable burble (which develops close in behind the ship during the landing approach). For landing and launch it was preferred to have about 30 knots of wind across the deck. If there is no "natural" wind, the ship must make it by steaming at 30 knots.

This causes the wind to hit the island (bridge area) of the ship–the wind deflects up and then comes back down just aft of the ship–causing a "burble" or downdraft right behind the back of the carrier. A mini-microburst of sorts. You had to put enough power on to get through it so you didn't go low. If you left it on too long, you would be high at the ramp. It's a quick, major maneuver–power on, lower nose, get out of burble then power off, raise nose, power back on. Bim, bam boom! We then flew back to Oceana for a few days ashore.

We put back out to sea again on 7 Mar 1972. The next day our first CAT shot was uncomfortably light since we only weighed 36,000 lbs–a terribly soft "shot." We just skated off the deck, almost skimming the waves.

L-R: TLA, JJ, Fish, Rony Dean, Knapper

CHAPTER NINE

... DON'T HAND THE KEYS OVER TO JUST ANY KID

Just living aboard ship was enough to tire me out–a lot of walking as well as climbing ladders while wearing about 30 pounds of flight and survival gear. And then there was the *noise*–a constant grinding noise. It sounded like iron chains were constantly being dragged across the steel flight deck. My overhead (ceiling) of my room was the underside of the flight deck right below the port catapult. I could hear and feel the planes go to full power and then kick in afterburner. It sounded like Niagara Falls from two feet away while a cannon was being fired at the same time. It felt like my room was being launched! Basically I was living under the takeoff end of a runway! When the holdback broke, releasing the plane, it sounded like a guillotine striking a wooden block. The thud and reverberation of the shuttle hitting the water brake at the end of the catapult stroke was like a steam engine freewheeling down a mountain into the side of my room and bouncing off after a good jolt. As the metal shuttle was being pulled back it sounded like a freight train with its brakes on being dragged backwards against its will, grating over an iron floor. Even when there were no flight ops, they constantly checked the catapult by firing a "no load." The shuttle, minus an aircraft, hit the water brake at the end with great noise and vibration. "No Load" became synonymous with certain people who were no good to anyone. We referred to the flight deck as the "roof."

The whole evolution of flying off the ship was very fatiguing. For me, the mental concentration and physical exertion created immense stress and many times resulted in complete exhaustion. And this didn't even include combat missions! No one can know unless they've done it. Pounding jet noise on the flight deck alone was draining. I felt like a punching bag. At night the flight deck was like being in the "twilight zone." On the way to the plane Boot would stick his head out the hatch leading to the catwalk and declare "negative light check" and fake turning around. Night was an impressive and scary thing at sea with nothing but intense black. By the time I was ready to launch I was usually soaked through from the heat, humidity and high exhaust temperature of other planes. Sweat ran down my neck and back.

On the flight deck at night, normal visual cues just did not exist. Out of the black shadows the silhouette of the taxi director appeared almost like an apparition. It was completely surreal. I could barely see his two little lighted wands he held in his hands. I just followed where he pointed the wands as he gave me directions and then passed me along to another director farther down the deck. I didn't look where I was going while I followed his commands until I arrived at the catapult. I had to have complete faith in 19-year-old kids. They were magnificent. While following the taxi director I spread the wings, lowered the flaps and went through the takeoff checklist. I had to be precise in getting to the correct position on the CAT so they could hook my nose gear and holdback bar to the shuttle that was attached to the catapult. The number on the weight board held up to me had to match the weight I had calculated earlier. That was to make sure enough steam power was loaded into the catapult to get me airborne. Prior to manning up, Paul and I would go to a different part of the Ready Room and figure what we weighed (i.e. weight of plane, fuel, bombs, racks that held the bombs, etc.). We'd then compare our numbers and use the higher of the two–no soft CAT shots for us! Although a catapult shot was better than any ride at an amusement park, it was still forced-forward violence. It was like being snatched on the collar by someone running and dragged along backwards, faster than you could keep up by kicking your legs, and then flung into an abyss.

There was a Navy recruiting ad in the magazines that showed an aircraft with the lines:

> *"It does zero to 150 in two and a half seconds so we don't hand the keys over to just any kid that comes along."*

The plane did in fact go from a dead stop to flying speed in two and a half seconds; that's zero to 150 knots in 250 feet! I'd pick out the gauges I wanted to watch because of the transverse Gs that plummeted me straight back. I couldn't move my head, and my eyeballs would cage so I couldn't move them either. At night, I'd have Paul hold his flashlight on the gauges because every now and then the instrument lighting would go out. As I was hurled off the ship, it initially gave me the feeling that I was climbing. The tendency then was to push the stick forward, which is not a good idea when you're only 60 feet above the waves. There was a painting in a military art exhibit in Washington, D.C., which accurately depicted this procedure. It was a canvas painted completely black surrounded by a black frame. The inscription underneath read:

This is what distinguishes a Naval Aviator from all other pilots–the night catapult launch.

Landing aboard ship had been referred to, especially by Air Force types, as a *controlled crash*. This was another reason why it was referred to as "hitting the boat" especially since the end result was very violent because we hit so hard and stopped so fast. But it took great precision to accurately get to that exact point on the deck, you just couldn't land anyplace on the flight deck and catch a wire. Trapping aboard was like walking along a path in the woods, daydreaming when someone smacks you in the face with a baseball bat. Ferociously, you were hauled back aboard ship with that same "forced violence" that launched you. I got it coming and going. As soon as I touched down, I went to full power while putting in the speed brakes. This was in case I didn't catch a wire; I would bolter and could get airborne again for another try. Of course, I was going forward at 150 miles an hour, giving it full power and then catching a wire, which was trying to stop me. I was basically trying to go in opposing directions at the same time.

Someone had done a great caricature showing a wide-eyed pilot with a death grip on the stick. Underneath it read: *An aircraft carrier is the only ship in the world that gets smaller and smaller as you get closer and closer.* The four wires were 20 feet apart, making the landing area the size of a tennis court. WWII war correspondent Ernie Pyle said it was like landing on a small block in Main Street during an earthquake and hurricane. Although it was a big ship it was a little airport with a very small runway.

Returning to the ship in the daytime, each squadron would rendezvous at an assigned altitude over the ship, flying in a big circle. Operations were done "zip lip" (i.e. no radio transmissions). The only broadcast you'd hear was "Charlie Five" from the tower. This meant that a plane had to cross the ramp for landing in five minutes. I had to look down and figure out where my wingmen and I fit in so that a plane landed every 45 seconds. More than just landing, it was bringing the plane *back aboard ship*–the sole reason for the existence of the carrier. One radio transmission to a pilot who was having a difficult time landing was "you've got to land here son, this is where the food is!" At night, the interval was one minute. I'd be placed in holding and given an approach clearance time. I would have to figure out my holding pattern via speed, angle of bank, rate of turn, length of pattern, etc. so I could arrive back over that exact point at the designated time I was to commence my approach. Many times half way around the pattern, the controller would change his mind and say, "Cleared for the approach!" Quickly swinging into a 90-degree bank and pulling four G's, I'd head for that point in space to begin the approach. If you varied at all from your approach time, you'd have to broadcast it i.e. "504 commencing 10 seconds late"–invariably some other pilot would come up on the air with a "Heh, Heh!"

*

The night Carrier Controlled Approach (CCA) was the ship-based equivalent of a Ground Controlled Approach (GCA). This was where a controller talked you down. Callouts would be, "Above glide slope, left of centerline correcting, etc." His last call would be, "Three-quarters of a mile call the ball" (your visual reference for glide slope). You would have to visually transition from your instrument panel two feet in front of you to refocus on the "meatball" (yellow light) three-quarters of a mile away, which looked about an inch high. Correct lineup and airspeed were also critical. However one night when the controller said "call the ball." I looked up to see the side of the ship! I was headed straight for the hangar bay. I could even see the planes in there. He talked me down into the side of the ship because the ship had turned! Of course, I pulled up and went around. During our previous cruise in the Mediterranean, I was asked to fly a senior officer from the ship's company ashore at Capodichino in Naples, Italy. As usual, it was one of those black rainy nights (aren't they all?). The Italian controller said quickly and repeatedly in broken English, "Too - a - high, too - a - high, too – a - fast, too - a - fast." They don't control they criticize! Finally the senior officer said, "Come right, son, I got the lights of the runway." *I thought I was doing O.K. for*

80

lineup, but who is a Lieutenant to question a senior officer? I started coming right and the controller excitedly shouted, "Hey - a hey - a you - a - go for - a - the highway you're - a - bad - a - boy you - a - listen to me." The officer made a coughing sound in his mic.

*

On one approach to the ship, Pri-fly (the tower) asked me, "Are you alone?"

"No, I have my B/N with me" I replied, trying to lighten things up a bit. It's a hairy profession and for me it was tough to make it fun. I was just trying to survive.

I don't know who it was but someone wrote: *"Being a carrier pilot requires aptitude, intelligence, skill, knowledge, discernment and courage of a kind rarely found anywhere but in a poem of Homer's or a half gallon of Dewar's."* I wondered if *maybe* I should start drinking Scotch! There were times when I got out of the plane after a few bolters and found that my knees were weak. One time, Chief Hickman of the flight deck Line division held up his hand with a tally written on it: Passes III Bolters II Bingos I. After landing, I was taxied forward and parked along the forward port side of the ship. I wasn't quite sure where I was parked but when I looked out my side of the cockpit after opening the canopy, I realized that if I had climbed out my side I'd have ended up in the ocean some 60 feet below! I had to climb across the B/N's seat to get out.

*

Every pass was graded by the Landing Signal Officer (LSO), also known as *Paddles,* which harkened back to the days when pilots were "waved" aboard ship by the LSO holding flags or paddles to visually communicate with the pilot, now done by radio. He was positioned on a platform on the port side of the ship near the landing area. I asked one LSO how he got the job. He said the senior LSO came up to him and asked him how big he was? "I'm six two and 220 pounds, sir."

"You'll do, you're big enough so as not to get blown off the LSO platform."

The help from the LSO saved more than one pilot. He could hear and see a mistake you were making before you realized it and he'd help you correct it. The motto of the LSO School was right on the mark, Rectum non-Bustus! After the recovery, the LSO would go from Ready Room to Ready Room and debrief each pilot individually. If anyone had a particular bad approach and landing, the tape of it was played over and over on the TV screen in the Ready Rooms–there was no place to run and hide. All grades were posted in the Ready Room. Everyone knew exactly where he stood within the Squadron, the Air Wing, the Fleet, and the Navy. When LT Bob "Trol" Tolhurst (who had the best boarding rate, i.e. highest grades in our squadron) would get ready to fly, we'd jump all over him. "Better man the Five Inch Guns–Trol's getting airborne", meaning that the only way he'd get back aboard ship was to shoot him down. This would start a 30-minute rebuttal by him. In normal conversation, Trol would ask us, "Hey did you see this or that movie or read this book?" We'd say, "No" and he'd continue to tell us the whole story. We put a stop to it when he inquired if we had read *War and Peace.* If we asked him the time, he'd tell us how to build a watch. A good guy, though. He recalled each and every pass he ever made at the ship. Years later when he retired, there was a CD (not available in stores) covering all his landings. The young sailors in his squadron were selling it for fun and profit.

*

One evening I flew from the ship back to NAS Oceana for the next day's Commander, Naval Air Forces Atlantic (COMNAVAIRLANT) Change of Command. Acting as an usher, I got to seat the guests and talk to the wives while the other guys were lined up in ranks. A few years earlier Esquire magazine did an article about what professions had the prettiest wives. Turned out it was professional athletes and Navy pilots. Father Ignatius at St. Benedicts taught us that the object of the intellect was beauty. Sure enough, I guess that made us Naval Aviators very intellectual! Another squadron had a ladies powder puff football team called "the Tight Ends!" One wife who fit the bill perfectly was Donna, who was married to a pilot who had been my classmate during A-6 training. Anytime we had a squadron function, she would come up to me and say in the softest, cutest, lingering southern drawl, "Fish, would you dance with me? My husband doesn't like to dance." Seemed all the good-looking girls were married to friends. B/N Hal King's wife Loren was so proficient in the demands of a Navy spouse that she could have been the mold used for creating the perfect Navy wife. She was also known for making a mean "garbage can martini".

A6 Blue Angel Flying

CHAPTER TEN

SARACROPOLIS

There was no day or night on the ship—just continuous operations and work with incessant noises and odors of its own. The ship defied the real world and produced one of its own. It seemed amazing to me that a city of 5,000 could steam on the seas and be an airport at the same time. Basically it was a Naval Air Station that went to sea. Anytime we'd have a discussion with people comparing us with Air Force pilots, we'd say, "Yeah, I guess it's a lot harder to land on a 9,000 foot runway that's standing still then it is to land in 80 feet on a ship that's moving, pitching and rolling with no runway lights." And we had to do it in the rain at night after being shot at!

*

We learned one of our stops on the upcoming Mediterranean cruise was to be "Saracroplis." That was our name for Athens, Greece, because of what happened on our last cruise. We had a boiler blow, which put a hole in the bottom of the ship, causing serious flooding. The Russian fleet, that wasn't there to help us, immediately surrounded us. They were just going to watch. We were down to one screw out of four and limped into Athens harbor. The ship was listing and actually in danger of sinking. The only thing left to do was launch the Air Wing and fly to NAS Rota Spain. Being launched from Anchorage was hardly ever done since there was no wind over the deck, and therefore the catapults had to be cranked up as high as possible to get a plane airborne. It was a real kick in the pants. After we launched, I kept telling Boot, "You watch that cruise ship on the right and I'll watch the one on the left." We had to stay low and fly in between them to build up speed in order to raise the flaps. The ship was only a mile or so offshore pointed right toward the beach and Athens International Airport. The controller in Athens tower kept yelling, "This is Athenia International Airport on Guard (a universal frequency) please - a - don't fly over my airport I'm a *seriously* please - a - don't fly over my airport I'm a *seriously*." An F-4 pilot with the appropriate call sign of "Ginhead" did just that, doing rolls down the runway in an F-4–there's always one! His dreams of becoming a Blue Angel were dashed that day.

We flew to Sicily to refuel. Flying into NAS Sigonella, I had a hard time understanding the tower and asked for the English-speaking controller. "I am," was the reply. *Great!* He had us land downwind, causing the Executive Officer (XO) and me to blow tires while trying to stop on the runway. Since there was only one tire on the base, the XO got it and proceeded on to Rota. We had to wait for the ship to fly in a new tire the next day. Sicily looked and felt like 1942 with old WWII trucks, bombed out craters, and bullet holes in some buildings. We went into the local town of Catania for dinner with wingman crew LCDR Don Lindland and LTJG Don Peterson. No one spoke English and we didn't know

Italian. We ordered by the point and pick method with the menu. At one point during the meal, Don Lindland said, "You're part Italian; what was your mother's maiden name?" I said, "Falco." The music stopped and everyone looked my way. Later on when we asked for the check, the waiter waved his finger back and forth, shook his head and said, "Falco." Must have been one of the local "families" at one time?

The next day a new tire arrived, so we continued on to Spain. For two weeks we flew low level hops terrorizing the countryside. We flew at 50 feet up rivers, by castles and monasteries (so much for contemplative meditation that day). We had a policy that if you got behind a plane from another squadron and took a picture, he would owe you a six-pack or a bottle of booze. An A-7 squadron was known as the "Bulls" of VA-37. Boot and I were screaming along very low when all of a sudden I said, "Boot–there's a bunch of bulls back there."

Boot answered, "Let's go get 'em."

"OK." I pulled up, made a big climbing U-turn and, diving down, started to stampede a whole herd of *real* bulls down a hillside. "Oh, those bulls!" exclaimed Boot. I could just imagine the next time a matador got in the ring and, if a jet flew over, would cause the bull to go crazy. At least it would give the bull more of a fighting chance.

The ship stayed in Athens for about a month while being repaired earning the name "Saracroplis". Then of course we had guys like LT Tom "Jack" Wharton who wasn't impressed with anything foreign. All he ever wanted was a slurpee and a hot dog. He thought the beautiful Dolomite Mountains in Italy looked like a pile of rocks. He got the moniker "Jack" because he would always ask, "So what's the story, Jack?" Boot even wrote a play entitled *Smilin' Jack Wharton's Worldwide Quest for a Seven Eleven Store.*

*

The rumors the wives put out were absolutely unbelievable. They were saying, "The Mediterranean cruise will now be 11 months; we're leaving early, not leaving at all, going to Vietnam instead." About that time, a wife in another squadron left her husband for someone else in the same squadron. Later on, somebody put out a bumper sticker that read "Honk if you've ever been married to Mary Jane."

Early on during our first cruise we found an easy way to find the ship. It was usually under a big thunderstorm or we could follow the oil slick, which in some cases was the best navigation aid on the Sara. Once during bad weather in the North Atlantic, when all the Navigation Aids on the ship were down, we were told to drop down to 200 feet and follow smoke flares to the ship.

*

During our workups off Florida I took new B/N LTJG Sandy "Rat" Sanford on his first ever night flight off the ship. Sandy, weighing all of about 105 pounds soaking wet, did in fact look like a drowned rat. His slight stature belied how tough he really was. His strength contained no meanness, but it did hold a great sense of humor. He always flew with a stuffed toy rat peering out from his flight suit. Later in the cruise it was "kidnapped" by the helicopter squadron guys and held for ransom. We were airborne about 20 minutes when I started to vomit violently! In order to distract me, Rat kept calling out, "Traffic 11 o'clock high", etc. even though it was only stars. I couldn't go back and land because I had to tank the F-4s who were flying home to Oceana. I couldn't bingo to a field ashore because of low fuel. We completed the mission–tank, throw up, tank, throw up, and then headed back to the ship. I told Sandy that I'd make one pass at the ship and if we didn't get aboard, that he should eject because I kept passing out.

Back aboard ship, Father Bernard Lamond, O.S.A., the ship's Chaplain, was awakened from sleep by the noise of the planes going around. As an Augustinian priest, he taught at Villanova, so he and I had a real connection. His parents emigrated from Scotland around the turn of the century mainly because his father didn't want to be pressed into the British military. They settled on a street in Needham, Massachusetts. They loved the area; however, they were unsuccessful with bearing children. His parents noticed that their neighbors all had five or six kids. The only difference was that they were Scottish Presbyterian and all the neighbors were Catholics. So they became Catholics. Out of their six children, three became priests and one became a nun! I told Father Lamond that he'd be a Presbyterian minister if it weren't for that street of Catholics. His father died in a factory accident while his mother, who sold buttons and ribbons in a store, was pregnant with Bernard.

The planes were unable to get aboard and kept boltering because three of the four wires were broken, leaving only a single wire to catch. The Padre went up to Carrier Air Traffic Control Center (CATTC) and asked, "Who's in the A-6?"

"LT Fischer," answered the controller.

"Oh he's a good Villanova Boy. Watch this pass."

I had a good pass, trapped aboard and threw up. Sandy said, "Boy, you are something." I passed out and a Corpsman got me out of the plane. I woke up the next day and was told I had food poisoning. I could tell you it was from the "mystery meat" that was served in the wardroom. It was a blob of meat covered in thick brown gravy. Just thinking about it makes me ill to this day. Not a word of "good going" by my commanding officer.

Early on in the cruise, the good Padre told me, "Carrier ops takes gumption and builds character whether you want it to or not!"

My parents and my 17-year-old brother arrived in Jacksonville on 16 March 1972. The next day the ship sailed for a Dependents' Day cruise. This was really great being able to show those we loved what we did. On the way out we had a nice breakfast in the officer's wardroom. At the table Mom looked at me and said, "Is this ship moving side to side?"

"A bit Mom."

The whole Air Wing was launched for an air show. On our way up to Vulture's Row to watch, Captain Sanderson, the commanding officer of the ship came down the ladder. Well, of course I knew who he was, but I was just one of 5,000 men. I introduced my parents to him, and my mother said, "You make sure Alan's eating OK." *Oh, man, there goes my career!* A year later I was up on the bridge in the middle of the Tonkin Gulf at 0200 during battle stations. The Skipper turned to me and asked, "So Lieutenant, did you tell your mother you're eating OK?"

"Yes, sir, yes, sir!" I couldn't believe he remembered. Lunch was served on the way back. It really meant a lot to have my family see what I did. My pilot father didn't move a bit and was really impressed with the flight ops. Little did I know that it would be almost a year before I would see them again. About this time, there was talk of a major cut of reserve officers such as myself, in July.

CHAPTER ELEVEN

TUMBLEWEED

During our previous Mediterranean cruise, Roger Lerseth and I launched off the ship on the 0130 launch in an A-6B. Roger was the kindest person I had ever met. Mark Twain would have called him "a man equipped with a right heart." A gentle spirit, he always thought of the other guy and had a big, easy-going devious smile and a twinkle in his eyes. Rog was always up to something. Ashore in Naples, he'd pull out a phone still hooked up to a wire from under his raincoat and say, "There's a phone call for you." The Italians really had a hard time figuring this one out. He did return the phone to the Ready Room–eventually.

The A-6B was the most expensive plane in the fleet–some $24 million and carried two anti-radiation missiles (Standard Anti Radiation Missile-AGM-78) known as STARM, valued at $100,000 each. At this time the Russians were in bed with the Egyptians, supplying surface to air missiles as well as arms and aircraft. We were going to fly offshore around Alexandria, Egypt hoping to get "locked up" by a missile radar site so we could get a reading of the radar frequency with our electronic gear. We were airborne about 30 minutes when things started to go bad–real bad. First our navigation gear, then all the instruments, and finally our radios and our lights went out. Unbeknownst to us, our CNI package (Communication, Navigation, Instruments) had failed. "Loss of Communication" procedures required me to fly left hand triangles of one-minute legs. The radar controllers back at the ship would hopefully see this on their scope and launch a plane for us to join up on and lead us back to the ship.

I said to Rog, "You know that if I join up on a plane and he leads me down through the goo to the ship and I bolter or have to go around, we could fly into the water because I'll have no instruments for reference."

"If we stay up here too long we'll run out of gas," he answered. "The Skipper will really be mad if we have to jump out of such an expensive plane." Roger had the smallest of radar sweeps left on his radarscope. He picked up what he thought may be Crete. "Let's go for it."

"By the way, Roger, the lights on the runway go off at 2200. Since we can't talk to their defense people on the way in, they might get angry. Just a few weeks earlier the Greeks had shot at two German NATO planes who had failed to make the correct radio contact.

"Roger, why don't you take out your survival radio and call the ship."

"I don't know if there's one in here–I had to borrow Ron McFarland's survival vest."

"Oh great! Since Ron's from Texas, there's probably a Colt 45 beer can, barbed wire and *tumbleweed* in there."

Luckily, there was a survival radio and Roger broadcast, "We're going into Crete." We flew over Crete where I thought Souda Bay, the Hellenic Greek Air Force Base Airfield, should be. The U.S. Navy used a portion of it. It sat in a valley surrounded by high mountains. One side had Mt Lefkei Ori at 8,048, feet and the other Oros Idi at 8,056 feet. The area was totally socked in with clouds and rain. I told Roger we'd spiral down into the valley trying to stay inside the mountain ranges. But if the spiral got too big, we'd become part of the landscape. Unfortunately a few years later, fellow squadron mate and good friend LCDR Bruce Cook did in fact fly into one of these peaks.

As Rog looked out the front windscreen, he asked, "Fish did you ever see that cartoon where a pilot asks the co-pilot, 'How did that mountain goat get in this cloud'?"

"Great Rog, I needed that!"

We shook hands and headed down, down, down in the black clouds, spiraling lower and lower as unrelenting rain continued to pound us. Ten thousand feet, five thousand, two thousand feet–still in the goo. No place to go but down. At one thousand feet, the thick clouds above us made it darker still. Five hundred feet-nothing, but at two hundred feet we somehow broke out, right over the runway with the lights on! Seemed that the Officer of the Day had gone to the O'Club and forgot to turn off the lights. The landing was OK, and later that day they fixed the plane and we flew back to the ship. My mother told me years later that she had sat straight up in bed that very night out of a sound sleep.

From then on, LTJG Ron McFarland was known as *"Tumbleweed"*, and years later opened a Sports Bar in Dallas named "Tumbleweeds." I told him I should get a percentage of the proceeds!

I asked our Skipper if he heard our call. He said all they heard was, "We're going in."

"Did you launch the rescue helo?"

"No."

Unfortunately, during our next cruise, Roger's luck ran out when he was shot down and captured in North Vietnam. Surprisingly, the Skipper did tell us that we did a good job in saving the plane. He made up for it a few months later, though, when the Air Wing held the Royal Hellenic bombing derby. The ship would tow a target called a "spar" about 200 yards behind the ship; it looked like a long telephone pole. We rolled in and fired 2.75 Zuni rockets at it. My superb airmanship, eyesight, hand-eye coordination and just plain dumb luck all came together on one run. I hit and cut the cable that was attached to the spar and it sank. This gave me the win and CAG gave me the "Rocket King" trophy (a 20 mm shell on a stand). The Skipper never said a thing.

*

My good friend from AOCS, Larry Kilpatrick, was in our Air Wing flying an A-7 with VA-105 based in Jacksonville at NAS Cecil Field. He and I were both Reserve officers, which meant that after our five-year commitment we could leave the Navy because we had a reserve commission. He used to say, "You can take my wife, you can take my car, but please dear God don't take my R," as in USNR. During the workups off Florida, Larry would graciously loan me his 1964 VW Bug when the ship pulled into Port, and I'd drive down to Fort Lauderdale. Having been continually worked on, it sported a few different shades of gray and one of purple. Since it was Spring Break, there were a million college students around. More than once, a kid came up to me at a red light and offered to buy the car. I had to explain that I didn't own it. "Cool, Man." When I returned the car his wife, Jane made me dinner. I always told her how pretty she looked pregnant. She loved hot fudge sundaes but was watching her weight during her pregnancy. Years later she reminded me that anytime I showed up, Larry would let us go get ice cream sundaes!

Larry and Wendi Kilpatrick on VW Bug

CHAPTER TWELVE

WHO WAS THAT IDIOT?

One day when the squadron was back at Virginia Beach, one of our pilots decided to take his B/N and visit his hometown area of Philadelphia–with an A-6! They were going up and down the main streets so low that women were covering their children by lying on top of them to protect them. They didn't lose their Wings, but did get fined by the FAA. Years later, I ran into the pilot and he told me how he was sitting in the gate area at San Francisco International Airport, watching an airliner taxi straight into the gate in front of him. A young man started to squirm around in the chair next to him so he asked him what was wrong.

"When I was a kid in Philly, a plane was flying low up and down the street. Ever since then I'm afraid when planes come close."

Another time, the B/N's sister was interviewing someone for a job at her company. She noticed that the applicant had been in Naval Flight training. She asked him, "Why did you leave?"

"I just couldn't believe all the stories they were telling."

"Like what, for instance?"

"Oh there was one where a Navy plane was buzzing downtown Philadelphia. I knew that couldn't be true!"

Of course, to this day they disavow their adventure.

Pop actually said good-bye to my mother during World War II in much the same way. At the time, he was based at Mitchel Field on Long Island. He never forgave the Red Cross because they failed to help him get leave to see his new baby daughter before he went overseas, even though he was just sitting around. He told my mother, "I can't tell you when we're leaving but you'll know." When the time came, they got airborne and Pop asked his radio operator, young Jerry Weiss, if he could get him to the George Washington Bridge. "Sure, Skipper. My apartment is right next to it." A week earlier an Air Force General actually went to the Weiss's household to talk to him and his parents about Jerry shipping out due to the fact that his brother had been lost earlier in the war. Jerry said he would only go if he went as a part of the Fischer Crew. The crew all had such faith in Pop. From the George Washington Bridge, Pop was able to make his way over to West Paterson, New Jersey. My mother's kid sister Joan was in the seventh grade at West Paterson's Number Four grammar school. It was a three-story building next to an open field on McBride Ave. Pop flew his B-24 alongside the school, level with the windows. He thought, *what could they do to me–send me to war? I'm already going. Maybe they'd make me stay home.*

The teacher got so excited she yelled, "Everyone, get under your desk–we're being bombed!" Realizing it was a U.S. plane, she then said, "Who was that idiot?"

"That's my brother-in-law," answered Joan.

The first stop on the flight to England was Goose Bay Labrador. Years later, his engineer told me they hit so hard on landing that he thought they would bounce to England! After refueling, Pop was number seven in line for takeoff. The first six planes took off and crashed into a hill at the end of the runway, at which point they cancelled the launch. Since the crews had all trained in the South, this was the first time they had turned the heat on in the planes. It was found out that faulty heaters allowed carbon monoxide to seep into the cockpit, causing the pilots to get drowsy and pass out right after takeoff. When they resumed the launch, they still had to battle the storms of the North Atlantic, resulting in even more losses over that great ocean.

*

21 March 1972–we went back to sea for more workups. I hadn't flown in five days, so naturally I got a night hop flying the tanker. There was a 500-foot overcast with lightning and storm cells all over the place. I took great pride in flying tanker hops, which in and of itself could be very dicey, yet gratifying, by helping a few planes low on fuel. Up at altitude it wasn't bad. I'd have a schedule of how much fuel to give to a couple of F-4s. After they'd receive the required amount, I'd hear LT Al "Taco" Cisneros say, "Hey Amigo, how about 500 pounds more?" Another pilot: "Fish, how about some more for the wife and kids?" I'd always give them extra until I found myself low on fuel. When the tower told us to "hawk the deck," we would drop down to 200 feet or lower and fly a close-in circle around the ship. If they said

the plane on final was low on fuel, I'd have to position my plane so that the plane low on fuel could plug in immediately after a bolter. Many times, I'd have to put on all kinds of power to speed up to get to that spot, only to slow up enough for him to tank. In weather like that, we were trying to fly visually in bad weather conditions. I had to be in and out of the cockpit to keep from flying into the water, while trying to pick up the ship and plane visually. There was even salt spray on the windscreen.

One has to be crazy to do this for a living!

I always felt that it was nutty landing in pouring rain with one-mile visibility and 45 knots of wind. During one approach, I couldn't see anything until three-quarters of a mile, and could barely see the meatball (glideslope) in close because of the rain. Another time the deck was pitching so much that the meatball went off the top, then off the bottom, then off the top again. This caused the LSO to say, "Go for it!" which was a license to kill. I'd have to spot the deck to get aboard. Times like that I thought I should have listened to my Italian grandmother who used to tell my mother, "Alan should have a nice little job in a store, selling shoes."

*

The only change during this time was lessening the landing interval to 30 seconds in the day and 45 seconds at night. This meant we had to be super fast in getting out of the "gear" (i.e. the cable I caught with my hook). This took some doing. I had to move out of the landing zone as fast as possible to make sure I didn't cause the guy behind me to go around. I realized that I had caught a wire only after a jarring stop–in fact, if I didn't have my harness locked, I would have gone through the instrument panel. A bit stunned, I came off on the power while a flight deck crewmember gave me the "hook up" signal. As the wire was retracted, I started freewheeling backwards. At the same time, I had to bring up the flaps and slats so I could fold the wings and look for a taxi director to get me clear of the landing area. It was like trying to cross Broadway against the light in the rain at night.

One F-4 stayed in afterburner for a few seconds after trapping causing the Captain of the ship to say over the radio, "You didn't make the ship move any faster." There was never any place to run and hide. Another time a pilot launched off the CAT with his brakes on, leaving two huge black marks of rubber. The Captain said, "That didn't slow you down at all!" And no one at home had any idea what was going on–the fast pace, the danger and the pressure.

Big ship, little airport!

*

101

Back in our room, Boot and I always had a hard time hearing announcements on the ship. This was due to a huge air duct that ran up the side of our room. We called it the "rumble machine," owing to its steady and loud vibrating noise. It would drown out any announcements, especially the ones about "sweepers, sweepers, man your brooms" at 0200, which was OK with us. One time we decided to open the door to hear what they were saying. When we opened the door, there was nothing but smoke–so we got out of there! One side of our room was actually the side of the ship. When a wave hit, it sounded like a muffled explosion caused by someone hitting the side of the ship with a huge sledgehammer.

*

Unfortunately, there wasn't much of a leadership example in our squadron in the form of our Commanding Officer. Listening to him was like being in a locker room full of 12-year-old boys. I don't mean to insult 12-year-olds. During one All Officers Meeting (AOM), he said in no uncertain terms what he would like to do passionately to another pilot's beautiful wife. He'd then do this little jig, shuffling his feet and laughing with a shit-eating grin. He was, in fact, an inspiration to me–he inspired me *not* to stay in the Navy. He was only out for himself and never realized that loyalty went both ways. He'd throw his mother under a bus to get ahead. One can always judge the character of a man by the way he treats those beneath him. In the meantime, he was running scared of CAG, and some of the Lieutenant Commanders run scared of everybody. Commanders sweat making Captain, and LCDRS sweat making Commander. We Junior Officers were just trying to do our best and survive at the same time. My friend, LT Harry Thaete, used to say that we junior aviators were only interested in four things: where's my rack, where do I eat, how to get to the Ready Room, and where's my aircraft? When we got to port, Harry would always add, "How do I get off this barge?"

The CO kept reiterating that how we did during the Operational Readiness Inspection (ORI) reflected on his fitness report, which in turn reflected on ours. If it weren't for the Junior Officers, the squadron would fold. The main thing some of the Heavies (senior officers) did was make the Navy one big paper chase with all the reports and forms, etc. Turned out that it wasn't how good one was, but how good he made things look measured by the amount of paperwork. I thought it to be sheer, unadulterated nonsense. I began to feel like Groucho Marx who resigned from the Delany club of Beverly Hills, a professional group stating, "Please accept by resignation. I don't want to belong to any Club that would accept me as a member." I didn't want to belong to a group that had this commander as a leader.

We ended up number one in the ORI. Of course the CO took all the credit. We flew back to NAS Oceana, totally exhausted on 30 March 1972–the same day the North Vietnamese army invaded South Vietnam, the Easter offensive had begun. The next day, the CO called me into his office. "Lieutenant, you are the Welfare and Recreation Officer. It seems the maintenance troops have been running a donut selling operation in their shop and there is some money missing. I want you to do a non-judicial court martial investigation on yourself." I didn't even know what that meant, let alone that they were selling donuts. *I'm going to court marshal myself over donuts?! The guy can't be serious!*

*

The following day, Boot and I were flying a low-level training hop out over the ocean. We were screaming along about 20 feet above the waves when all of a sudden there was a loud explosion. Maps, dirt and broken glass swirled violently all over the cockpit. I instinctively pulled back on the throttles, popped the speed brakes and started to climb to slow the plane down. Boot had his hand on the ejection handle. It got real cold real fast. My teeth were chattering so much I could barely talk. I looked over to

A6 Convertible - it got real cold real fast!

Boot's side, and over the Intercommunication System (ICS), I said, "There's only a crack in the canopy." Boot put his hand out the side and it blew backwards in the wind stream. All that was left was a little piece of glass in the corner–the rest of the canopy was gone! Our airspeed produced a 150-knot wind to whirl around the cockpit making the plane a bit difficult to fly; however, we got the plane back in one piece. Boot's helmet had a huge crack in it where a piece of glass had hit. As usual, the Skipper didn't say a thing. He felt it was our fault.

CHAPTER THIRTEEN

DON'T ANSWER THE PHONE!

"Don't answer the phone!" I called to Sarah as she entered the kitchen to pick up the receiver. The day before, on 7 April 1972, LTJG Jerry "Moon" Mullins and I had paced back and forth in our Squadron's Ready Room. We were waiting for an "up" aircraft for a weekend boon-doggle. Our Squadron had a liberal cross-country policy that allowed us to take a plane over a weekend, enabling us to get needed flight time and additional experience. "Boot" had a picture of himself in an A-6 with the inscription: *LT Paul Wagner in government subsidized private jet.* It was our version of a company car. Jerry had agreed to fly with me on a trip to Albuquerque for a fun weekend. It was a great way to get flying time and visit a few friends–girl types–at the same time. The way I looked at it was that we were "self-employed." Taxes paid our salary and we paid taxes. The call finally came up from Maintenance. "501 ready for LT Fischer." We were out by the plane in an instant, doing a pre-flight check. I had both engines started when our plane captain found a bad hydraulic leak. Two hours later, and a lot of work and luck in finding the needed part, we were back in the plane. We started to taxi out and Jerry said, "We're on our way."

"Don't say another thing until we get there, Jerry."

Our one refueling stop was Tinker Air Force base in Oklahoma City. It was a great place for a quick turnaround. They had all the necessary equipment hooked up before you even shut down both engines. Besides, you could order a nice box lunch to eat on the next leg of flight. I tried calling Sarah but there was no answer–for all I knew, she was out on a date. We went to seventh and eighth grades together in Cedar Grove, New Jersey, and dated a few times in high school. She was now living with her younger sister, Michelle; both of them were teaching the Indians in the mountain villages. After refueling, the left engine started normally but the right wouldn't even begin to start. Jerry and I looked at each other, the same thought running through our minds. We didn't want to get stuck at Tinker. We began discussing the benefits of renting a car to drive the last 500 miles. Jerry climbed out of the plane and started hitting a few things with a screwdriver. I don't know what they taught him at "Banana School" (BNAO: Basic Naval Aviation Officer School), but it worked and the engine started.

With mountains rising up to 10,000 feet near the airport, flying into Albuquerque International Airport at night can get your attention real fast. My final approach into the runway was less than spectacular. It was a right downwind approach. Since the B/N sat on the right side of the aircraft, he totally blocked out my view of the runway. As I turned final, I decided to play "airliner" and put on all my landing lights. Since I had overshot the centerline to the far side, I had to bank far right then back to the left for correct line

107

up. My landing lights swept the tower one-way and then the other and then back. It was like someone trying to find a seat in a movie theater with a flashlight after the picture had started. The tower controller said, "Nice!" with a laugh in his voice. There was a small portion of Albuquerque airport used by the Air Force and designated Kirtland Air Force base. They sent out a "follow me" pickup truck to help me taxi to the correct parking space. We parked the plane and who got out of the truck but Sarah, all tanned in a long flowing Hawaiian dress–and barefoot! After I got out of my flight gear, she gave me a big hug and kiss. I asked her why she didn't do that when I first got out of the aircraft. She said that my torso harness of straps and buckles (which connected me to the ejection seat) looked like a big jockstrap–good enough reason for me. We climbed into her pickup and arrived at her little adobe house about 11:00 pm. Her kid sister Michelle arrived a half hour later. Sarah made a great Mexican dinner, but a little spicy–so much so that I haven't had any problems with my sinuses ever since.

The next day we all piled into Sarah's pickup and headed out. Jerry and Michelle rode up front while Sarah and her 8-month-old German Shepard, Ralph, and I rode in the camper shell. He was a puppy that had paws as big as a catcher's mitt and a heart to match. Our first stop was the corral where Sarah kept her two horses–a mare named Belle and her colt Mariah. Since Jerry grew up in Philadelphia before going to the Naval Academy, it was quite an experience. It was the closest he had been to a big animal, let alone a horse that tried to bite him. We drove up into the Sandia Mountains, visiting the Ghost towns of Cedar Crest, Madrid and Cerrillos. There was a pinkish color to their granite peaks. In Pueblo mythology, these mountains were considered sacred. In the small town of Madrid we ate at a bar where a sign read, *No dancing on Sundays.* There were Native American families living nearby. I watched as mothers, with small children clinging to their skirts, cooked outside in small adobe ovens. They were too proud to beg for aid. I looked back over their bark-covered Hogans and thought, it's really sad that they lived better 300 years ago than they do now. We continued up into the Sangre de Christo Mountains, the southernmost sub-range of the Rocky Mountains. The Spanish explorer, Antonio Valverde y Cosio in 1719, named them. The reddish hue of the snowy peaks at sunrise and sunset reminded him of the blood of Christ. Looking out over the desert, I could see as far as my eyes could physically take me. Sarah mentioned that it wouldn't surprise her to see God Himself walking out there. The view was so breathtaking that I think I did see the Almighty. Sarah is a very deep, sincere person. She loved teaching school to the Native American children in the mountains and really enjoyed life. Her genuineness and warmth were ever present.

"What's that sound?" Jerry asked as he leaned his head out of the truck window listening to a tire leaking air. It was a good thing we were near a gas station in the middle of nowhere and able to get our tire fixed. *I was beginning to wonder what else would happen that weekend.* Just before we left, on Easter Sunday, the North Vietnamese invaded South Vietnam with a full force of 20,000 troops and Russian T-54 tanks across the Demilitarized Zone (DMZ), which separated North Vietnam from South Vietnam. Known in the West as the Easter Offensive, and the Nguyen Hue Offensive by the communists of the Democratic Republic of Vietnam (North Vietnam), they also attacked the western flank of South Vietnam through Laos where they had prepositioned their forces following infiltration along the Ho Chi Minh Trail. Since they knew that we would never invade North Vietnam, they were able to muster all their forces and send them into the South. All along Highway One, the Communists intentionally shelled innocent children, women, and the very old who were trying to outrun them. Their onslaught was held off at Dong Ha by 600 ARVN (South Vietnamese) Marines and a handful of American Advisors. Marine LT COL John Ripley spent three hours under fire packing 500 pounds of explosives under the bridge that crossed the Cu Viet River and blew up the bridge. This small group stood firm against the 20,000 troops, heavy field artillery, and 200 Soviet-supplied T-54 tanks. American air power was non-existent due to bad weather and an ongoing rescue of a downed airman that took 11 days. Their orders were "hold and die" and they did both.

There were rumors in the wind concerning what ships would be deployed, including the Saratoga. No East Coast ship had gone to Vietnam in five years. We were all dressed up and ready to go dining and dancing in town. Sarah was standing in the kitchen when the phone rang. I immediately shouted from the other room, "Don't answer the phone!" I just had that certain feeling since the only ones who knew I was there was the Navy.

Without thinking, Sarah answered the phone. "It's for you, Alan."

"LT Fischer, this is Sergeant Mahan at Kirtland AFB. Your Commanding Officer called and said take off at sunrise." Jerry said my jaw dropped about four inches.

"What time is that Sergeant?"

"Zero four thirty, sir."

I called Boot back in Virginia Beach. He was eating pizza and drinking beer with "Jack" Wharton.

"Is this for real, Boot?"

"Yup. Better come back."

We all went out for a quiet dinner. Afterwards, Sarah and I went for a long walk and stayed up most of the night talking. What a strange feeling. I tried to get across to Sarah that even if I didn't make it back that I truly believed in what I was doing. It was especially rough on her because her brother Ed barely survived being machine gunned in Vietnam a year earlier. Jerry and I and the girls were out at the aircraft at 0400. During the pre-flight, we found a hydraulic leak that in normal times would have kept us there for another few days. We also had a hard time starting the right engine. Once again, after about 10 minutes of banging with a wrench, Jerry got the thing turning. Soon after takeoff, our radios failed, but we just kept going.

We landed back at NAS Oceana where there were all kinds of people running around our squadron spaces in the hangar. Personnel from all the other squadrons on the base were helping out. LCDR Jim Kennedy, our maintenance officer, pointed to an aircraft from another squadron and said that we needed "that generator, that engine," etc. and he'd get it. Our maintenance operation would have been dead without Jim Kennedy. He had been on leave with his family, camping out in the Great Smokey Mountains of North Carolina, when the recall went out. In the middle of the night a Forest Ranger came into his camp. Waking Jim, he asked, "You Kennedy?" Everyone made it back except for one Air Wing doctor who was never found before we left.

When I walked into the XO's office, he said, "Thanks for bringing the plane back; you have an hour to pack, pack for a year– we don't know where we're going and you can't tell anyone."

*

I had been living with Ken Knapp until, true to his word, he went back to Illinois to marry Stephanie. So I needed a place to stay. The problem was solved when another good friend, LT Mark Brady, went to join his squadron already on cruise in the Mediterranean. He said I could move into his apartment with his roommate Ray Sandelli. Since he was from Jersey too, we hit it off immediately. We had a good time rooming together. One day I came home with 2x4s and a piece of plywood and carried them into my bedroom.

"What are you doing, Fish?"

"I'm building a desk. I know the Navy is planning to cut back on officers around September so I want to apply to every airline in the world." I did just that, saying I would be available in October of '72.

Ray was meticulous in all he did. The apartment was spotless with everything in its place. One night I wrote down a phone number on a piece of paper and left it on the coffee table and went into my bedroom. When I came back the paper was in the garbage can. He kept his motorcycle in the living room and his corvette was so clean that one could eat off it. He bought it at Pensacola Buggy Works, which was the highest grossing Chevy dealership in the U.S. due to the sales of corvettes, aka "Ensign Mobiles." That was the problem with becoming an Officer and a Gentleman–it gave you expensive tastes. He was equally fastidious with his military bearing, always keeping his uniform crisp and neat. He was just as precise with his military duties (years later this would help him become the PR guy with the Blue Angels). I drove back to the apartment and found Ray washing his corvette. "Ray, I need a hand packing, I think I'm going to Nam." I hadn't completely unpacked my cruise box from our last cruise to the Mediterranean. Going through my drawers, I couldn't decide what to bring, especially if we ended up going to the North Atlantic. I still had my doubts that we'd end up in Vietnam. Ray looked at my

Blues and said, "Don't think you'll need that uniform or the tennis racket," and I tossed them aside. I repacked the cruise box and dropped it off at the Squadron.

I called home and told Pop that we were going off the coast for maneuvers, but if I was gone for more than two weeks that he should come down and clean out the apartment and get my car. Pop said, "You're going to Vietnam, aren't you?"

"Can't say Pop."

That night on the national news they showed the Saratoga being loaded for a year's duty in Vietnam. Some secret!

"Wait a minute, Ray I don't want to be gone for a year. I just got back!"

That evening I was on the phone saying goodbye to family and friends. Someone said, "I saw the Saratoga leave on TV, and I'm glad to see you didn't have to go."

"Wrong–I am going. We'll be flying out to the ship tomorrow."

Ray had two tickets for an Elvis concert for that Monday night. He called his date and said, "Sorry but you aren't going", and took me instead. Elvis was fantastic! Riding back to the apartment, I saw people in their cars, laughing and having a good time. I wanted to say, "Hey don't you know there's a war on? Let's pull together and win this thing." They were completely oblivious to what was going on. It was like having a disease and everyone else was enjoying good health, totally unaware and unconcerned about your situation.

Another call was to Joanie. It had been almost two years since I first met Joanie, a Navy nurse, at Friday night Happy Hour at the Dam Neck Officer's club. We had talked a bit that evening and I promised I'd call her after my return from a week at Survival Escape Resistance and Evasion (SERE) School. I knew what she was thinking, *sure another line.* I left the next morning for fun and games in Maine. When I got back, I called Joanie. "How was it, Alan?" She asked.

"Oh, it was all kinds of fun, especially the prison camp. I knew I was in America and that I was going to be released, but it was so realistic that I would have killed anyone of the guards if I had gotten my hands on him. Since we hadn't eaten the whole time I found out what it was like to be really hungry. It was sort of like breaking a leg, so I'd know what it would feel like if I did break it." Actually I knew I was better prepared if I got captured.

Joanie and I had spent a lot of time together. She and her roommates worked at the Naval Hospital in Portsmouth, VA. I'd meet her for dinner when she worked the night shift and make the rounds with her. One night she walked into the room of one of her patients and quickly swiped an unlit cigar out of his mouth with one quick move of her hand. "Give me that!"

"Yes ma'am little lady, yes ma'am little lady" he said as he sharply saluted a few times, while winking at me. I just rolled my eyes.

"Joanie, do you know who that is?"

"Yes, he's my patient."

"He's General Chesty Puller, the most highly decorated Marine of World War II and Korea!" He was known as "Chesty" not only for his bull chest but also for his fearlessness and devotion to duty. His gruff, give 'em hell attitude, was admired.

"Doesn't matter–he shouldn't be smoking."

He died in 1971, but his name still lives on among the men and women who serve. At any Marine base around the world, the close of the day is often greeted with, "Goodnight, Chesty Puller, wherever you are."

All she said was, "Alan, I'll pray for your safe return."

In our cockpits, Primary Flight and Advanced Flight training

CHAPTER FOURTEEN

DESTINATION UNKNOWN

Ever since we received word that we were shipping out, the entire normal military BS was non-existent for the time being. It was absolutely incredible how the whole base and the other squadrons gave 110% in helping us prepare to leave, while the Navy bureaucracy just plain disappeared.

The next day, 11 April 1972, I was fast asleep on the couch in the living room, since Mark had just returned from cruise and got his bedroom back. My sister Lory called at 0530 to say "goodbye" again. Years later, I would have a son born on that very day. The local Jacksonville newspaper had the headline; "Saratoga Sails-Destination Unknown".

Ray drove me out to the Squadron where Boot and I briefed for the flight to the ship, which had already left Mayport, Florida and was about one hundred miles east of Jacksonville. Ray carried my gear out to the plane and helped me strap in. It really meant a lot to me especially when he tapped me on the helmet and said, "Good luck, old buddy."

I was number two in a four plane flight. We were held on the ground for a lengthy amount of time waiting for our clearance. Since the weather was marginal with rain and clouds in the area, we had filed an IFR flight plan. Finally we were told that Washington center radar was "down." Our Flight Lead decided that we'd go VFR. Take off and rendezvous went OK, but as we headed south, the ceiling got lower and lower. The Lead then decided to climb up and through it! We started at 8,000 feet and by 15,000 feet were still "Popeye" (in the soup). He decided to do a 180 and go down below. We three wingmen could barely see him, which made it difficult to stay together. Prime conditions for a mid-air collision! Despite all this, and beyond all belief, we found the ship.

As we checked in with the ship, Pri-fly (Primary Flight control -the tower) requested the names of each pilot for the LSO. Roger Lerseth was flying with LCDR Don Lindland, by far the best pilot in the squadron with a personality to match. Roger radioed, "Lindland," but the ship wasn't receiving him well and kept stating, "Say again."

Roger replied; "Lindland. I say again, Lindland."

Frustrated, he decided to use the phonetic alphabet, which uses words to identify letters. "I spell - Lima, India, November ah D, L, A, N, D." Roger couldn't remember all of the phonetic alphabet. It was a great diversion after trying to fly wing for two and a half hours in bad weather. All planes trapped aboard with no problems. Unbeknownst to me, Paul Wagner had come aboard with two bottles of Liebfraumilch Glockenspiel wine! Good thing he had them wrapped up. We all met in the Ready Room and saw on the bulletin board a chart of Southeast Asia. Our Spooks (Air

Intelligence Officers) put it up there, along with a sign that read, "Would you believe?" I wasn't sure whether I could believe it or not.

*

My morale and that of the Air Wing was excellent with spirits high. I had joined the Navy because of the war, and felt it was the best way to help out. I believed in it and wanted to fight in it, this is exactly where I wanted to be. Even while in college I felt bad because other guys were fighting a war while I was in class–it just didn't feel right. We had grown up believing it was our duty as Americans to do our part and fight for our country. I also felt that I owed those who had already risked everything by serving in the war. It had been very frustrating to be playing war games during the Mediterranean cruise while my friends were involved in the real thing. I bet Boot a case of wine that we would get turned toward the Mediterranean before we got to Africa. This was a play on the old reverse psychology for me. For the first time ever, I felt my life was my own, and since I alone was totally responsible for myself, it gave me a great sense of being alive.

If I had only known what awaited me.

With the Air Wing aboard the ship headed 110 degrees at 22 knots, with a 15,000 mile trip around Africa ahead of us, I knew that it should take about 30 days. I was literally on the proverbial "slow boat to China." I remembered that a Latin word for *journey* meant *day*. That was in the time when a trip to anyplace took a day –this would take a lot longer.

The Captain of the ship came up on the 1MC (ship's PA), which is transmitted throughout the entire ship, to tell us that no matter where we are going we have to be back in time for an October Yard date for the ship's overhaul. I'm thinking *that's not bad.* Every few days after he finished with his official announcements, he would always mention about the October yard date. He stated once that the date was set up 15 years in advance and that it can't be changed. Now I began to wonder if he was right. The days were filled with briefs, lectures, and studies–trying to get us up to speed with "war stuff." Our first and only stop will be the Philippines around 8 May 1972. I was sure our movement had been sent by the Russian Intelligence Gathering Ship (AGI) that was sitting off Mayport.

Each day, we would go up on the flight deck and run or work out with weights in the forecastle. Two squadron mates were notably conspicuous by their absence: LT Tom "Jack" Wharton and my B/N. Boot said that he felt he was allotted just so many breaths in life, so he didn't want to waste them by working out. I still couldn't believe we were actually going to Vietnam. I really wanted to get my two cents in. I had a lot to learn! We had All Officer Meetings (AOM) in the Ready Room every day, and so many of them that someone made a patch of "100 AOMs" for our flight jacket. Some days we would have up to five hours of lectures. These included different target areas, escape and evasion, types of ordnance we would carry, as well as their defenses. North

Vietnam was heavily defended with more AAA guns than in the Ruhr Valley of Germany in World War II. Add MiGs and surface to air missiles (SAMS) and we had some big time opposition. This fact was written up in an article in Newsweek magazine in 1966, offering a detailed summary of the incredible defensive array that the North Vietnamese had assembled, thus labeling it the most heavily defended area in the history of aerial warfare–and since 1966 it had gotten worse! We were learning all kinds of new words. One such was WBLC–water-borne logistics craft. Pronounced *wiblick,* it is any small boat the bad guys use to resupply. Another topic was the many names the enemy was referred to. They were the Viet Cong (VC), Charlie, Gooks, and Gomers. Since our friend Dick "Gomer" Havenaer was from North Carolina, it caused someone to ask, "We're fighting North Carolina?"

*

We were told about the Rules of Engagement (ROE), which were absolutely ridiculous. Third country shipping was off limits even though they were carrying arms and ammunition to the enemy. MiG airfields were also off limits meaning their fighters could come up and shoot us down but we couldn't prevent them from taking off. However, the VC had attacked Tan Son Nhut Air Base near Saigon as well as Bien Hoa Air Base in south central Vietnam blowing up many planes in the process. So they could attack our air bases but we couldn't attack theirs! SAM sites were out of bounds while they were being built and manned by

Russians. You had to be shot at or somebody shot down by one before they could be attacked! This gave great advantage to the enemy. There were too many rules of engagement to make this effort viable. One pilot asked if we had to check in with Hanoi's air traffic control center before we attacked them. Handcuffed by idealistic and oblivious politicians, and Hollywood, we were forced to play by paralyzing and suffocating rules, while the Communists who didn't, laughed and took advantage. It seemed that the devil led the unbridled enemy that taunted the United States, while lives were being compromised and lost.

*

At the end of each AOM, there was a chance for anyone to make "slashing attacks or cutting remarks" when you could ping on anything or anyone. These were always good for a laugh. B/N Dick Schram even hammered himself when he made Lieutenant Commander. He showed up in the Ready Room with a bandage on his forehead. He said he had a lobotomy–that they had drilled a hole in his head, removed his brain and filled it with BS. He said it should help his career! Previously, Dick had been the announcer for the Blue Angels. While announcing the Air Show at Reading, PA, his father known as *The Flying Professor*, was killed when his plane crashed due to a mechanical problem. Dick was credited with keeping the crowd calm in the midst of this personal catastrophe. Dick was married to Sharon, an American Airlines flight attendant. On one of her flights, the Captain was Pop. On this particular trip they were riding in the crew van to the layover hotel in downtown San Francisco when Pop mentioned something about a hippie who was standing by the side of the road. Sharon said, "You sound like my husband."

"What does he do?"

"Oh, he's a B/N in an A-6 Navy Squadron." They put two and two together and realized that Dick and I were in the same squadron.

*

It was very noticeable how well everyone in the Air Wing was getting along. Even the all-important "self-investigation" court marshal into myself over the donut fund was dropped–by me–and no one noticed. So much for the "donut caper."

One day up on the catwalk, a group of enlisted troopers danced to polkas they played on a tape deck. They were quite good. Meanwhile, a group of Puerto Rican boys were really doing a job playing the bongos. The diversity among the men who stepped up to duty represented well–this melting pot that is the great country we live in. After dinner, we would adjourn to the "porch"–an area on the catwalk–and watch the sunset. I had to wonder at a few fellows who said, "Gee, when I joined up I never thought I'd be going to war–I don't think I like the idea!" *What were they thinking? This isn't a bowling team.* I mentioned that this was what we trained for and if they felt differently, they should turn in their wings. Later on a few did. I had very strong convictions as to what our job in flying for the Navy was. Besides, when we took the oath we had freely taken upon ourselves the obligations and duties involved with loyally serving our country. But actually none of us knew anything of the realities of war.

At sea, the beauty of the night heavens was absolutely inexplicable–from the way the bright white stars covered the whole sky, to the vastness of the darkened sea stretching out in all directions toward infinity. The Milky Way commanded the sky with a pathway paved with stars. Due to our southerly position, the sky looked different from what we were used to, and for the first time we saw the Southern Cross constellation. During night at sea, there was a sense of complete detachment from the earth feeling suspended in time and space. With no signs of any other ships I felt that we could be the only ones left on the planet and not even know it. One WWII writer correctly stated that a Navy ship "becomes like a planet orbiting in space–a world in and of itself." In the heavy seas, I felt like a cork bobbing around in the ocean, and knew I never ever wanted to go to sea on anything smaller than a carrier.

I'd go to the ship's library and check out books on patriotism, as well Norman Vincent Peal's book on the Power of Positive Thinking, and H. Lidell Hart's History of the Second World War. In an attempt to get into the right frame of mind and find some courage, I also read Vatican II's Writings on Waging War. It states, *"Those who are pledged to the service of their country as members of the armed forces should regard themselves as agents of security and freedom on behalf of their people. They are making a genuine contribution to peace."*

124

We UNREP'D (Underway Replenishment) from the USS Detroit each day. This involved her steaming alongside and sending over food, fuel and supplies. It was quite an evolution. She stayed with us as far as the Cape of Good Hope in South Africa, and then turned back. Every two days, we set the clocks one hour ahead, or roughly one hour per 15 degrees of latitude. Of course, it was done during the night so we kept losing an hour of sleep! Some guys figured that if you slept an extra hour a day, it would cut a year's cruise short by some two weeks.

CHAPTER FIFTEEN

A DIRE PORTENT

LT Jim Lloyd, an A-7 pilot from VA-105 out of NAS Cecil Field, was telling me how he learned about our deployment. It had been raining hard for two days so it came as no surprise late Friday night when Jim got a phone call at home from the Squadron Duty Officer. "Jim, we need you at the Squadron ASAP." Jim told his wife Ruth that he'd be back as soon as he could–that they probably wanted him to move a few airplanes because of the weather–same as he'd done before. Since Jim was the Maintenance Control Officer, he figured he and a few other Maintenance types would be all that was needed for the job. He was really surprised when he arrived at the squadron spaces in the hangar to find practically the whole squadron there. Everyone was talking in excited tones.

Jim asked, "What's going on?"

"We're not sure but the Skipper wants to talk to us. Here he is now."

"Attention on deck!"

"Take your seats, gentlemen. Well, as you all know the North Vietnamese have invaded South Vietnam full force. There are two carriers there now but they need help–and we're it! Now we have to round up the whole squadron and be ready for sea within 48 hours. Do what you must, and be back here at 0600 tomorrow. Dismissed."

Jim grabbed LT Larry Kilpatrick and LT John Cabral. "Let's go back to my place and discuss this. That way, it won't bother your kids, and it's on the way anyhow." Jim's wife knew immediately that something different was up by the look on the men's faces. They explained that they were to go to sea in a few days for extra maneuvers and that was all they knew.

"Bullhockey! You're going overseas!"

"We don't know for sure, Ruth. Only time will tell—how about some beers?"

The rest of the evening, Jim, Larry and John discussed what had to be done in their department to bring the Maintenance shop up to speed. Since they had just gotten back from the Workup, things were still in pretty good order. Jim was wondering how his parents would take the news. Only a year earlier, his brother John, who was his mirror twin, had been seriously wounded in Vietnam. John was serving with the Army's Special Forces when a sniper hit him in the back. The shock had been so powerful that the forceful blast threw him into the air where he caught up with his own blood spray. Since he was rescued right away and flown to the Hospital ship, Mercy, Jim had no inclination that he had been hurt. John said the closer to the battlefield the kinder the care. The medic on the battlefield saved his life. He'd never forget how the helo pilot braved heavy gunfire to land and rescue him and five other wounded comrades. The helo pilots were mean tough hombres, but took great care of him while they flew him to Ben Hoa airbase. At the same time, another Army pilot radioed that he was bringing in some wounded. When he landed and after they took off the wounded the ground personnel went around to thank him. When they got to the pilot's side of the helo, they noticed he was slumped over. The pilot was dead. He too had been wounded but never mentioned it. The last thing he did was save these men. This was a man who knew that *"There is no greater love than this, that a man should lay down his life for his friends."* Yet he didn't even know the guys he had saved, let alone being his friends. Wisdom of love made visible. John said the nurses at the hospital ship were like angels. Nurses in Japan were fair, but when he finally got to Letterman Hospital in San Francisco, they barely talked to him and found him as just another patient. They were terrible. John ended up getting out of the service before Jim was scheduled to leave. They both knew that they wanted to eventually be in the forest service. John had done a drawing showing his M-16 stuck in the ground with his helmet on it. Footsteps in the snow led off into the woods at the foot of a mountain. The saying underneath read, *wait Jim's not here yet.* And now he may never be.

Back at the house, Jim noticed that at times Larry was totally lost in thought. It was as if Larry knew something he couldn't tell anyone about. Larry stayed late, talking about all the possibilities with John and Jim. When he got home, his wife Jane could feel a difference in Larry. He was subdued. Larry was actually an eternity away–he was looking over to the other side with his thoughts. Larry had been very pensive, so much so that it caused Jane later to say to a friend that she felt that *perhaps he knew these were to be his last days with them forever.* He wasn't so much concerned about dying, but more about how his family, especially Wendi, would react. His love for his little 2-year-old daughter was profound. He would miss seeing her grow up. It gnawed at him, that unfathomable fear that many a combat pilot would come to know. He knew full well that he wasn't going to make it back, and yet he went. "Take care of yourself and know that I will always love you," he told Jane." Larry had a heightened awareness of everything around him; the grass and how green it was, the flowers with all the different colors. He also had an understanding or maybe a "non-understanding" of other people: *I have to go and they don't. They have a great chance of surviving – living to old age. I have a great chance of not making it back at all.*

The next morning, Jane called her parents and suggested they drive from Atlanta to see Larry off because, "You just don't know." They were very close to Larry and considered him a real "son." Larry felt the same toward them. While Larry was packing his cruise box, he started giving things away to his father-in-law telling him he wouldn't need this or that. He also asked that he keep an eye on Jane and little Wendi. Undoubtedly, he felt the hand of death on his shoulder.

John was the more focused one, so much so that it was hard to break his concentration once he had prepared to do a task. During the last at sea period, this had been a problem. At one point he was given a "wave off" and landed anyway–so intent was he on getting aboard ship. The CO came within a hair's breadth of pulling his wings. He was still in the process of debating it when all the commotion took place with this rapid deployment. All three men would meet a very violent fate.

*

18 April 1972 at 0334, we crossed the equator at 34 degrees 40 minutes West Longitude, and of course Latitude was 00 degrees 00. It began as a very hot, sun-burning day. For days, the Captain would broadcast *messages* from King Neptune (Neptunus Rex) that had been sent via "seaweed communication in Kelp code," warning us about disturbing his realm and domain with a boatload of Pollywogs (Wogs), those who had never crossed the equator. They were messages from beyond the horizon and across the seas of time. One read: *"For you must know that any craft who'd fain cross the Great Sea Lord's Special Domain, must pay the tribute that King Neptune wishes, and be received by mermaids, bears and fishes. We will see you on the morn, and any who resist will wish he had not been born."* The time-honored traditions of "crossing the line" have always been around, passed from the Vikings to the Anglo Saxons and Normans. Early on it was used to weed out the weak members of the crew. Now it is a big party for the crew. Those who had previously "crossed the line" were called "Shellbacks" and were in charge of the action. Neptunus Rex, with his personal emissary Davy Jones, arrived with Queen Amphitrite

among sailors fully dressed in their part as pirates. A "Jolly Roger" pirate flag flew from the mast.

The "ceremonies" consisted of crawling on our hands and knees on the flight deck. We were not allowed to look up at the Shellbacks who were running the show. All we could see were their legs walking alongside us. They were using a flat piece of a thick fire hose to help us move along by hitting us in the backside. Talking to one pair of legs, Bruce Cook asked, "You Kennedy?" referring to the words used by the Forest Ranger to find our Maintenance Officer Jim Kennedy. *Whack! Ouch!* Yes it was Jim.

We were smeared with all kinds of rubbish while a combo lunch was shoved in our mouth. After kissing the greased belly of a 250 pound black chief dressed in a big diaper as Baby Huey, we got to crawl through a tunnel of garbage and then dive into a canvas pool of trash. Next was a "chunky haircut" and a great hosing off from the fire truck. All in all, it was great fun and a proud moment in becoming a member of the Ancient Order of Shellbacks.

*

We were currently 0400 degrees South and 38 degrees West. I wished the heck we'd get there, but it would probably be over before long. I wanted to do some damage up in North Vietnam. *Such naïve bravado!* This sentiment went back through all the wars. I recalled reading that when one Union regiment received orders to join the fight in the Civil War, the men rushed around celebrating like a bunch of schoolboys let out early from school. That all changed when the first rifles and cannons were fired. I found that to be very true.

22 April 1972–24.42 South 02.52 West. I called the Navigation (Nav) Shack for our position to keep track of our progress on a map I had. Many times I was told, "this satellite stuff isn't working–call the bridge–they're shooting the sun–they'll give you a more precise location." And they did. I got three shots today, including the Black Plague vaccine. My arms really hurt, and a little later I almost passed out. I felt terrible. I lost another hour's sleep during the night. That combined with the shots and going from winter to summer to winter to summer, and my system is screaming, "What's the story Jack?"

23 April 1972–29.06 South 04.50 West–about 1800 miles south of the Equator. Overcast, cool, fall-like weather. It reminded me of going to high school football games and Sunday rides with the folks. That was our entertainment as kids. We'd drive up to the country, looking at the trees in their autumn colors. We'd hike in the woods behind Pop's childhood farm in Camp Gaw, New Jersey that was named after the camp of Indian Chief Gaw. He told us how there actually had been a Lenni Lenape Indian family living on their property until one day they were just gone perhaps to the deep woods of Pennsylvania. We did find some arrowheads in the area they camped. Pop would bend over a young birch tree so we could climb on it. We'd hang on as Pop let it go–it was a good ride. Later in the day we'd stop at Verducci's in Singac. It was a bakery in an Italian residential area. Mom would buy an almond

coffee cake and a long loaf of Italian bread. She'd slice the bread, put butter on it and toast it in the oven. That comprised our dinner. The coffee cake was the dessert. Since we didn't have a TV, my sister and I would lie on the floor in front of the radio listening to *The Lone Ranger, The Shadow and Sergeant Preston of the Yukon.* It really built up our imaginations and I learned that the good guys always won.

*

We're about halfway there, and I was amazed that we hadn't seen any other ships other than the Detroit. During one AOM, we were handed a small booklet by the Medical Department of the Saratoga. It started out with the words "Make up your mind that you will live through it." Part of the procedure for wounds said, "Maggots will clean the wound (eats only dead flesh). Do not cover if maggots present."

25 April 1972–we rounded the Cape of Good Hope and were able to see South Africa and her hills some 15 miles away. It was a real choke point with lots of shipping, including two Russian AGIs and a submarine. This was most of what I had seen so far. The ship pitched and rolled with continuous thirty-foot swells. The USS Detroit turned and headed for home. The next day we were at 35.39 South 25.18 East–approaching the Indian Ocean where the water had become an emerald green. I found out that day that combat pay was a whopping $115 a month. I wondered how much that was a mission. Probably won't get that many missions in anyway. Guess again!

CHAPTER SIXTEEN

IT ALL FIT TOGETHER

I always have agreed one hundred percent with the war. I didn't see any difference between the way the Communists took over Eastern Europe and now the current attempt to take over Southeast Asia. In fact, I had a great contempt for any regime that oppressed people and had a rule-by-terror government. They destroyed all religion as well as the family unit and the rights of the individual. I loathed Communism. I knew that great cruelties were perpetrated by godless communism and that it had an infinite capacity for evil. As early as 1919 Winston Churchill warned about Communism. "A ghoul" he called it. "It descends from piles of skulls." He also stated, "It is not a creed; it is a pestilence." In 1927 humorist Will Rogers wrote, "It seems the whole idea of Communism, or whatever they call it, is based on propaganda and blood."

I never liked the way they overpowered the little guy, plus I felt I had a score or two to settle for my friends who were lost in Vietnam. Unknowingly at first, I grew up with this great hatred of Communism. In first grade I had a classmate, Angelica from Lithuania. Her parents told us how she had to hide under the floorboards of their car as they escaped the Russians who flooded the tunnel just after they drove through. My eighth grade teacher, Mr. Bob Davies, read us James Michener's *The Bridge at Andau.*

The story told of a bridge the people tried to escape over from the Russians while attempting to get out of Hungary in 1956. Young boys with grenades ran into Russian tanks, trying to stop them. My friend Gabor Menyhart's dad was one of those freedom fighters. They so wanted help from America—it never came. In college I had classmates from Cuba. Their dads had been very successful doctors, airline pilots, and architects. Castro took their homes and their jobs before they were able to escape. In 1968 the people of Prague held off the Russians in their quest for freedom. The last radio call from Prague was "Help, Help, Help! But there was no help from America or anyone else in the free world. Today the locals there will point out a statue of the Russian soldiers and explain, "This represents the Russians liberating us from the Nazis. Then they came back a few years later and liberated us from *liberty*." In South Vietnam, the Viet Cong is the military front for the Communist National *Liberation* army. How does their idea of *liberty/liberation* resemble anything near the truth? They had totally destabilized the very words "liberation and liberty." Once again 'bad guys' liberated freedom and replaced it with cruel oppression. They weren't interested in liberating anyone; they just wanted to take over another country.

On January 31, 1968 the VC Guerillas as well as North Vietnamese regulars had attacked areas in South Vietnam in violation of the Tet Lunar New Year Truce. Even though it was an enormous defeat for the VC, it was portrayed by the U.S. media as a loss for America. After the 1968 Tet offensive Newscaster

Walter Cronkite got on TV and said, "This is a war that can't be won." So the North Vietnamese pulled back their peace feelers they had in place with the British Embassy in Hong Kong. This, even considering that they had gotten decimated in the Tet offensive and that the hoped-for rise-up of the South Vietnamese people against the Americans didn't occur. The antiwar movement was critical to Hanoi's victory. The Western media wrongly portrayed the offensive as a U.S. defeat and never corrected it. They and the politicians harmed us greatly. No one had the big picture as far as Communist expansion went. They just didn't get it or perhaps they didn't care? The protestors simply ignored the sacrifices made by fellow Americans.

Of course there are always those who ask, "Why fight for a country that can't fight for itself? We helped England and France in both World War I and II because they couldn't continue to stand-alone. The same could be said of helping South Korea to survive. It was honorable intervention against communist aggression that was giving the South Vietnamese a window of freedom. There were valid reasons to help South Vietnam with the moral objective of saving people who needed help. The purpose was to help South Vietnam remain independent. We also were members of Southeast Asia Treaty Organization (SEATO), an alliance to contain any communist aggression in the free territories of Southeast Asia in general that put South Vietnam under its protection. There were many valid reasons for us to try and help this new democracy.

Marine Brigadier General Paul Kelly (also a Villanova graduate) later said, "We went there (Vietnam), I think in a good conscience. Certainly in a military way in good conscience." "To those who say the Vietnam War was an internal civil war," the General said, "it was never that. It was an invasion of the South by the Communists of the North," he said. "It was violation of the constitutional rights of the people of South Vietnam. They asked the United States for assistance. Although many of us seemed oblivious to our impending sacrifices, we still went to maintain freedom for people we had never even met." Aviation pioneer Gil Robb Wilson summed it up best when he said: *"He who dedicates himself to a great ideal, himself becomes great—not by his own effort, but in the light of the thing for which he stands."*

Also over the years there were daily accounts and TV news footage of those trying to get over, under or through the Berlin Wall, people who were shot down by gunfire and left there to die. They only wanted to escape communism and be free.

When the Berlin Wall finally came tumbling down in 1989, B/N Paul Wagner wrote:

The Falling Wall
They split a town
With steel and stone
To shoot men down
Who climbed toward home.

They built the miles (in 1961)
So high and wide
That Lenin laughed
And Goethe cried

But walls of stone
Can never grow.
They have no bone,
No life to show.

A wall is dead,
Not like a tree
Whose limbs can spread
So high and free.

When walls fall down (in 1989)
And trees rise,
The world looks up
With joyful eyes…

Paul said that the fall of the Berlin Wall, without a shot fired, was nothing short of Divine intervention when it took over 60 million lives to stop Hitler. President Reagan together with Margaret Thatcher and Pope John Paul II had done a great job. Even someone with a superficial knowledge of history could see that an evil empire had imploded. It was noted in 2017 that in the hundred years that communism existed 100 million people died because of that perverse ideology.

Thomas Paine remarked, "Where freedom is not, there is my country." Add St. Augustine who said, "War is God's answer to a neighbor threatened by force," and for me it all fit together.

At night it was amazing to look straight *out* and not *up* to see the Big Dipper. The water had become a turquoise green. Rain showers popped up often and every now and then small boats and coconuts floated by. Some native actually paddled by in an outrigger canoe! The color of the sky and the water, along with towering pure white cloud buildups rising up from the cobalt sea was actually awe inspiring. Together with unbelievable sunsets it begged the question, *how, with such magnificence of the Lord, could there be a war on?* Such incongruity.

The Boot - the best!

CHAPTER SEVENTEEN

SHIPMATES

Still underway at 34.30 South 45.10 East, the days were becoming warmer as we headed back up to the equator. At night the water reflected the full moon. It would have been a very romantic night if it weren't for the five thousand guys I was with. A favorite sidelight was timing flying fish that leaped out of the water from the side of the ship to see how long they stayed "airborne." The record was 32 seconds. Sometimes we'd take in some sun on the flight deck commonly referred to as "steel beach." Since it was Sunday a Holiday routine was declared which only meant more inoculations–some hell of a holiday! I got to listen to some real "down home" music down in the hangar bay. Six of the troopers were playing and singing country western music. They had two guitars, a banjo, a fiddle and a Hawaiian guitar. Each one took a turn singing. This went on for four very enjoyable hours. At 2400, we became part of what I considered the *"real"* Navy–the storied Seventh Fleet!

*

Living in such close quarters was a real lesson about patience, tolerance and understanding. My collateral duties in the squadron made me the Power Plants Branch Officer, which put me in charge of the Aircraft Engine Maintenance shop. The shop had twenty men from varied backgrounds who worked on the engines. There was a Puerto Rican kid from New York who believed that anything north of 184th street in Manhattan was upstate New York, a backwoodsman from Kentucky, and a college grad from Ohio. One of the boys in my shop owned the Red Barron bar in Virginia Beach and had a brother who was captured with the U.S.S. Pueblo. He said that when his brother was caught making a fire to keep warm, the communists made him stand in a block of ice, barefooted, until he melted all the way through it. Then when he was released he was asked if a friend of North Korea could visit him in America! One sailor from Nebraska told me that his grandmother had won the "skillet toss" contest as well as the "hog and husband calling" contest during the "Days of Swine and Roses" at the county fair. I also had a sailor from Louisiana. A tall lanky easygoing guy, he explained how his father would plant the farm by the position of the moon, the stars and the planets. The shop was a real cross section of America.

The Chief who ran my shop was a good ol' boy from Georgia, which meant I couldn't understand him and he couldn't understand me. He told me, "Don't worry sir, I'll take of everything" and he did. There was truth in the axiom that the Chiefs run the Navy. I always liked what was written about rank:

Lieutenant:

Is run over by locomotives

Can sometimes handle gun without inflicting self-injury
Makes high marks when trying to leap building
Dog paddles
Talks to animals.

Chief Petty Officer:
Lifts buildings and walks under them
Kicks locomotives off their tracks
Catches speeding bullets and chews them up
Freezes water with a single glance
He is God.

My Chief was always chewing on an unlit half-smoked cigar and reminded me of the old Navy Chiefs in WWII movies. One afternoon we were leaning over the catwalk in the middle of the Indian Ocean and I mentioned, "Boy, Chief, there's a lot of water out there."

Taking his cigar out of his mouth he said, "Yes, sir and that's just the top of it."

One A-6 had *LT Al Fischer* painted along the canopy rail. The troops from my aircraft power plants shop had painted, "Big Al" under it. They wore green turtle neck shirts that said "VA-75 power plants" on the front and "Big Al's Boys" on the back. The hatch going into the shop read "Big Al's Shop." I told them it was insubordination–and that I loved it! But my CO was very jealous of it. They also had painted on the hatch a sign saying, *if we can't fix it, it ain't busted.*

I'm still gung-ho over going to war hoping we'd get there in time–what was I thinking?

*

Now, as news reached us of the many successes of the North Vietnamese, we began to wonder if we would make it in time to do any good. The peaceniks and the politicians like Senators William Fulbright and Ted Kennedy were selling out another country to the Communists

That night at 2400 when we entered the Sunda straits between Sumatra and Java, the Captain mentioned we might want to go up to the flight deck. We were passing to the south of the volcano Krakatau. When it erupted in 1883 with such force (200 million kilotons); it produced brown sunsets around the world. The release of the gas and dust into the atmosphere disrupted cloud cover and global weather patterns for years. Since the visibility was fantastic we could make out red lava coming out of this big mountain. It was the first land we had seen in two weeks.

The next day I was on the Flight Deck with Chaplain Father Robert Witt. I asked him "so Padre when you were 'in country' did you sleep with one eye open?"

"I used to sleep with BOTH eyes open." He went on to say, "This war isn't going to end until they bring the B-52s up North, all they understand is brute force. The only way to talk to a Communist is with one foot on his throat. You can't negotiate with

143

evil." When I asked him for his blessing he said, "It's not Robert's blessing, it's the Lord's" (I was still learning about my religion) and blessed me.

*

3 May 1972–still steaming at 12.09 South 96.00 East–a hot, sticky day. We got two shots of 2 1/2ccs each of Gamma goblin that is supposed to build up your system's resistance. Unfortunately, the huge needles also build up a big egg on your backside. Some guys had snuck on beer when we left. During the night some of them decided to have a "dumpex" where they would throw a few bags of empty beer cans off the front side of the ship. Just as they did so a gust of wind caught the bags and blew them into the open hangar bay doors causing the bags to split open when they hit the deck. It was quite a sight to see a bunch of officers in shorts and flip flops trying to pick up the cans that were making a racket rattling around on the hangar bay's steel deck.

Around this time the Commanding officer of the ship announced that the 5-inch guns would be "exercised" i.e. test-fired, "just in case we have to fight the ship." A floating target was placed in the distance and when the guns opened up, it sounded like a freight train going through the sky. There were more misses than hits, and I was hoping the ship didn't have to fight to defend itself! On an earlier cruise, a ship fired at an airborne target that was being towed by an airplane but the bursts were going off around the plane instead of the target. Right before the pilot jettisoned the target, he radioed something to the effect that he was "pulling the target not pushing it."

*

The ship was ordered to go directly to Subic Bay with no Singapore stop. Having burned most of our fuel it made us so light that we were riding high in the water making the ship top-heavy causing her to roll more. They were taking fuel out of the planes to burn in the boilers. The ship received a message from Admiral Thomas Walker, Commander of the Naval Air of the Pacific Fleet (COMNAVAIRPAC)–"Good luck and good hunting." I was proud to join the ranks of other family members who had served our country in time of war. Pop's Uncle Bill was a doughboy in WWI. Grandfather Falco lied about his age in WWI, being too young, and again in WWII, as he was too old. A wireless operator in the merchant marine, "Sparks," actually was on the ship that landed his son Alphonse (my Uncle Sonny) on D-Day. Uncle Sonny was exempt from the draft because of a football related injury to his knees. He still wanted to do his part and enlisted in the Army Air Corps anyway. Although he was an office Clerk, they gave him a gun on D-Day and said, "Go!" He spent the first three months of the War in a foxhole in France. After landing the troops on D-Day, my Grandfather's job was to pick up the bodies of the men lost–my mother said that he was never the same after that.

All of my uncles on both sides of the family served, and of course Pop flew B-24 missions over Germany. Something like 12 family members had served during wartime. Growing up, I knew

145

of only two men who didn't serve in WWII. Mr. Wayne was born with no toes on one foot, and my Uncle Eugene lost his hand working in a defense factory at age eighteen. He had already signed up for the Marines.

I didn't need John Wayne movies for inspiration. I had grown up with evidence of service and heroism all around. Mr. Byce had lost a leg in the Battle of the Bulge when a German round went right down the barrel of his tank—Pat Buttram who was Gene Audrey's sidekick in the movies saved him. Mr. Knox and Mr. Dilley both had been wounded. Mr. Ruggerio lost his leg as a 17-year-old tailgunner in a B-17. Mr. Byers fought in Italy. All were wonderful men and great role models. The ones who had served in the Pacific refused to ever buy anything made in Japan. One gentleman refused to eat rice because "it was Jap food." Even with their lingering injuries, they would help my dad literally dig out a farmer's field each year to be used for our Little League games. I believe my love of country and the importance of serving my country was inculcated at an early age from just being around these men, especially Dad.

Years later, I heard of a few men who had had enjoyed draft deferred jobs. Of course if they wanted to they could still have signed up. This allowed them to stay behind with the women and children and live a life without fear or danger while safely earning good money. In the last analysis they could go home at night to a BBQ, a beer and play with their kids. Pop also had a

146

draft-deferred job building aircraft engines at the Curtiss Wright factory, but this didn't prevent him from volunteering.

*

We had the "Minor Olympics of CVA-60" and the Captain's Cup. I took third place with 80 push-ups in one and a half minutes. I lost to two little Marines who weren't going all the way down. Our CO didn't say a word about my effort. We had a good relay team with two of our young sailors really moving out and we took first. Again the CO didn't say a thing.

Of course, we made up some of our own "competitions." For example we had the "kick-ass and take names later" event featuring B/N LTJG Paul "Vids" Hvidding. He was a fair-skinned blond haired guy who looked like a mild-mannered 18-year-old who didn't even shave. Even with such a gentle nature, he would go on to fly the most demanding missions. A former college football player in the squadron didn't match up to him. The English pronunciation of his Norwegian name is Vidding with the H silent. His wife was expecting at the time. He said if she had a boy they'd call him Victor with an H.

7 May 1972–we were about five hundred miles out of Cubi. The USS Sellers came out from the Philippines for UNREP giving us much needed fuel. During the night, our fighters went to 30 minute alert since the Chinese had gone on the alert.

8 May 1972–After 28 long days we arrived at Subic Bay, Republic of the Philippines. It was on fabled Luzon Island. I asked

my Chief if the small gunboats in the harbor were there on maneuvers. "No, sir, they're there for the pirates."

"Pirates, as in arrgh?"

"Yes, sir!" I could barely believe it. In fact a few months later pirates did land on Grande Island seizing the local resort and robbing the vacationers!

Subic Bay was a beautiful setting with tall, jagged, jungle-covered mountains completely surrounding it. It was right out of a South Seas movie. We docked on the NAS Cubi Point side of the Bay that had a runway parallel to the dock. Locals on the pier welcomed us with their native dance called Tinkiling.

The soaring heat and intense humidity would be the drill for the rest of the cruise. If you were walking along and one raindrop fell–it was too late to look for cover. The torrential downpours of the Monsoons and Typhoons would soak you through and through. As it turned out the 1972 Pacific Typhoon season had no official bounds. It rained year round. Typhoon is a corruption of the Chinese *t'ai-fun*, or *great wind*. Some gusts rose to 115 mph. And we were right in the middle of it!

The Hancock was in port as well, leaving the carriers Kitty Hawk, Midway, Coral Sea and Constellation still *on the line* in combat. I wished we were there. Man, was I naive!

CHAPTER EIGHTEEN

JUNGLE TRAINING and REUNIONS

The Cubi Point Officers' Club sat high on the side of a hill with a beautiful view of the bay and the surrounding mountains. Dinner was excellent and cheap. The surroundings were plain and simple a tropical paradise. With such contradictions it *was still hard to believe there was a war on.*

The Officers' club was divided into split level two floors. The upper part had a beautiful, highly polished Koa wood bar. The wall was lined with plaques of the squadrons and ships that had passed through over the years. A wide staircase with ten deep steps went down into the formal dining area. Drinks were ten cents, but during Happy Hour they dropped to five cents so the fun began early! Guys would come in and order a hundred drinks at a time. The CO of a squadron would pay for the glasses ahead of time.

On the upper level, tables would be lined up in a row and wet down with beer. To simulate catching a wire someone would take a running start, dive and slide on his stomach along the table, trying to catch with his mouth a rolled up table cloth held by two guys on the other end. Another bold, dumb soul, buoyed with liquid courage, would sit on the table top in a chair that had coasters or wheels. Buddies on both sides would place a towel behind the chair for power. A "catapult officer" would give the signal to launch. The chair and its pilot would be flung along the table into the air over the stairs and into the dining room below with the hopeless, impossible idea of landing straight up on all four wheels. Besides interrupting diners, guys would end up with broken arms, legs or worse. This precipitated the building of the Catapult (CAT) room.

The CAT room was a cement walled bunker out back and below the O'Club where nothing, except maybe one's reputation, could be broken. For $1.00 you could ride the "slide for life." A pneumatic charge fired a small cockpit built from a banged up refueling tank. There was enough power to propel the cockpit to 15 mph in the first two feet with the same G forces as the World War II hydraulic catapults. You got one chance to drop the hook and catch the only wire. When you missed, you ended up in a pool of water 3 ½' deep. If you managed to do it, you got a bottle of champagne and your name on the Wall of Fame. One who did was NFL Quarterback Johnny Unitas when he was there on a USO tour. As the night wore on and drinks flowed, more and more people would show up. Finally the local American teachers would try it just wearing their underwear.

*

On a very hot day on 9 May 1972 at 0630, we left for Jungle Environmental Survival School (JEST). In spite of my initial trepidation, it turned out to be a fantastic experience. Since the trees in the jungle in Vietnam are triple canopies high you had to learn to lower yourself down in case you landed on the top of

150

one. It required us to rappel from a tower set on the upper edge of a deep ravine. We were showed how to take a long flat rope (that was carried in the survival portion of the aircraft's seat pan) and run it through a D-ring that was attached to a clip on your torso harness. You held the rope up with one hand and when you lowered your hand, you slid down the rope. The first time took some prodding from the instructor—actually more like a push. After the first time, we ran back up the hill to do it again!

We then went into the jungle with the Negritos, or "little black people," which was what the Spanish called the short black people they saw in Southeast Asia. The men were barely five feet tall. I had read that they were ancient people who were the very first to come to S.E. Asia. The Malaysians even called them the *"orang asli"*–the original people–who came with the first wave of people to leave Africa. Their fathers were headhunters and they loved Americans. Unfortunately, these original aborigine Filipinos were scorned and treated just like the American Indians. These guys were the guerilla fighters of WWII and still had their original call signs. Our guide was "Sharon," who was all of four feet six inches tall, wiry and tough, a great little guy. When a Japanese patrol would go into the jungle, the Negritos would sneak in and slit the throat of every other Jap as they slept. After a while there were no more patrols. The only weapon they carried was a foot long machete like Bolo knife. The handle came from the horn of a caraboa (domestic water buffalo considered the national animal of the Philippines) and the blade was made from the steel spring of a jeep that was so sharp it had to be carried in a wooden sheath. It could cut right through bamboo and they were very adept at throwing it. When we finished, "Sharon" gave me his Bolo knife with his initials engraved in the blade

*

The Skipper told me to throw a party for the squadron on the beach. As always, my Chief said, "Don't worry, sir; I'll take care of it." That was the same thing he told me when I was put in charge of the Christmas party back at Oceana! We had held it at the Enlisted men's club on the base. It was co-ed with wives and girlfriends invited. Part way through the night, an upturned hat went by me with money in it.

"What's that for, Chief?"

"It's for the go-go dancer, sir."

"A what?–You can't have a go-go dancer at a Christmas party–that's sacrilegious!" Next thing I saw was a girl in a tan raincoat being hustled through the crowd. All of a sudden she was up on stage dancing her heart out. I had to admit that her little red and white fluffy Christmas bikini outfit was done in good taste. The Skipper ended up on stage dancing with her. *Man I dodged that bullet!* This time the Chief told me just to show up on the beach the following day. I got there just as he pulled up in a jeep with a big piece of machinery in the back.

"What's that, Chief?"

"A portable generator, sir. We can make frozen Daiquiris right here on the beach."

"Where did you get it?"

"Don't worry, sir, the Marines will never miss it."

"By the way, nice jeep–where did you get that?"

"Don't worry sir, the Admiral's not back until Tuesday."

Oh great!

*

10 May 1972–We put out to sea to get in some flying. It was 95 degrees and very humid. It really was the tropics. Sweat soaked right through my flight suit and canvas gear as well as my rubber oxygen mask as I sat in the cockpit with the canopy closed. The heat was stifling.

We launched off the ship and did a sightseeing tour of Luzon, which included flying over Corregidor with its rich, sad, violent past. I thought of the brave men from another time who were at Corregidor and Bataan, places that had such miserable, brutal histories. I can't even imagine how rough the fighting was followed by years in prison with all the unbelievable brutality. There were some 72,000 Filipinos and Americans on the Bataan Death March, but only about 7,500 survived! Of the 12,000 Americans, only 1,500 made it home. The mountains were covered with thick jungles that went right up to a lake formed by a volcano. We recovered back at Cubi Point NAS so we could fly each day before heading into combat.

*

Back at the O' Club I ran into Jim Higgins, a classmate of mine from Villanova who was flying A4s off the Hancock. This was just the beginning of running into old friends. There were a lot of good guys out here. My friend Jim Kiffer from the Vigi squadron ran into his best friend from High School and then his college roommate. He told them "we're either all going home together or we're all going to die." The next day I ran into an instructor from my AOCS days, LT Bud Morris who was an F-4 RIO (backseater) on the Constellation. He said he was in a real quandary. He had called his wife from Japan, telling her that the ship was on the way back home and not to worry. When the North Vietnamese invaded South Vietnam, they were sent back into combat. Hangar bay three was completely loaded with motorcycles that the guys bought in Japan. When they pulled out they were all pushed over the side. Back on the line, Bud had shot down a MiG and he was wondering how he could explain this to his wife. He said that Chicoms (Chinese communists) and North Koreans flew some of the MiGs and that they knew our pilots and which ones were having marital problems. Turns out they had a good spy network in the U.S.

Down the bar was LT Kevin Moore, a high school classmate from St. Benedicts Prep in Newark, N.J. It was like old home week. A few weeks before, flying off the Coral Sea, he barely made it out of his F-4 that had had a major mechanical problem. The plane was violently thrown into a spin. Navy guidelines were such that if an aircraft is uncontrollable at 10,000 feet, it becomes government property and you leave it. Kevin was barely able to punch out at 6,000 feet! The next few times he got airborne he was jumpy to say the least; however the following week he bagged a MiG-17 in a rough dogfight over North Vietnam. Another crew in his squadron had been the wingman of the same pilot when they got their MiG. Now everyone wanted to fly as this guy's wingman. Although they were glad they got a MiG they actually felt bad because they didn't see a chute. Kevin and I talked about our high school days and some of the guys. One classmate didn't know what he wanted to do after high school so his parents sent him to Columbia University to take a weeklong battery of tests. When the results came back the instructor said, "You should be a hippie." And he did! Kevin reminded me that some guys in our class had the record for the most time in detention or Justice Under God (JUG). In fact, at our senior assembly the class rock band played and sang a song "Why must I be a teenager in JUG?" to the tune of "Why must I be a teenager in love?" by Dion and the Belmonts. We both knew that classmates Mark Judge, Bill Meister and Ed Brady had been killed in action in South Vietnam. Mark was trying to rescue a "lost battalion" when they were ambushed. Ed was only a few days away from meeting his wife in Hawaii for R&R when he stepped on a mine. Bill was lost fighting as a helo door gunner, while trying to save wounded troops. Kevin said that schoolmate George Cooker, who had been shot down in 1966 and listed as MIA for some four years, was now officially declared a POW. We realized about 15 classmates were over here. They were living up to a few lines from our school's

Alma Mater; *Our loyal hearts to thee we bring.... for God, for country, and for thee."*

CDR Mickey Mefort, XO of RVAH-1, was at the bar having a contest with a Marine pilot, drinking "flaming hookers." This was basically a glass of brandy on fire. The idea was to quickly take a drink and put the glass down with the flame still glowing. Mickey took a drink and put the glass down still on fire. The Marine matched him and slammed down his glass with a guttural "harrumph!" Mickey picked up his glass . . . and *ate it!* He won. Mickey started his career as a Blimp pilot, which allowed him to wear only half a wing on his uniform. He said one time it took him three days to go from Lakehurst, New Jersey to Philadelphia because of the high wind–a distance of some 50 miles. Now he was flying an A-5 that went 1,200 miles per hour!

*

The Coral Sea pulled in–old number 43 was built in 1946 and had three MiGs painted on the side, which represented what her fighter planes had accomplished. I wished we'd get to the war zone soon! Such a fool! What false illusions! I should have known better what to wish for. And more 5cc gamma goblins shots for me! Once again those BIG needles produced BIG bumps on the ol' backside.

Worst of all was when a plane, usually an A-6, just "disappeared", never coming back from a solo night low-level mission. There were no planes escorting the A-6–you were all alone. No one saw you "go in." Sure enough, about this time, word came through that Marine Captain Dave Leet and his B/N were lost. Dave and I had been in Meridian together. He was a gentle, easygoing farm boy from Wisconsin. His wife Cathy was as pleasant as she was cute. He was flying an EA-6A out of DaNang. He had set up an orbit off the coast of North Vietnam with his electronic counter measure plane to jam the enemy radar. He checked in at 0415 as "RM08" but was never heard from again. He was a real good guy.

We heard that the Air Force dropped the Than Hoa Bridge. It spanned the *Song Ma* River and connected rail shipment points from China to Vietnam. Thirty-five planes were lost over the years trying to destroy it. Known as the dragon jaw or *Ham Rang,* the Vietnamese said this was the bridge that held the world together and that after it fell, the war would end. *Better not end before I get there!* More dumb thoughts!

Manning up

CHAPTER NINETEEN

ON THE LINE

18 May 1972–Sailing off South Vietnam, Dixie Station, in the South China Sea–on the Line (Combat Ops) for the first time. Only the senior officers went over the beach into MR IV (Military Region 4). Flying close air support they worked with a FAC (Forward Air Controller) hitting troop concentrations whose location was discovered by the FAC. I flew a tanker giving fuel to two F-4s that were low on gas. I was able to see land and could actually see some fighting on the ground. I also heard Vietnamese gibberish on the radio, "Yankee, Saratoga," as well as a warning of MiGs being launched out of Hanoi.

Earlier, we had been briefed on the more sophisticated and accurate SA-4 and SA-7 missiles, which the gooks now had–all compliments of the Russians. The Russians later acknowledged that they had deployed over 17,000 missile technicians and operators/instructors in 1965 while North Vietnamese missilemen spent six to nine months of training in the Soviet Union. They supplied approximately 7,658 SAMs to North Vietnam. From 1965 through 1966 nearly all of the 48 U.S. Aircraft shot down by SAMs were downed by Soviet missilemen. North Vietnam also received large amounts of military aid from Cuba, China and North

Korea. As usual the Russians were using a surrogate country to fight their battles since they knew they couldn't take us head on. Basically they were making the "cold war" hot. Even the South American communist terrorist Che Guevara stated, "He wanted to create 'two or three Vietnams'." In 1962, the Chinese started supplying North Vietnam with military supplies as well as anti-aircraft crews and engineers to repair damage done by American aircraft. Eventually, over 320,000 Chinese troops served in North Vietnam. Just another case of a Communist onslaught to take over a small country.

The Viet Cong would use a downed pilot as a decoy, set up a flak trap, shoot down the Search and Rescue (SAR) aircraft and then go in and kill the pilot. I felt no need to rush home when there was a job to do there first. I had no qualms or hang-ups about bombing the communists–I'd stop bombing if they if they'd stop fighting–but I knew they wouldn't.

*

5 May 1972–We flew our first close air support combat hop with the XO (CDR Earnest) and LT Bob "Trol" Tolhurst going into MR IV about 300 miles distance from the ship with fourteen 500 pound bombs (Mark 82s or MK82s) each. When we checked in with the Forward Air Controller (FAC) we told him we were three A-6s with 42 MK82s, our playtime (time we could stay around) was 45 minutes and we could drop two bombs a run. The FAC *politely* threw off any F-4s he was using since they didn't have much of a bomb load and weren't too proficient (or fond of)

doing the "air to mud" work as they called it. They wanted to bag MiGs.

We worked with a FAC with the call sign of Covey 270. Some FACS flew the slow, vulnerable Cessna O-1 Bird Dog that was nothing more than a Piper Cub. These Air Force and Army pilots were really cool and calm, all the while getting shot at like crazy as they flew down among the trees looking for targets. These guys had guts! Other FACS flew the O-2, or Oscar Deuce, with a call sign of Covey or Nail. This was the Cessna push-pull two-engine Cessna Skymaster. They flew out of Pleiku or Nakhon Phanom, Thailand and would locate and spot targets while handling battle coordination. The FACs used two radios at a time–talking to the guys on the ground and to us at the same time. They carried 17-pound white phosphorous (WP) rockets which gave off white smoke to mark locations of targets. They would also participate in the battle by firing Zuni rockets, shoot an M-16 out the side window, or drop grenades. One FAC I knew figured the best way to drop a grenade was to pull the pin and put the grenade in a paper coffee cup. That way the safety latch wouldn't release until the cup hit the ground and the grenade rolled out. They were really good, I mean REALLY good!

The FAC was especially glad to see us. We bombed along both sides of a canal, very close to a friendly outpost (OP) or fort, making it a little tight. We'd ask where the friendlies were and the FAC would answer, "A tee, tee away," which was something akin to "across the street." You got good real fast at bombing because the last thing you wanted to do was hit the wrong guys. The enemy could be a half klick or a klick (kilometer -1,000 feet) away. Our dive-bombing was done in 50-degree dives. We were able to put 100% on target hitting enemy bunkers. If we hit what the FACS wanted us to, it elicited calls of "You got 'em, nice hits," and "Shit hot!" It was a good feeling to finally get into the war and do something to help out. The Mekong Delta area was very flat with winding rivers all over the place. We always had to have the FAC in sight before making our bomb run. Many times he would say, "I'm over the squiggly river." An F-4 pilot said, "If the FAC mentions one more time he's over the squiggly river, I'm going to shoot him down." From 15 thousand feet every river looks squiggly.

Dropping our bombs in the daytime attacks was a big misnomer. It wasn't like a WWII movie where the B-24s were dropping their bomb load during a straight and level run–which in and of itself was suicidal. There were no "smart bombs," so our delivery was a precise dive-bombing run. We would figure our gunsight mil setting, dive angle, altitude and airspeed at release. For example, an *ideal* "drop" would be at 5,000 feet 500 knots and 50 degree dive angle, pretty much a vertical dive–just throwing ourselves straight down at the earth at great speeds. Since none of this could be counted on unless conditions were perfect, you had to make up with some Kentucky windage (i.e. if you were in a shallow dive you pickled lower, faster-pickle higher, etc.). You started out by rapidly rolling inverted and then pulled through so your nose was pointed straight down in front, short of the target, while still upside down. Quickly rolling upright, your speed would build up in the dive run, causing the nose to start rising up to the target. When everything came together–after dodging gunfire and missiles–you pickled off the bombs and pulled 5gs or more to pull out of the dive. The Gs would cause me to weigh almost a 1,000 pounds and my head about 60 pounds! My helmet would swivel down and forward on my head, covering my eyes. I'd have to push it back up with my left hand as I pulled back on the stick with my right hand. Blood was rapidly drawn from my brain with the sensation of someone sucking on a straw, quickly resulting in *tunnel vision*. My view was limited to looking down a tube. This continued to a *gray out,* where all color was removed from my vision. My whole body was being crushed. After most hops I felt like I'd been beaten up in a boxing match. Each time stinging salt sweat ran into my eyes as well as down my back.

I had the same ritual before each mission. I'd take the Browning 9mm automatic pistol that Pop had given me out of my safe and load the gun, as well as two extra 13 round clips. My philosophy was that I wasn't going to try and hold off a battalion of gooks, but if it was me, a few of them and the helicopter, I was going to get to the helo. I wanted the option to be mine. I had mentioned to Warrant Officer Jerry Waldon, our ordnance officer, that I didn't have many bullets since the 38 was the Government Issue. The next day there were about 20 boxes of 9mm shells in my room.

CHAPTER TWENTY

BOOT

Normally crews didn't share the same stateroom, but Boot and I did. In case of a shoot down, the remaining roommate would send home the personal effects. Since we were bachelors, we didn't care all that much who got what. Paul was born during World War II in Germany. Boot's mother told him that when she was dating his father he would go up into the mountains to get her an edelweiss flower. They were few in numbers, very high up and hard to get so that if a boy gave it to a girl it truly showed that he loved her. His father was wounded on the Russian front and died about a year later because they didn't have access to any drugs to ward off infection. His mother buried anything of value in the backyard and took off with Paul and his two siblings, running and walking through Eastern Europe to stay ahead of the Russians. She would steal potatoes out of the fields at night to feed her children. His Grandmother had to stay behind. The Russians came and told her she didn't deserve such a big farmhouse and that she was only rubbish. They filled the house with a bunch of Communist riff raffs and relegated her to one bedroom where she eventually died. Paul realized how lucky he was to get out of Eastern Europe when so many others were killed or enslaved, and he was free. He always felt that if he could keep someone free for one more day, he'd feel good. He believed the cold war was worth fighting even if it happened to take place in Vietnam. Boot said he was glad he was able to help repay the goodness America showed to his immigrant refugee family. They settled in Tallahassee, Florida where his mother worked waiting on tables in the cafeteria at Florida State University. One of Paul's jobs was going to the neighbor's for ice. One day his sister said, "Paul, come see. We have a refrigerator." That was a big day. His older brother went to West Point while Paul went to the Naval Academy. Kiddingly, he said he had gone to Florida State, complete with beautiful coeds, for a year and then murdered someone. The judge offered him life in prison or the Naval Academy. The letters between him and his mom were all in German. Years later, Paul would spend all his time devotedly taking care of his mother for three years as she slowly and painfully died from brain cancer. Being a true German he believed in a balanced life; his mother had taken care of him as a child and then he took care of her. He told me that along with flying in combat with me, taking care of his mom was the most rewarding thing he had done in his life.

For years I thought he got the nickname "Boot" from being the Boot Ensign at one time (i.e. most junior). But years later, during reserve duty at NAS Willow Grove, Pennsylvania I ran into Bill McDermott, a fellow Villanovan who had been a pilot in our squadron during our first cruise. He told me that he was from the Germantown area of Philadelphia and that the local soccer star was Helmut "The Boot" Wachenhover. Since Paul Wagner's middle name was Helmut, he called him *Boot* and it stuck. Paul was by far the smartest person I had ever met. He knew everything about everything, especially history. His intellect was matched by his dry sense of humor and he used both to write skits for the squadron. Very well read, he could answer any question and spoke three languages fluently. He kept his own counsel, always keeping to himself. I would mention that I had heard about something and he'd say, "I heard that two days ago." I responded with, "You don't tell me anything. What's next, Boot? 'Oh yeah, Al, by the way–the war's over. Been over for three days'." It's sort of like telling your wife you heard our favorite restaurant was closing and she says, "Yes, I heard that last week!"

His letters to me after the Navy always included, "O.G.A." for "Oh good Al," and "You never tell me anything." He'd end with "n.t.t.y.a" which meant, "Nice talking to you Al." This was long before text messaging. In fact, to this day he doesn't have a cell phone or computer.

He wasn't even supposed to be on this combat cruise. He had already made two cruises and was up for shore duty when our emergency deployment happened. The Navy Detailer from DC who was responsible for assignments came out to the ship in Westpac. Boot talked to him in the Ready Room asking him what was going on, why he kept getting extended on sea duty. The only answer he got was, "We don't have all our nickels and dimes together yet back in Washington, plus you are single." From then on, right before we launched off the ship when I asked him if he was all set he'd answer, "Yup, got all my nickels and dimes together." I always wanted to write a Broadway Musical Comedy with him! On the top of the mission cards where it had "Crew"– Boot would write *Der Fisch und Ich*.

Years later, he would write me: *Don't you think that sort of experience in the middle of life is an anchor for an entire life? This was a defining time in our lives. We were a great team. Never downed an airplane when we could have downed one every night. I was very lucky to have you as my pilot.* He also mentioned to me "as you look back on life you don't realize at the time what the good Lord is doing for you–he put me with you–we fought in a war worth fighting. How lucky I was," he also said that he "felt that the Lord waved a magic wand that dictated that he should fly with me."

He was right about never downing an aircraft. A squadron policy was that we weren't to go over the beach unless we had two generators on line. We needed both to make sure the instruments that warned us of threats (such as AAA and SAM radars) worked. Many times we launched with just one generator. However, there was one pilot who would "down" an aircraft if the windscreen was dirty. I recall the time he radioed the air boss that his plane was "down on deck." When asked what the problem he said, "Radios." I don't think he ever flew a night low-level mission–which meant someone else had to fly two! He was sacrificing someone else's safety for his own survival. He really endeared himself to the ordnance troopers because they had to manually download the seven tons of bombs they had just loaded on his plane. This happened more than once. Some crews referred to this as the pilot hearing "night noises." We actually got in one airplane that he had "downed" and flew a very successful mission.

During a tanker hop when the F-4s joined up on our wing to take on fuel, Boot took off his flight boots and socks and put his feet up on the instrument panel. Instead of his helmet he put on a baseball hat with the bill turned up, while wearing a flashy Hawaiian shirt. He then proceeded to eat a sandwich while waving a can of beer in his hand. Before they left, he flashed a centerfold from Playboy, which really drove the F-4 guys crazy.

Boot paid me a great compliment when he told me later that I wasn't one of those "sweaty palm" pilots. He had a calm, unflappable air about him. He was cool, calm, proficient, and very professional. If I had to classify one person as completely fearless, it would be Boot. He was one helluva Bombardier/Navigator and I couldn't have had a better one. He was simply the best and he kept me alive during two cruises. He was also a kind man, and in my eyes he can do no wrong.

Der Fisch und Ich

CHAPTER TWENTY-ONE

SO FAR AWAY

21 May 1972, Sunday–During the sermon, the Padre added, "Not like you heretics from Villanova or Holy Cross (where helo pilot LT Bob "Dunner" Dunn had gone)."

We both replied, "Hey. Watch it Padre!"

He told me later that it was to keep us awake. His sermon was right to the point:"We, as Catholics, have no right to kill anyone; but, if someone is an unjust aggressor, and when we try to stop him he is killed, then he has died because of a fault of his own. It is not because of us that he has died. For example, a Quaker will not kill, but if he heard someone in his chicken coup, he'd say, 'I'm not supposed to shoot anyone but you're standing where I am going to shoot'."

For me, there was a good moral argument for us being there. We were trying to help these people, though we had nothing to gain personally. There had been too many good people who have died because of the aggressors from the North. Hopes and dreams of Vietnamese as well as Americans had been spent trying to stop these Communists.

We didn't get *fragged* (i.e. the mission assignment) until 2400 for a 0400 go. A frag order is a *fragmentary* order–a brief outline of the mission. The schedule was slipped under our door at about 0100 and the sound of the paper sliding in was enough to wake me. Arriving at the Intelligence Center, we were given the particulars of the mission. Then we began the planning and follow up with a major brief in the Ready Room, which included the strategy we were going to use.

*

22 May 1972–We flew on Dick Engel's wing to MR IV to work with FAC Covey 270 again. We were the first Air Wing to show up in this area so they were especially glad to see us. We bombed along a canal 110 miles southwest of Saigon-14 MK 82s per aircraft. I asked the FAC to have the "Friendlies" send up a smoke from their outpost, which was basically a triangle of logs. A whiff of white smoke came up from the middle of the compound. I told Boot, "My God, it looks like something from 'Drums along the Mohawk'." The FAC told us to bomb along the perimeter because they were coming over the walls. There was no margin for error. As we left, he relayed that the guys in the OP were really happy since this was the first time in three weeks they weren't taking fire. That felt real good. On another mission we asked, "Where do you want us to bomb?" "Bomb the smoke, they're being overrun!" They had hunkered down with hopes of taking out more of the bad guys. It still was a horrible feeling to drop bombs on our own troops. We later found out that many of our men had survived.

Our Flight Surgeon, LCDR Bob Randolph, walked around with a ball cap on and a white pullover turtleneck that said "CVW-

3 Quack"–something right out of *MASH*. When I took the "Combat Quack" up on a tanker hop he showed up with a big gun, crisscrossed bandoliers of bullets and a huge knife. He could pass for a Mexican revolutionary and hold off a battalion, even if we weren't going over land. I said, "Doc, if we have to punch out, you're going to drown."

24 May 1972–We flew strike lead into MR 4–some 44 miles southwest of Saigon. Working with Covey 226, we dropped 14MK 82s to hit enemy emplacements. Rolling in on target, the whole ground erupted in what looked like sparklers or flashbulbs. I thought it looked neat until I realized they were actually muzzle flashes from all the guns shooting at me. They also had Soviet-built SA-7 Strela shoulder fired anti-aircraft missiles that carried a high explosive warhead. One FAC was hit with 50-caliber gunfire, but was able to make it back safety.

On one of the close air support missions, I flew with Bruce Cook as Ace Lead, while I was Ace Two. We were tasked with hitting gun emplacements along the shore. These batteries would open up on a downed airman in the water and also prevent rescue forces from coming in. At one point after a bombing run, we became separated. Bruce asked, "Ace Two, say your posit (position)." Since we were out over the Gulf there were no physical points of land to use. I was looking all over the place trying to find some sort of landmark or even a boat to use as a reference. Below me was the ocean and all around were huge cumulous clouds. Still looking around and totally bewildered I

170

answered, "I'm by the cloud." But then again there were clouds *all* around my position. Trying to be more precise and help distinguish the different clouds and after some more thought quickly said, "I'm by the *big* cloud." These immortal words proved that fact could become legend as well as one of the celebrated sayings of naval folklore, especially in VA-75. The XO jokingly threw his helmet at me in the Ready Room when I returned. Years later, when they disestablished the squadron, they did a skit commemorating this event which included a helmet being thrown!

*

There were days that were so beautiful they were almost magical. Some nights a full moon would seem to just pop up out of the ocean and shine across the sea like a spotlight producing a wide ribbon of gleaming light across the sea. But many times a beautiful day would turn into a black tropical night that produced a thick foreboding dimness on the flight deck. On one hand, night was an ally. When I flew over the beach, it kept me out of sight of the gunners and hopefully below their radar. But while night should be soft and relaxing, it could quickly turn into a malicious enemy with intrinsic dangers. Night was now harsh, filled with unending gunfire from radar-controlled guns, SAM missiles and the invisible presence of the land with solid karst ridges jutting up to smack you.

28 May 1972–An A-4 pilot off the Hancock was shot down. We heard him on his survival radio say, "Gooks are all around and they got my other radio. Tell my wife I love her and

call off the SAR." He was never heard from again. The beautiful sunset on the way back to the ship just accentuated the absurdity of it all. However the weather was really violent with little let up. It was always very hot and humid and the heat on the flight deck was searing. The massive thunderstorms were unbelievable with the sea literally boiling from the storms. Some nights the thunderstorms were way in the distance. All you could see were bolts of lightning dancing on the horizon in a chorus line of quivering greenish stick figures striking the ocean. They were so far away you couldn't hear any thunder. It was an eerie stage show. I dropped VA-75's one-million pounds of bombs–in only 12 days!

1 June 1972–We left Dixie Station off South Vietnam and transited north to the Tonkin Gulf and "Yankee Station" off North Vietnam. We were now officially members of the *Tonkin Gulf Yacht* club and got another patch for our flight jacket to prove it. We had a steak cookout on the "Steel beach" of the flight deck, but since I was really tired, I just tried to rest.

4 June 1972–19.00N 118.00E. During an afternoon hop near Vinh, Tom "Jack" Wharton and B/N Don "Low Drag" Peterson had a SAM fired at them. Boot and I went up that later night in an A-6B trolling to try and get them to paint us with their radar, but the SAM site stayed quiet. Vinh even kept the city lights on and we had lightning flashes all around us. Took off and landed back on ship while being battered by rain. Tom Wharton is now known as "SAM" Wharton and his B/N, Don "Magnet" A. Petersen.

In honor of their exploits, Boot wrote:

Sam, Sam the missile man
Dodged a SAM and away he ran –
That's the last time he will fly
Close to Vinh
Low or high.

*

The Air Wing caught a Chinese Communist (CHICOM) ship unloading supplies into a smaller craft, those water borne logistics craft we referred to as wiblics. We seeded the area around the ship with mines. Since it was a "third country" ship, we couldn't bomb it even though it would have been easier and smarter. The U.S. guidelines were so complicated that it was extending the war. I didn't feel the U.S. even had a policy for winning. You would think the Generals and Admirals would speak up. Seems it was feared that if a SAM site were hit killing Soviet technicians, the war would escalate. I always felt that the Russians and Chinese didn't need an excuse to start a bigger war. In the meantime, these guys could kill us. During the day a merchant ship would go by us with SAMs on the flight deck that they would fire at us that night. We should have just sunk them or turned them around. It was deplorable that the British Merchant Navy crewed the SS Ardrossmore, which carried arms and other supplies from China to North Vietnam. There were too many politically protected

173

targets, such as the airfields providing sanctuaries for the enemy. The Rules of Engagement (ROE) for this war were outrageous. And we bailed out the Brits in WWII? Whose side are they on? As Junior Officers, we may have been above politics, but we were certainly affected by it.

During that time, a popular song back home was Carole King's "So Far Away," which really fit the bill–everything and everyone dear was so far away, indeed. With people back home we were just plain *gone*. For us we were not only *gone* but also *away*. Away from everything in life that was "normal." And as far as our loved ones were concerned, though endless miles separated us, thoughts of them were only a heartbeat away.

CHAPTER TWENTY-TWO

"THEY'RE TRYING TO KILL ME!"

6 June 1972–19N 107E. Three more Alpha strikes today. An Alpha strike is when the whole Air Wing (of about thirty planes) hits a target. We attacked petroleum, oil, lubrication storage (POL), and bridges N.E. of Haiphong that were defended with a boatload of SAM sites and a lot of AAA.

7 June 1972–19.57 N 107.00 E. Once again the Air Wing flew three more Alpha strikes. We flew cover for a strike into the Hon Gai Railroad yard complex northeast of Haiphong in the A-6B carrying the STARM missiles. This was my official first mission to North Vietnam.

If the enemy were to lock up our planes with their surface to air missile radar site, Boot would get the reading of the frequency of their radar and program it into our missile. Even if they shut down their radar the missile remembered where it was. The Standard Arm missile was fifteen feet long and weighed 1,400 pounds with a warhead of over 210 pounds. With a fifty-mile range it could provide standoff capability. We sat south-southwest of Ille Da Cat Ba Island in Haiphong Harbor and saw about thirty ships unloading war supplies. Again, they were off limits! Our mission called for us to sit outside the SAM and AAA envelope out over the water. We'd fly a figure eight pattern so we were almost always pointed toward the land where the threat would be. On this particular mission we were to cover the strike force against SAM missiles. If the bad guys came up with radar to launch a missile, we'd fire a Standard Arm at the site. The strike force got in and out with no enemy radar observed at all.

Additional plans called for us to cover the A-5 Vigilante (Vigi) as it came through the target area to take post strike damage pictures. This was known as a Recce (reconnaissance) mission. Of course the Vigi had to wait until the dust and debris from the attack cleared so they could get good pictures. This gave the gunners, who were by now warmed up and mad, time to rearm. I thought these A5 guys were crazy! We were then to follow the A5 south to Vinh where he was to take pre-strike photos.

I saw the Vigi coming out the mouth of Haiphong harbor. As he passed far below us, I told Boot, "OK, we'll turn and start heading south to follow him."

All of a sudden the F-4 Recce Escort radioed, "The Vigi's been hit; I've got one chute!"

I turned north in toward shore and said, "I've got two chutes."

At that point, the F-4 said he was low on gas and was heading back to the ship. I moved in closer to shore overhead the crew and started giving the downed crew's position to the ship and any rescue helos that may have been coming in. Pilot Chuck Smith and RAN Larry Kuntz had luckily gotten into their rafts.

Serenely, Boot said, "That's it!"

"That's what?"

"I've got a good lock on the radar site."

On my glare shield I saw indicators, lit up in red, *Target Acquisition* and another *Missile Ready*.

I hit the pickle switch and watched in amazement as the Standard Arm missile dropped down and ignited. It flew along with us for a few minutes to build up speed and then shot out front and zoomed up leaving a smoke contrail.

"My God, it looks like Apollo 15!"

"Well you better start moving because there's one coming back the other way!" Boot calmly exclaimed.

"What do you mean?"

That's when I heard the high-pitched *deedle, deedle, deedle* in my headset that sounded like a French Police horn. At the same time a flashing red light lit up on my glare shield with one word– *Missile* –meaning a missile was locked up on us and heading straight toward us at 1,500 miles an hour!

I saw what looked like a telephone pole with fire coming out of it. It was right on track for us. I broke to the right and the missile went the same way, I broke left and down and it did the same thing. I was running out of airspeed and ideas real fast! Trying to out-maneuver the missile, I rolled and dove–going from about 18,000 feet to 12,000 feet. It finally exploded, trying to turn with us. All of a sudden red-orange fireballs that turned into dense black smoke surrounded the plane.

"Boot, call the ship. I think A-7s are dropping air burst bombs on us."

"I don't think so; there are no planes above us–I think it's triple A–anti-aircraft fire, flak!"

"You think so?"

"Yup. Are you dropping chaff (metal strips to confuse their radar) Al?'

"Yea."

"Good."

We struggled back up to 18,000 feet and fired a missile. They fired one back and then hosed us down with more AAA. This went on until we unloaded the two standard arm and two shrike missiles. Sweat was pouring into my eyes and the constant G forces were beating the heck out of me. Extensive violent anti-aircraft fire repeatedly blanketed the aircraft. We then dropped down and flew low along the beach trying to divert the gunfire from the enemy troops along the shore who are shooting at the guys in the rafts.

In the meantime, a helo came in with rescue diver ADJ1 John Wilson who had 18 rescues to his credit. Just a few days earlier he had been part of an ill-fated top-secret mission code named "Operation Thunderhead", which really played heavy on his heart for many years to come. Standard operating procedure was to drop him at 10 feet and 10 knots. All of a sudden the door gunner said, "There he is." John jumped at 100 feet and 100 knots! As soon as his swim fins hit the air stream, he went horizontal.

When he struck the water, his pistol broke a few ribs and collapsed a lung. He came up and Larry Kuntz (the RAN, backseater from the A-5) was in his raft trying to fight him off with his survival knife because John was dressed in black. Later John told me "He tried to stab me!"

"I'm one of you!" yelled John. Larry pulled John into the raft and asked, "Are you OK?"

"I'm supposed to ask you that!" answered John.

Larry's chute had billowed in the water, giving the shore batteries an ideal target. John said the water geysers from the exploding shells reminded him of a big white sail. As they had drifted closer to land, the enemy troops on shore were able to zero in on them especially since Larry's helmet was white with bright yellow stripes. John hunched over him trying to conceal this nice target.

The second helo came in and did a running pick up where they just hook up and go. Consequently, the guys were spinning as they sped away. John said he'd see the ocean, and then the guys shooting at them from the beach, then he'd see the ocean, then the guys shooting from the beach again, etc. as round and round they went. Thankfully both Larry and his pilot, LCDR Chuck Smith, were rescued. Chuck said he heard a warble (from the enemy's radar), dropped chaff, broke and then was hit.

When we landed back aboard ship the ordnance men looked at our plane in disbelief at the empty missile racks. Boot and I were the first in VA-75 to fire a Standard Arm missile. We

ended up firing a total of 13, which made us members of the millabuck club since the missiles went for $100,000 each. I mentioned we didn't get any radar

LCDR Smith, LT Kuntz enroute to the USS Saratoga after their rescue in Haiphong Harbor

signal indication from the bad guys. Top-secret message traffic was intercepted. In it the missile control officer, whose name they actually knew, stated that he had visually tracked "an A-3J bomber (the original designation of the A-5) aggressor aircraft." At the last minute he provided radar guidance, hitting the plane. Fortunately the warhead didn't explode when the missile hit the plane.

ADJ1 Wilson, ADJ2 McCARTHY, LT. Kunz
Returning to USS Long Beach

Rescue diver John Wilson and the results of his courageous action

On the way to the shower, I passed our Skipper in the passageway. He asked, "Do you feel more comfortable now?"

I just wanted to yell, "My God they're trying to kill me!" I thought, *this was my first real mission in the North and I didn't even get over the beach yet they shot the heck out of me and I'm probably gonna be here for a year!*

I said, "I know what to expect sir."

On the blackboard in our Ready Room, one of our sailors had drawn a caricature of me hanging out of the cockpit firing my 9mm pistol at the SAM sites.

My previous letters to Ray Sandelli included the comments such as, "This isn't bad" when we were flying close air support. Now I wrote, *"They got real close. They're trying to kill me! Help!"* Ray later told me each time he heard an A-6 was down; he'd visit the chapel and say a prayer for me.

*

About a month later, rescue diver John Wilson was also instrumental in the rescue of LCDR Smokey Tolbert. Smokey had been a Blue Angel, got out of the Navy and flew for American Airlines before getting laid off. He came back into the Navy and was flying A-7s off the Midway. Named Baie du Brandon by the French we knew it as Brandon Bay while the Vietnamese called it Vung Phu Dien. It's just north of the city of Vinh. Heavily armed Hon Mat Island sat just to the north of the bay. It was heavily fortified to protect the transshipment point of Vinh for war supplies headed south. Part of the defenses was a radar-controlled quad mounted 23mm AAA gun. The gunner, whom we thought to be Russian, was really good. If you got near him, he got you. Smokey did just that and was shot down, but made it out over the water where John Wilson, jumping from the helicopter, rescued him after he had ejected.

I ran into Smokey the next time we were in Port. He still had his arm in a sling and was limping due to his injuries.

"I'm gonna get that son-of-a-bitch."

John Wilson later told me that this was the very same thing he said when he saved him.

"Smokey, let it lie; he'll get you again."

The next line period Smokey went after the gunsite. He was heard screaming all the way down because he was trapped in his aircraft and couldn't get out. Seems like a bunch of guys who had gotten out of the Navy and came back in after being laid off from the airlines were either killed or captured. I remember thinking, *if I get out of this, there's no way I'm coming back.*

*

The presence of danger abolished any idea I may have had of the thrill of adventure and replaced it with an alarming fear. Any so-called glamour gave way to the grit of combat. All the bravado was gone when the realities of war finally hit home and was replaced with cold terror. I especially felt bad for Pop because I knew that he, perhaps better than anyone, understood clearly what I was going through. He must have been terrified knowing how easy it would be to lose a son. When I returned, a co-pilot of his at

American said, "Your Dad flew each and every mission with you." One time Pop told me that the reason some people don't go to church or pray was because they had never had to ask for "help" in a big way.

During one particular brief, CAG said, "We'll be in Indian country (deep in North Vietnam) so if you get shot down we'll make one pass to make sure you're O.K., but we can't get you out."

In between Alpha strikes, we'd fly STARM missions, tanker hops and night low levels. There was never any let up.

On the way over I had made a tape for my parents telling them in a kind of light-hearted way what was going on. Now I made another one but when I played it back I could hear the fright in my voice and never sent it to them for fear of worrying them.

Standard Arm Missile (STARM)

CHAPTER TWENTY-THREE

BIDDEN OR NOT BIDDEN

We put on a very funny skit in R/R for the Skipper's going away party. The CO wrote himself up for a Bronze star medal for continuous leadership–and got it! Later on in the cruise, LT Jim Lloyd was shot down deep in North Vietnam and evaded all night before being rescued and he got a Bronze Star. The next day was our CO's change of command–happy to see this skipper go. He would do anything to get ahead and was utterly clueless to his own blundering incompetence and proved that one could be wrong with authority. Admiral Nelson once said, "You can't be a good officer without being a gentleman." I didn't know he knew this guy. CDR Charlie NMN (no middle name) Earnest took over. There couldn't have been a more opposite set of values. CDR Charlie Earnest was a considerate man who truly cared for the troops. He was more concerned for their welfare than for his own advancement. He knew that his advancement was based on how efficient he was and not on whom he kissed up to. His mere presence was a motivator. Years earlier, as the pilot of an A-3D (to some it stood for "All 3 Dead") flying off USS Hancock, he suffered a cold CAT shot causing him to crash into the water in front of the ship. He recalled watching the carrier pass overhead before he went out the top hatch to safety.

We were in our plane on the flight deck getting ready to go. The Sara was operating in the same area as the Kitty Hawk and Coral Sea with all the ships of their battle group passing us by.

Boot mentioned, "It looks like WWII."

"What are you talking about? You were on the wrong side in WWII."

"Who were the Germans fighting?"

"The Russians."

"Who are we fighting now?"

"The Russians," I answered.

There was always a Russian AGI, that intelligence gathering ship, near us. It would send signals ahead as we launched, notifying the enemy that we were coming.

I found out later that a Carrier in the South China sea and the Tonkin gulf in the course of a cruise would steam some 10,000 miles back in forth while carrying on combat operations. Heck we could have almost made it home with all that steaming!

In-between missions, we stood at 15-minute alerts! There was very little down time. The whole squadron was involved in flying missions in the same lousy weather with the constant thunderstorms.

Since we had now flown combat missions over the Red River valley of North Vietnam, we officially became *River Rats*.

The certificate of membership read:

"For successfully striking targets located in the Red River Valley of North Vietnam, the most highly defended area in the history of aerial warfare. For gallantry in facing MIGS, SAMS and GUNS defending those targets. Alan G. Fischer, LT, USNR is hereby honored by membership in the 'River Rats' Association."

The Red River Valley Association was formed in 1967, first as a social group and then later on as a philanthropic activity. It provided comfort and support for the family members of those who were KIA/MIA and later on scholarships to their children. Their foundation says it all:

"From Unprecedented Aerial Warfare Came Unheralded Sacrifice Through Spirit, Pride and Professionalism." Another patch for the old flight jacket!

*

13 June 1972, 0030–We flew a tanker and also took on fuel from an A-7 three times. At 0900 we went on an Alpha strike carrying 14 MK 82s with about 35 aircraft and hit the Phu Ly RR yards, storage buildings/barracks. Heavy AAA. My biggest fear was putting my bombs in the river that ran right along the target area. We did OK getting all bombs on target. Flying by Kien An airfield, Boot could see the gunners on a 37mm gunsite. I heard him say, "You didn't get me you bastards." Evading SAMS and pulling G's is just beating the hell out of me.

One of the worse things before a strike is the apprehension. How much AAA, how many SAMS will there be? How will my dive be? Heard MiGs were up the day before and bagged two guys. We'll be far inland–where to go if we get hit?"

"But the waiting time, my brothers,
Is the hardest times of all."
(Sarah Downey, Psalms of Life)

*

Our nightly bomb load usually consisted of a mixture of bombs. We'd have eight 500-pound iron bombs with snake eye retarded fins to hit a "hard target" such as a bridge, power plant or warehouse. Since we were flying the missions at 200 feet or lower the bombs had four stabilizing fins that sprung open to slow the bombs decent. This prevented us from getting blown out of the sky by our own bombs. We would be given a target ahead of time. Paul would spend hours pouring over maps and charting our course to the target. This would include checkpoints, headings, time and distances. It usually took him three to four hours to plot a mission and he was always very precise. The A-6 had very sophisticated systems which could give you a synthetic representation on your instruments of what was ahead of you thus enabling you to fly low level in the dark of the night. However, I never saw that once in combat and could never use the fancy stuff. The systems were just too hard to maintain at sea. Basically, we would start around 200 feet above the ground flying headings based on Paul's calculations and a constant airspeed, say 360 knots. Over North Vietnam while operating the attack navigation radar system Boot would find the target and "lock it up" by adjusting the cross hairs on his radar screen. As we made our run he would "sweeten up" (precisely refine) the target "lock up" giving accurate commands to my instruments. Being so low and fast, and with the undulations in the terrain, we were only a quarter of a second away from hitting the ground.

The rest of the load consisted of six Mark 20 rockeye (CBU or cluster bomb units)–a container with 247 shaped-charged bomblets, like small grenades. These were good for troops, trucks and POL storage. I spent about 35 seconds looking for trucks at night in the rain at 200 feet. You just couldn't see them! Consequently, I would return to the ship with the rockeye bombs. The last thing I wanted to do was just pickle them off over the beach with the chance of hitting some kid asleep in a hooch. I didn't jettison them in the ocean because they were an expensive piece of property. This meant that I had to dump fuel to stay below the maximum landing weight back at the ship, which gave me fewer chances to get aboard. Plus I was landing with bombs still aboard my plane!

The next night punishing rain soaked us through and through before we even made it to our plane. There was imminent peril just going up to the aircraft and manning up in a deluge of rain. The depth of the darkness made the Taxi Director's yellow-lighted wands look like an invisible person, a phantom of sorts, was using them. Ghostly red glow of the deck lights weaved up through the hot mist of the vapor steam of the catapult making it another "twilight zone" hop. Looking ahead off the CAT, I could see absolutely nothing. It was like being in a foggy coal mine. When we came back to land, the weather was even worse! The weather as usual was just plain angry.

Single plane night low-level hops were always terrifying and this was no exception. Gunfire erupted the minute we went "feet dry" over the beach, and chased us every step of the way. There was no hiding, especially from the fan song radar that controlled the surface to air missiles. No matter how little time I was inland, it felt like a lifetime. We hit the target and got the hell out of there. For me the war had really begun in earnest. Somebody said that flying into combat for the first time was like playing Hamlet on Broadway without a rehearsal. What I would have given to be near Broadway–even the Bowery for that matter.

Before some missions, official word would come over the squawk box in the Ready Room saying, "Cancel event four (the two a.m. go) the weather is too bad, except for the A-6s." On the way to man up we'd go by the F-4 Ready Rooms and the crews would be in there watching a movie and eating popcorn. The enemy had a price on our heads, offering so much for a captured pilot. I told Boot I'd turn him in, get the money and then take off. He didn't go for that.

After a mission, any feeling of accomplishment and survival was all too short-lived. I knew I would have to do it all over again in about six or eight hours. My nervous system was a riot of emotions. I recalled that "Bidden or not bidden, God is present." I certainly hoped so!

CHAPTER TWENTY-FOUR

INTO THE HAND OF GOD

14 June 1972—We flew a night STARM off Vinh. There was a Chinese Merchant ship (MERSHIP) sitting off shore. Since we had finally mined the harbors and river mouths, the only way they could get war materials to shore was to offload them into "lighters" the small boats we called "WIBLICS."

As always, third world country shipping was ridiculously off limits, even though the missiles they were offloading would be fired at us later that day! However, once a small boat was five hundred feet from the mother ship, they were fair game. This set up "MERSHIP surveillance." Two A-7s would "birddog" the ship twenty-four hours a day. At night one A-7 would make a low pass and drop a parachute flare to light up the ship. The second A-7 would fly over the ship and take a look at the operation to see if anything was being sent ashore.

Our job was to sit overhead in the A-6B and watch for any radar activity from inland that would indicate a possible SAM launch at the A-7s. I watched from above as one A-7 flew by and dropped a flare, illuminating the ship. LT John Davis of VA-37 then called "in" to make a visual report. In the best of conditions, flying at night under flares was like being ushered into an unlit auditorium with a searchlight on you. I saw a small flash from the back of the ship and then a huge explosion. I told Boot that John must have dropped an airborne blast bomb.

His wingman called "Canyon Passage Two say your position?" Complete silence. Then the unsettling "Mayday, mayday, number two has been hit." A Rescue Combat Air Patrol (Rescap) was launched to no avail. The enemy had deviously set up a small anti-aircraft gun on the back of the ship. That small flash I saw was the muzzle flash from the AAA site on the ship. John stood out under the bright light of the flares, an easy target. But the ship was "off- limits" and prohibited to be attacked! Bit by bit, I was losing my sense of humor. John was married with four kids.

Freedom is a light for which many men have died in darkness for.

The fact of the matter was that he didn't give up his life for *our* freedom, but for a people that he didn't even know, which made it even more sacrificial.

*

Over the beach there were violent level six thunderstorms that were considered "God's finger." Seemed more like a fist to me! There was furious, pouring rain that continued all the way back to the ship. The radar controller talked me through my approach and said, "Three - quarters of a mile call the ball." Because of the hard rain being thrown out of the pitch-black night, I couldn't see the meatball and had to call "Clara" to the LSO, meaning I had no glide slope or anything else for that matter.

The LSO said, "Roger, I hear you, keep it coming."

Oh great, I can't see the ship and he can't see me!

At the very last second, I saw the meatball and the landing area and trapped. Boot reached over and patted me on the back saying, "Good shot Al." Man if he only knew! I had to pull from deep within to get aboard without killing us both.

The normal scan for coming aboard ship was: Meatball (for glide slope), lineup (for centerline), and angle of attack (for correct speed). Captain Ron Williams, an F-4 Air Force Exchange pilot, was with VF-31. He called the meatball the *light* and his scan was, "water, steel, water, steel, steel, steel, steel." He was a real good "deck spotter."

We stopped bombing north of 20.30N perhaps due to President Podgorny of USSR's visit. More political BS. A few days later one of our pilots turned his wings in, but then regretted it.

*

16 June 1972, 2300–While taxiing up to the catapult, I heard an A-7 from VA-105 that had just launched report, "Roger that, Cherubs 10 (1,000')." Then nothing but deafening silence.

LT John Cabral had impacted the water a few miles ahead of the ship. He probably ejected underwater because they brought him back wrapped in his parachute. Years later in *Approach*, Naval Air's safety magazine, there was an article entitled "He flew into the water holding Kathleen in his arms." He was probably overly tired and maybe distracted by his thoughts.

192

In 1902 George Hoar had written in his Book of Patriotism:

"Let all American girls learn to give her husband, and her brother, and her son, high counsel, so that he may never be tempted to fail in any hour of trial by thinking of her."

John was one of the guys that had been with Jim Lloyd and Larry Kilpatrick the night before we shipped out.

The very next night, 17 June 1972, I had dinner with Larry also of VA-105. He said he was really scared to go tonight after what had happened to squadronmate John Cabral the night before. His commanding officer said it'd be OK for him to stand down and take a few days off. But Larry said he couldn't face his fears by running away. After dinner, I flew a night STARM off Vinh and Larry flew a recce hop, looking for targets of opportunity in North Vietnam. As always there were huge thunderstorms over the beach. When we got back we ate another meal together.

"Do you feel better now Larry?"

"I think so."

The following day, 18 June 1972, we flew a night low level up near China where I felt we were the targets at a shooting gallery. At the same time, as 'Canyon Passage 406,' Larry was flying an armed reconnaissance mission deep in North Vietnam near Nhan Loc. He and his wingman had flared a bridge in order to bomb it. I heard Larry call that he was rolling in "hot" to bomb the target and then "clear, turning left" off the target. For some reason he also broadcasted, "watch your altitude" because of the hilly terrain and at night it's real easy to break an altitude and get too low to pull out. I didn't know if he was talking to his wingman or himself, but after that radio call there was nothing at all! Maybe he got too low, knew it and ejected or was shot down. Either way, the world just swallowed him up. His wingman didn't see an explosion or a fiery crash on the ground. For days we would fly and broadcast on our emergency channel, hoping against hope that he could hear us on his survival radio and he would then contact us. But there was nothing. We never saw any wreckage or a chute He had launched on the same cycle that John Cabral had the previous night. Although Larry knew all along he wasn't going to make it back, he went anyway. A great man of true moral convictions, he went with faith, alone into the darkness.

God Knows
And I said to the man who stood at the gate of the year:
"Give me a light that I may tread safely into the unknown."
And he replied:
"Go out into the darkness and put your hand into the Hand of God.
That shall be to you better than light and safer than a known way."
So I went forth, and finding the Hand of God, trod gladly into the
night.
And He led me towards the hills and the breaking of day in the
lone East.

(Minnie Louise Haskins)

Larry was a friendly, warm-hearted man who courageously stood firmly for what he believed in. It wasn't just a passing thing but an indwelling of fortitude that enabled him to go on fighting even while fearful. His steadfast spirit of quiet courage remained unbroken. He had a gallant heart that was loyal and faithful. AOCS classmate C.L. Overman said he was the penultimate Georgia "Gentle" Man, class act, good southern man and hero.

As the Book of Wisdom says, "The just man, though he die early, shall be at rest. For the age that is honorable comes not with the passing of time, nor can it be measured in terms of years."

I could hardly believe that I had lost a very dear friend who left behind his wife and their 2-year-old daughter, Wendi. All of a sudden, he was gone–just plain gone, disappeared off the face of the earth! We fought hard, prayed hard and cried even harder. Now it seemed too often as well! Although these were justifiable emotions, my heavy heart was mourning and I was crushed. It was heartbreaking and the sorrow was bottomless and sad enough to make an angel cry. This was getting real personal real fast! He too had been with Jim Lloyd and John Cabral the night before we shipped out. One of the worst things about losing your buddies was that there was no one to talk to it about. In the Wardroom, if you said, "I really miss Larry," the guy sitting next to you would say, "I miss him too." You didn't dare write home about it so as not to worry the folks. You just had to keep it in inside which in many cases was worse than the grief itself. This could eventually overwhelm you. It was heartrending. What else could happen?

CHAPTER TWENTY-FIVE

THE FLEET WHITE FEET

One day Boot and I were planning to attack a target around Ninh Giang in North Vietnam. Our Ops Officer LCDR Don Lindland came by and said, "You're not going there you'll get shot down." About a month later, we were looking at the same target when LCDR Bob Graustein came by and told us the same thing. They were really concerned about us. Later on in the cruise because they thought the target a necessary objective they went on to attack it. Sadly both of them were shot down near that same area.

21 June 1972–Alpha strike before heading to Port. I was finally going to get some down time. On this last mission, CDR Sam Flynn and LT Bill John of VF-31 bagged a MiG 21 and said he was very good. The MiG had first been on squadronmate Dave Arnold's tail firing three missiles at him barely missing. When Dave got out of his plane, his face was white. Sam did a traditional victory roll coming by the ship.

Larry Kilpatrick is now officially listed as MIA. All I can remember is how many times he told me how much he loved Jane and Wendi. I knew I would always keep an eye on them.

After a tough mission, the "Quack" would come in and ask if we needed anything to calm our nerves. He'd hand out small bottles of booze for medicinal purposes. I logged about 90 hours and 38 missions this line period.

*

22 June 1972–We flew ahead of the ship to Cubi Point and spent two hours touring the islands and hassling. The jungle was very thick with a small clearing here and there with a little hut or two. We flew over the area of Baguio up in the hills before landing at Cubi. Our ship had docked next to the heavy cruiser USS Newport News (CA-148). It did my heart good to see a real warship in the thick of the fight. The Black Shoes (Surface Navy guys) were doing their part. She'd come into Port with the paint on her 8-inch guns blistered from so many firings. Her nickname, "The Gray Ghost from the East Coast" was given to her after taking on 28 shore batteries in North Vietnam without being hit. She certainly lived up to her call sign "Thunder." I ran into Father McElroy who was chaplain at Pensacola when I was in AOCS. His advice to us the first week was "Don't quit!" He was now on the Newport News. I remembered that one Sunday he said, "I never say anything about those who come and go because there are so many who do but I have to say something about LT Roger Staubach who is leaving this week. He first came to me plebe summer at the Naval Academy and asked me what time daily Mass was. I said I wasn't even going to tell him because he couldn't make it. For the next four years he was there at daily 5 a.m. Mass."

A few years earlier on July 4th, Father was based "in country," saying Mass for the Marines outdoors. His clerk, who was acting as his altar server, looked up, and said "Padre, I'm hit." He fell dead from a sniper's bullet. Father Lamond would later write a poem about the heartrending incident called "Freedom's Boy." The other Chaplain of the ship was Father Mark Doyle who had been Chaplain at Chase field when I was there. I affectionately called him the "Rabbi." He told me that one night the North Vietnamese sent PT boats out after them. Father said, "The ship lowered their eight inch guns and it was beaucoup firepower–a mosquito couldn't have gotten through." Neither did the PT boats.

I went for a swim and called home. It took about four hours of dialing to get the overseas operator, only to get cut off. I finally got through but toward the end of the call I could tell my mother was getting emotional. I'd say, "How's the Woog? (Our dog)."

She'd say, "Oh, he's fine."

I'd quickly say, "Goodbye, love you," and hang up.

We all ordered our "I've been there" belt buckles with our names and wings on the front. By now we had "Combat" in front of our nicknames, so I was the "Combat Fish." One wife got one that read, "Combat wife."

On base, I saw a young Marine with a T-shirt that said *we piss off more hippies by 9 a.m. than you do all day.* Later that evening I took Navy nurse LT Kathy Rourke out to dinner. She had been Joanie's roommate when we dated in Virginia Beach and was now based at the naval hospital at Cubi Point. I affectionately called her *Rourkie* while she called me her *WESTPAC brother.* Whenever we pulled into Port, she loaned me her car, a big, lumbering 64 Dodge, so I could get around the enormous base. It sure beat having to ride in the local cabs or jitneys. Made from leftover WWII jeeps, they were gaudily decorated and provided very uncomfortable seating for about 12 people. We went to the O'Club at Subic Bay, which was calmer than the one at Cubi Point —mostly Black Shoe officers.

The nurses' quarters had all kinds of autographed pictures from ships and squadrons. The one from the Kitty Hawk read: "To the Fleet White Feet of the Fleet." They are the most dedicated people I have ever met. They'd stay with young wounded and sick guys until they were healed or passed away. One Marine who had been in a coma was always asked if he wanted anything, but would never answer. And then one time he suddenly said, "Get me a beer," and then died. Another young Marine died during the night from a bug bite he got "in country."

There was no way you could ever "snow" a Navy Nurse out there; they'd heard every cheap line there was. One day I was at the Nurses' quarters with a few guys from the Heavy One squadron off our ship. There was a picture of a P-3 from the local Patrol Squadron on a table. All of the squadron members were signing it in order to present it to the nurses. Of course, we signed our names as well. One of their pilots laid into us, saying, "Hey, only the Skipper signs in red and the XO signs in green!" We had done both and we weren't even in their Squadron. We had a good laugh over that. These P3 guys really had some nice duty being shore based and flying very routine patrol flights keeping track of

Russian subs. Many had their wives living there with them. I felt that anytime someone got a good deal in the Navy, I was all for it. They all had flashy, bright colored "shit-hot" flight suits to show how cool they were. It caused an amused attack pilot to say, "I didn't know the P-3 squadron had a bobsled team!" Our flight suits looked like Omar the Tentmaker had made them. A real combat pilot in his flight suit looked an unmade bed. Of course years later some of the younger guys in our squadron had colorful bowling shirts made that read on the back "World Famous Custom Demolition–anytime, anyplace, any weather–Call VA-75 at 1-800 Bah Boom."

On the door to our stateroom, Boot put up the following:

If I go out and don't come back
First of all please check my rack
If I cannot in there be found
Look beneath a paper mound
But if I do get killed or shot down
And have to go to Hanoi town
Please open this and peer inside
I wrote it all before I died.

CHAPTER TWENTY-SIX

OR AT THE MEXICAN VILLAGE

25 June 1972–Reveille at 0500 after getting to bed at 0200 with an announcement that the ship expected to get underway ASAP in advance of typhoon Ora. I had to get all my flight gear and go out to Ops on the base to fly the aircraft out to the boat. About 30 planes were still at the air base and were to be flown out to the ship later in the day. The storm arrived sooner than expected, shutting down Cubi Point's airfield. We frantically tried to find enough chains to tie down and secure the planes against a fierce level five-force storm. Without a 13-point tie-down, the planes were bound to suffer major damage. An indifferent, lazy Base Ops officer, sitting comfortably in his office, kept saying there were no more chains available. CAG Bordone "borrowed" a jeep and after a visit to the Admiral's house arrived back with a key to the storage hut filled with new chains. We were able to chain down all the planes and retire to the O'Club where CAG bought us all a round or two of Martini's, which he referred to as "Tinis." Winds reached 85 miles per hour that night and caused 131 causalities in the islands.

At the BOQ, I took a sauna and got a massage (called a rubdown in those days) for $1.50. I was so relaxed that afterwards I felt like a heap of potatoes tumbling and rolling out of a burlap bag that someone had sliced open with a razor blade.

It's a known fact in the Navy that you run into someone you know either at The Mexican Village restaurant in Coronado, California or the Cubi Point O' Club. NAS Cubi Point was correctly known as the crossroads of the Western Pacific. Sure enough I ran into former flight Instructor Denny Gillease, Mike's brother from AOCS, flying A-7s off the Coral Sea. Instead of a peace sign hanging around his neck (we called it the footprint of the great American chicken), he had a pendant that said, "War" and carried a big knife with the inscription "Buck communism." I literally walked into Marine Captain Bill Holverstott (VT-4 Roommate), who was flying F-4s out of DaNang with Captain John Blackman, my classmate in flight training. Bill was fond of saying "stay on the step" which was an aviation term identifying the time and place when a plane and the pilot were exactly in sync. Then there was LT Jim Mast (flying A-7s off Oriskany) who had been my final instructor in advanced jets, which meant he had helped me get my wings. In jest I said, "If I get killed, it's your fault." It devastated him and he looked forlorn as he silently walked away. I really felt bad. If I had to make a list of guys I wanted to see just one more time, I would have seen them all there already–the fact actually scared me. Maybe my time *was* up?

*

The Cubi Point base was right in the jungle with huge lizards and monkeys all over the place. I was walking in an alley between two buildings when I stepped on a huge roach, which proceeded to chase me down the alley! We were required to carry our sidearm if we went off base because of the Hukbalahops, or Huks, the Communist terrorists of the Philippines. I asked a friend how he did with golf that day. Said he shot 84 and two monkeys because they kept running out and taking the golf balls. Some of the guys joined the "Baloot Club," usually after a "few" drinks. A baloot, or balute, is an incomplete chicken fetus. The egg is split open and everything is eaten–partially formed feathers, eyeballs, feet, beak, etc. Somebody ate six of them, and probably still isn't the same. These guys would also eat "Monkey on a Stick"!

Of course, others would go off base to Olongapo city known as 'The Po,' a place that made Tijuana look like the Vatican. It was a real Honkey-Tonk town with every sort of cheap, tawdry *entertainment*. Its seedy nightclubs raised sleaze entertainment to a whole new level. One B/N volunteered to become part of one such *show*. He did such a good job that it earned him the call sign "Dirtman." Whenever he walked in the Ready room everyone would sing "dadadada dadadadadadada, Dirtman!" to the tune of Batman. One of the few guys in the Navy with a theme song! I preferred to stay on base, besides it was safer.

Some of our squadron wives were staying there in rented houses with cooks, maids and butlers, which cost next to nothing. They called themselves "The Olongapo Babes." Even 46 years after our return, the "Babes" still hang around together and have a getaway each year. A fun group, they refer to themselves as TWSOP–*The Wives who Survived Olongapo.*

CHAPTER TWENTY-SEVEN

THE OTHER GUY MIGHT BE ME

2 July 1972–Back into combat on Yankee station. We briefed for
an Alpha strike to Hanoi but, due to weather, had to divert to Vinh
Sohn, N.W. of Vinh. They opened up with heavy 85mm while we
were still far from the target. Multiple red-orange fireball shell
bursts turned into black clouds while throwing out hot shrapnel in
all directions. The concussion caused by the explosions was
enough to flip a plane over or move a plane weighing 50,000
pounds a quarter mile out to the side. I was bracketed with bursts
going off behind, in front, and to the side of me. I tried my best to
throw off their aim by jinking hard and erratically changing
heading and altitude while at the same time trying not to lose too
much airspeed. Fireballs exploded right in front and to the sides of
my airplane. Any closer and we were goners! Through my rear
view mirrors, I saw furious bursts that chased me from behind. I
was being precisely tracked. For a split second it reminded me of a
story my Aunt Marie told me about mirrors. My Uncle George and
Aunt Marie had bought an old farmhouse outside of Albany, New
York. She asked the owner about the mirrors that were facing
outward by each door. The Old Russian woman explained that it
was to keep the devil away that came in the form of lightning.
After my Aunt moved in, she took the mirrors and put them in the

barn. That night they got hit twice by lightning! One came down and blew up the light over the kitchen table where her visiting parents were sitting. She put the mirrors back up. I hoped my mirrors kept away the AAA devil.

Continuous huge bursts of fire were still going off behind, in front and on both sides of me—jinking didn't help too much. I was beginning to feel they "got my number." Gritty puffs of black smoke-shockwaves slammed into the plane, while hundreds of razor-sharp pieces of steel hurled through the air. I rolled in and dropped my 14 MK82s. I figured that the gunners knew we always pulled off toward the sea so I planned to fake them out and go the other way. I did just that and *boom*! A big burst went off in front of the aircraft—I went the other way with the same result. With bursts all around the plane, I was thinking *I can't get out of here!* Finally, I was able to break free but to this day I don't know how. On the way back to the ship, I was still so scared that I had a barf bag out ready to throw up. I looked over at Boot and he was sound asleep! I hit the missile alert test and he sat straight up and mentioned something about shooting me the next time I did that. Coming downwind at the ship, I could feel my heart actually skip a beat. Back at the ship I asked my friend LT Brian Dempsey of Heavy One, "What was that place?"

"Oh, they call it the Vinh Sohn gunnery school because there are so many guns there. The site has bagged the most aircraft of the war!"

I've seen enough fireworks to last me a lifetime. The gunfire at night made the Fourth of July seem like a lightning bug at high noon in summer. I doubt if I'll ever enjoy fireworks again.

*

We UNREP bombs, fuel and supplies every night. I received a call one night in my room from the Bridge at 2215 saying they had a personal message from a LT Boecker and to contact him on the #1 Unrep station in the hangar bay. Jerry Boecker was a classmate of mine at Villanova and was the Engineering Officer on the USS Haliakala, an ammo ship. I spoke with him over headphones while he was standing across the way on his ship. Really a good guy and was wonderful to speak with him. His folks saw my name in the VU Alumni news and told him. We talked about classmate Jerry Keohe from Villanova, an easygoing pleasant guy. He volunteered as an Army Officer and was killed in action after being "in country" only a week. A few days after that, I got a letter from him saying he was with a good outfit and felt secure. They had all been wiped out in a grenade ambush. Also he said classmate Jerry Rinder, a Marine Captain, was landed ashore in Vietnam from a landing craft commanded by LT Brian O'Toole, his roommate. Villanova is here in force.

Coming back from our mission on July 4th, we had some friendly banter with a picket ship, call sign Oswald aka Ozzie, on duty in the northern part of the Tonkin Gulf. When we checked in, they invited us down for some surf 'n turf as well as baked Alaska for dessert to celebrate Independence Day! We told them we had to return to the ship but would take them up on it if we run into them in port–which we did about a month later!

*

In the cockpit, we had the Radar homing and warning system, the ALR45. It consisted of a small radarscope on the instrument panel that warned us of the fansong radar used to paint us (pick us up on their radar) and guide the SAMs. As the enemy searched for us with radar, an eerie fluorescent chartreuse green line would flicker on the screen. This neon light was accompanied by a staccato *did-dit-did-dit* sound in our headset. Quick, short chirping sounds, these abrupt tweets coincided with the detached dotted lines on the small scope. Once they locked us up, the sound became a steady legato and this unnatural green phosphorescent dotted line became solid, giving us the relative direction to the location of the site. The longer the line, the stronger the lock. We used to say that the line went off the scope and up and over our heads in the cockpit, the lock-up was so great. Many times, the scope was filled with a cluster of lines coming from all directions indicating multiple missile sites had us in their crosshairs!

*

Life magazine was really irritating me since it depicted us as the bad guys, but never showed pictures of the communists' tanks rolling into a Church at An Loc and killing everyone. The terrorism caused by the communists was unbelievable. It was barbaric. In Hue, they slaughtered 2800 locals. During the Easter Offensive, the communists would intentionally fire their 130mm artillery into the fleeing civilians. They would literally destroy thousands of mostly young women and children who were trying to outrun the onslaught. The level of butchery was unbelievable. After the battle at Con Thien, dead Marines were found to have been staked out alive on a cross like Christ. The demonstrators back in the States demanded a U.S. pullout–*how about demanding a Communist pullout?* The western press with its distortions and misinformation and ill-informed demonstrators were killing us. Every nutso who hated America was played on gook radio to our POWs. The absence of criticism of Russian and China was profound. His captors told POW Admiral Stockdale "we can't beat you on the battlefield but we will defeat you on the streets of New York and Chicago." John Steinbeck, working as a war correspondent, wrote, "The media was only interested in the "immediate and the dramatic" and that the real war in Vietnam was not being communicated to the people back home." It seems no one realized that the battle-hardened North Vietnamese communists and Viet Cong were evil; bad people, not just some lowly farmers.

Many times while airborne we'd hear a SAR effort going on. The emergency beeper on the survival radio went off automatically or could be turned on manually. This was hopefully followed by voice contact with the downed airman. Too often our plaintiff calls on our radios requesting "Beeper Beeper, come up voice" came to no avail. Years earlier, a pilot had ejected near China-owned Hainan Island. He sent out emergency signals from his raft for eight hours before permission was given for a rescue try because of the rules of engagement and politics. By then it was too late and he spent seven years in a Chinese prison!

*

At times I felt a sheer and utter sense of gloom. I was beginning to think this whole thing came down to how much luck one had. *Am I getting closer and closer to the edge?* My nerves were shot and my body was totally fatigued. I couldn't rest enough to work up to being just weary. Trying to rest always resulted in a frustrated fitful sleep and at best I'd catch maybe three hours of sleep at a time. It became the sleep of the damned, a type of tired that even sleep couldn't help. Also there were many times I was too hungry to sleep and too tired to go get something to eat.

Stuff just happened, you could be flying next to a plane one minute and all of a sudden he'd get hit and there was nothing but debris consisting of only dust and smoke. No chute, no nothing. Surprisingly you'd hear the pilot talking on his survival radio on the ground! Other times you could see a guy punch out, land, run and never be heard from again!

I have so many complicated emotions. War resets your metabolism to something like fast-forward in a zigzag sort of way and where all the years of a lifetime are compressed into minutes, even seconds.

They say it always *happens to the other guy* but I was beginning to realize that the *other guy* might be *me*

209

CHAPTER TWENTY-EIGHT

AND IT WAS NIGHT

6 July 1972–Alpha to Phu Ly cancelled due to weather–went Armed Reconnaissance (ARREC) in Route Package 3 (RP-3) looking for targets of opportunity. Hit RR bridges with eight MK83 (1,000 pound bombs). Dick Engle led. Ken Knapp was getting ready to roll in on the bridge when I saw his plane (that was across from me) totally engulfed in fire and smoke from AAA fire. He was inside one big, deadly cloud filled with shrapnel. I said, "Keep it moving Ken. They're shooting at you!" He missed the bridge but hit in the tree line that sent up a secondary explosion some 2,000 feet in the air–he hit their weapons storage area. Dick rolled in and obliterated the gunsite.

LCDR Bob "Mom" Graustein was on a low level when he got hosed down by AAA at Nam Dinh–very frightening. Seemed they were getting closer to Bob, but he continued to fly dangerous missions like everyone else. He's a good guy, but since he came from the S-2 (prop) community, he was always trying to play catch-up with the jet group. He worries about every little thing while trying to get ahead–earning him the call sign of "Mom."

One of our B/Ns turned in his wings. He was in the wrong line of work to begin with and probably would have killed a pilot and himself. However a poor private fighting in South Vietnam didn't have the option to just up and leave.

*

Boot and I tried to sleep during the day because we were just plain worn out. The stress and strain of combat, day in and day out was tormenting the heck out of me. My nervous system was outraged. I was scared *all the time*, more than scared–*terrified* would be more like it–in combat, out of combat, on the ship, off the ship, in port, out of port. There was no refuge and no reprieve. Even when in port it was always in the back of my mind that I had to go back into combat. The feeling consumed me and this type of fear could take away your very existence. However:

It is only in the face of death that we truly understand life.

(Dostoyevsky)

Coming back from one mission, it was so dark and the rain so violent that I couldn't see a thing on approach, and I boltered (missed the wires). After getting the crap shot out of us, I had to land in this ink black void. Instead of windshield wipers we had high-pressure air from the engines to blow the rain off the windscreen. Next pass I told Boot, "OK, turn on the windshield air; I can't see a thing."

Boot said, "It's been on for the last half-hour."

It looked like Niagara Falls was hitting the windscreen. There was just a small clear area about eight inches square in the upper right hand corner of the windscreen. I had to stretch and crane my neck to look up and out that little hole and fly the plane.

211

At the same time I could barely reach the throttles on the left side of the cockpit. We trapped OK, but it totally wore me out. Our plane captain climbed up the ladder to the cockpit and asked us how it went that night. I told him it was really quiet–we didn't get painted at all by enemy radar of any sort. I saw nothing on the ALQ 100, which was the equipment that warned us of enemy radar activity. He reached over and turned it *on*!

*

Weather continued to be hot and humid. It was downright steamy day and night, making it very uncomfortable. *You would think they could find a place with nice weather to hold a war!* Then I remembered that Pop said that after 15 minutes at altitude on their way to Berlin, the coffee in their thermos would be frozen. The temperature got down to 40 or 50 degrees below zero and there was no heat in the plane. Then, when they returned, their quarters in the Quonset hut were damp, cold and dismal. That changed one night real fast when the hut got hot and bright when a crewmember went up on the roof and fired a flare from his emergency signal pistol down the chimney into the potbelly stove in the quarters just for laughs!

In WWII, accidents and midairs caused by the constant fog and bad weather in England accounted for 20 percent of their losses. So weather was always a major factor in combat flying.

I carried plastic baby bottles filled with water so I could evade longer if I got shot down. I'd end up drinking them before even leaving the flight deck. On a CAT shot, hot, salty sweat from under my helmet would rush down my forehead and pour into my eyes, burning the hell out of them. The rubber oxygen mask would soak my cheeks as well.

We were all so jumpy that at night some pilots would call "SAM lifting three o'clock" when in fact it was a planet rising.

Before each mission, Boot and I would decide what altitude, for example 200 feet; we would fly our night low-level at. During the attack, he would have his radar in search mode and if there wasn't a return, it meant there was something ahead of us so we'd climb. The only problem was that it didn't pick up cables, fences, trees or barrage balloons! I'd watch my radar altimeter to get the correct reading of my actual altitude above the ground. Boot backed all this up with a chart showing the route with the headings and time to the target. As always, he spent two to three hours planning such a route. The Air Force F-111s flew the same type mission, but they did it on autopilot, while we hand flew it which is why it made the mission unique to the A-6.

*

Since 1 April 1972, there were 1663 SAMs fired–April 750, May 430, June 330, and 153 first week of July. Free ammo from Russia! The SAMs traveled at 2,000 miles an hour and were good out to 22 miles and 60,000 feet! Hard to run and hide from these guys!

I recalled in my senior year in college watching TV in the living room of our rental house with my roommates. President Johnson came on to say he wasn't running for re-election and that we were going to stop bombing North Vietnam. That was March 31st of 1968. I couldn't believe it then and I couldn't believe it now—a unilateral agreement with nothing in return from the North Vietnamese enemy! We didn't bomb North Vietnam for four years, while our troops were fighting in the South. It's like fighting Canada while they send their troops into the States and we don't attack Canada. This is akin to trying to step on a swarm of ants one by one instead of leveling the anthill. Also you would think that the powers-to-be would have learned from WWII that bombing alone does not win a war. In 1944 with the heaviest bombing of the war the production in Germany was the highest. You have to invade the place to win. Now, four years later, we were some of the first to go back North after they had all this time to resupply, rest up and get ready. They increased their Soviet supplied air defenses and moved troops and supplies into place near the DMZ in anticipation of the invasion of the South. During the lull in bombing the guards would tell the POWs that their country didn't even care enough to attack them. There were still politically protected sanctuaries. Inviolate airfields were left undisturbed, permitting the enemy free access to get airborne and attack our strike forces!

Filipino stewards waited on us during meals, but sometimes the conversations were hard to understand.

"Manrique, what's for breakfast?"

"Wabbles, sir."

What's a wabble? A waffle maybe?

At dinner we speculated what was for dessert.

"Banella ice cream, sir"

OK, now is that banana or vanilla ice cream, or both? But every now and then, we'd have Filipino night in the wardroom– quite good–lumpia and all.

Once again, we mourned our loss–a MiG bagged LT Bob "Gull" Randell and LT Fred "Bat" Masterson of VF-103–no chutes were seen. Just a few days earlier, Boot mentioned how lucky a guy Gull was since he was winning at slots at the Cubi O' Club. The next day we switched from the 1000-0100 schedule to the 2200-1400 one, which was very hard to get used to. As usual, I slept only two to three hours at a clip, with the days and nights converging. We went days without even seeing the sun. We joked that we were growing mold behind our ears and began to feel like moles.

*

12 July 1972–Day seed (dropped mines) at a river mouth at Hoang Xa–bad weather enroute. The idea of mining Haiphong harbor actually went back to February of 1965 when then CAG CDR Hank Glindeman of USS Coral Sea recommended it after seeing Soviet freighters loaded with trucks going up the Tonkin Gulf to Haiphong Harbor. Approval was recommended all the way to Washington. The reply came back stating something to the effect that "we're only retaliating (for the Tonkin Gulf incident), not declaring war."

It had to be a low delivery to stay out of the SAM envelope. I was at 50 feet and the Skipper was below me and off to the left. While making our mining run up Haiphong harbor, sampans in the gulf were taking pot shots at us while gunsites were shooting down on us from the ridges that lined the harbor. That makes four missions in 24 hours–*does anyone know what year it is?*

Hanoi Hannah (Trinh Thi Ngo), the Tokyo Rose of her day, made English-speaking broadcasts from Hanoi putting out propaganda daily. She said they had a pilot. We were hoping that perhaps it was Bob Randall. She also knew names of some of our pilots on the ship and where they were from!

When the blackness of the night closed in, it was different than it was back home. The dimness literally rose up from the sea and was not the warm, soft and encompassing kind that attracts you to restful, calm sleep. Instead there was cold fury and danger about it. The nights were so solid that the darkness was almost overpowering. The storms at night made it even more sinister and vengeful with heavy seas. The murky nights were suffocating. Combined with furious rains, it seemed the night was just waiting to snatch the life from me. Night became a hostile environment when it should be one of comfort not death. Night itself was being tortured. During night missions the intense anti-aircraft fire ripped the sky apart, piercing the darkness and opening jagged holes in the night. There was no sanctuary from a night heavy with gunfire. Bullets were coming at us from all sides. Perhaps it corresponded with the gospel of John concerning the Last Supper as Judas left to betray Jesus–"*… and it was night.*" A whisper's echo emerged, would my *night* come? On the way back to the ship, there were a million stars all above and around straight down to the horizon. I recalled that the Irish refer to the stars as 'holes in the bottom of heaven.' Weird and wonderful, it seemed to calm things down a bit. I remembered a line from a poem by my friend, Gayla.

"*And strange it seems, that overhead-are the stars I loved back home.*" My God, I wish I was back home!

*

14 July 1972–We flew a night ARREC up through the hourglass area to Hanoi hoping to "just happen" to drop on Jane Fonda and Ramsey Clark. When we dropped our bombs, we broadcasted they were for Jane Fonda who was visiting Hanoi. There were pictures of her in newspapers back in the States showing her sitting on a North Vietnamese gunsite. The caption read, "Jane Fonda in North Vietnam to encourage the Soldiers fighting against American Imperialist Air-Raiders." She was quoted as saying, "I wish one of those suckers would come by so I could shoot him down." She was shown on news footage stating that the POWs, according to the Geneva Convention, "were criminals and should be tried and executed." North Vietnamese Colonel Bui Tin told the Wall Street Journal, "Visits to Hanoi by people like Jane Fonda gave us confidence that we should hold on in the face of battlefield reverses. She basically was giving aid and comfort to the enemy. A bumper sticker said it all: *Jane Fonda Communist at Heart Traitor by Choice.*

Knowing that the enemy listened to our radios, Boot read a poem over the air during one of our night low-level missions:

Jane, Jane with thoughts of sin
Left the States for old Nam Dinh
When she got there it was dark-
So out she went to look for Clark
Who said after a prolonged kiss
We can't go on meeting like this
But that's the last thing that was said
Cause A-6 Rockeye killed them dead.

We figured later that since the enemy monitored our radio transmissions, they put this poem out in paperback form and make a million dollars.

Far left standing Skipper Earnest far right Don Linland - both lost

CHAPTER TWENTY–NINE

GATEWAY TO OBLIVION

One night coming back aboard ship nothing was registering in my brain. I was looking right at the instruments and could tell our wings were level but it just didn't feel right. I felt like we were in a turn. It was like looking at the hands of a watch and not being able to recognize what time it was. I had the worst case of vertigo ever and was totally exhausted as well. I kept asking Boot, "Are we level, are we level?"

"Yup, keep it coming Al." Thanks to Boot I made it aboard. Astronaut Eugene Cernan said landing on the moon was a piece of cake compared to landing on the ship at night.

Ron Lankford came back with his plane on fire and had to take the barricade to get aboard–he and his B/N started to nonchalantly climb out of the plane. When they lowered the B/N's ladder, it fell to the ground completely burned off. Seeing this and all the smoke, they jumped down and ran like hell. It was the plane with my name on it! It never flew again. A few days later Dave "Poppin' Fresh" (a generous sized man like the Pillsbury Dough Boy) Warren came back with the VDI (flight instrument screen) on fire. Since he was the B/N when Ron Lankford had the fire, we were now offering fire extinguishers to all pilots who have to fly with Dave.

Of course, combat action led to more than a couple of new expressions. Someone developed the "Falcon Codes." Instead of broadcasting a whole sentence, all you had to do was transmit a number. For example, Falcon code 101 meant, "you've got to be shitting me!"

Code 113–"Let me talk to that SOB."

Code 232–"Just out of curiosity, Gator (navigator), where the farg are we?"

Code 901– "If it's such a good farging deal, send someone else."

We had one thousand of these numeric codes, number 1000 being "Cool it, the Padre is here."

One night, we were diverted by Screwtop (E-2 radar plane) to a target that was different than the one we had planned. We were all elbows and alligators in the cockpit with charts to figure where we were going. Going across the beach we saw 40 trucks heading north, 50 miles in land on route 15. Then there was another 100 trucks and we hit them with 8MK 80s and 6 MK82s resulting in three secondaries. There was a SAM strobe out of Vinh just to the south of us on egress. Seems all these missions are hairy.

The Hourglass area of North Vietnam was basically a flak trap. They'd put a light on–you rolled in and got hosed down. The hourglass shape is formed by two rivers, the Red River (Song Da) and the Black river (Song Vi), which empty into the gulf of Tonkin (Vinh Sac Viet) near the town of Tang Chau. At night, the bad guys signaled ahead using strobe lights or small rockets, giving away our direction of flight as we flew over–then they put up barrage fire. This was easy to do since all the ammunition came free of charge from Russia and China. And then came the MiGs– one high with his lights on, and one low flying with them turned off.

Our ordnance guys painted on one of my bombs, *"If you can read this you are one lucky son-of-a-bitch."* Another bomb read, *"Excedrin Headache #2."*

*

During one mission, we hit Shipyard number three in Haiphong. The next day former Attorney General and current peacenik, Ramsey Clark, was surveying the damage. Whatever happened to aiding and abetting the enemy? He had given me my diploma from Villanova four years earlier! I'd like to shove it down his throat right about now!

CAG was a great guy who flew two missions a day as the lead. Affectionately having the call sign of "Guinea One", Commander Deke Bordone was a born leader with a mild mannered approach to leading his flyers of Air Wing Three. Many pilots would say they'd follow him to downtown Moscow with a cap pistol. Besides being a competent warrior, he always stood up for his men. He understood that loyalty went both ways. On one mission that he was leading, he actually bypassed the target by mistake. I heard someone say, "CAG, target one o'clock, CAG target three o'clock, CAG target is behind us!" at which point he turned the strike force and we hit it coming from a different direction. In his de-brief he said, "Did you notice how we faked them out?" Another time as he led us out from a strike there were so many SAMs in the air he radioed, "Aces (our call sign) go low," in order to avoid their radar. We were so low that we were pulling up for dikes. One of the planes on his wing called, "CAG trucks nine o'clock high!" We were below trucks that were on a road! A plaque was later hung in the ready room with that radio call. We could use all kinds of codes which the enemy could figure out, but if we said, "Come right to 090," they couldn't understand it!

The USS America was over here now and later on in port I saw more old friends–many of whom I had gone through the A-6 RAG with, were now in VA-35 on America, Dick "Gomer" Haverner, Bobbie Day, etc. When she got on the line, the America blew two boilers and went into port for repairs. This extended us from a 17-day line period to a 30 day one.

All our crews were interesting individuals; a good example was B/N Tom "Slick" Vance and pilot Bob "Chis" Chisholm who also roomed together. Before each mission, Slick would play the song "Miss American Pie" by Don Mclean which includes the line, *"This'll be the day that I die."* Slick also went by "CLO" for Combat Line Officer.

Over the beach on a night low level, Chis would ask Slick, "How we doing?" If there wasn't an immediate answer Chis would pop up another hundred feet! With all the gunfire going off around them, Slick would say "we ain't dead yet." We didn't know it at the time but Chis wore glasses and had a hard time seeing the ball

222

coming back aboard ship. So Slick would "call the ball" and always tell Chis he was a little low. Years later my wife asked them, "How did you get aboard ship?"

Slick answered, "It was the Chis and Slick show!" They were a good team.

Chis was so easy going that I am convinced he didn't know he was in a war! He was the type of person who could say, "I try to worry but I just can't." He'd have to get overly excited to make it to Zen. Years later after he got out of the Navy, he was flying DC-3 freighters in the Caribbean. One time his Captain overdosed and died on a flight. Coming back into the States, he was detained by the authorities for some time and interrogated at length. Seems someone had taken his identity and committed a murder. Chis said it was all just a big mistake. On a trip to Europe, he and his wife Bobbie had rented a "do-it-yourself" barge for a canal trip in France. One evening, he tied up the barge with a rope strung across the canal. During the night, a jet skier came by and decapitated himself on the rope. Again Chis ended up in jail but was eventually released. Anytime we mentioned we couldn't wait to get home, Slick would answer with, "What's the rush?" He would go on to say that nothing would change, no one knew or understood what we did. Nor did they want to. And he was right.

Years later Slick wrote me: *You are respected by me, as much or more than anyone, as one of the trusted warriors in our squadron along with Helmut. You were there to fight, as I believe that Chis and I were, and willing to and eager to do our duty, taking on the tougher jobs presented instead of finding an excuse to defer.*

Things happen fast at the ship really fast. Leading a four-plane formation back to the ship, the radar controller said "signal buster," which means use max speed to get back to the ship. Approaching the ship at 350 knots, I radioed that we were eight miles out. The air boss said, "Roger, spin two, drag one and you land straight in." I was all over the cockpit trying to slow down enough to get into the landing configuration while at the same time sending hand signals to my wingmen telling two to do a 360 turn in place while the last one loitered enough behind in order to drag it in after them.

During the previous night's mission, I was completely and utterly exhausted. When I climbed down the ladder on the side of my plane, I just kept going down to the deck. My legs wouldn't hold me up. I had no strength in my back and legs. My plane captain helped me to my room. My back was killing me from the long missions as well as pranging my plane onto the ship. Later in my rack I even tried giving myself a backrub.

This combat stuff could be a gateway to oblivion. Perhaps eternity was just over the beach?

CHAPTER THIRTY

R&R

17 July 1972–Heavy seas enroute to Cubi and arrived at 2100. Anchored out–hell of a ride on a U (utility) boat to shore. Saw nurse friend Kathy and she said it had been raining for 22 days straight. Average yearly rainfall was 700 inches.

Foreign policy dictated that we had to go to port in the P.I. before we could visit another port like Hong Kong for Rest and Relaxation (R&R). This was so that we were not considered a combatant ship when entering a foreign port. Some of the married crews were allowed to fly ahead via a commercial plane through Saigon so they could get there a few days early to meet their wives.

20 July-27 July 1972–R&R in Hong Kong. Out of the last 125 days, we'd been in port only six! We arrived at 0600 and anchored some four miles out, requiring a 30-minute ride to shore in the whaleboat or the officer's gig. *A Serviceman's Guide to Hong Kong* stated, "If you would like to extend your stay in the Colony, then take a weapon into Hong Kong. The going rate is about eight years in prison for carrying a loaded weapon. Even firecrackers are good for three years." There were no dock facilities, so all ships anchored out and were offloaded by smaller boats (wiblics). There were boats and ships all over the place from junks to yachts. The partially-sunk burned hulk of the Queen

Elizabeth lay on her side in the harbor. Something like one thousand ships a week came and went. It is a beautiful city and lovely harbor where three or four generations of the same family live and work on their junks and sampans. I shopped in the morning at the Fleet Club of the Royal Navy buying jewelry, jade, ivory and silk for the home front.

The first night in, I stood Shore Patrol Watch with the Brits andAussies. They told me, "Don't worry, sir; we'll take care of the Blokes." One of the Aussies asked me what type of plane I flew.

" An A-6," I answered

"That's a big Tinny," he replied.

He went on to tell me about Aussie football or "footie" as they say. It's as tough as American football but they don't wear any equipment for protection. He said that in America when a football star retires he becomes a TV announcer. Not so in Australia because the guy is all broken up and has an eye hanging out, etc. When one player got up in the morning his mate had to grab him by the shoulders and shake him in order to align the bones in his body. There was also a contingent of Gurkhas from Nepal, short, thick soldiers who also guarded the Queen. I asked if I could see one of their knives. Known as the Khukuri, or Kukri, it had an inwardly curved edge and was mean looking. "Sure" one said and nicked himself on his thumb–legend has it that anytime they pulled their knives, they had to draw blood. I was just glad it wasn't mine. The knife was acclaimed in a unit's situation report in North Africa in WWII. "Enemy losses; ten killed, ours nil, ammunition expenditure nil." It felt like WWII with allies. I wrote four letters home and my watch was up.

Later that night, I went to the Hilton's basement bar hideaway called The Den. Turn-of-the-century China coast décor and service by Cheongsam girls made it a special place. I sat next to a few guys surrounding a young lady, Donna, who was traveling with her parents. I said hello and she answered, "Oh an American!" in a most condescending, disappointed way. That evening I changed her from a pacifist college kid to a believer. We were inseparable for the next few days and actually became lifelong friends.

We had a party in our room until 0530. One B/N kept calling room service for more Scotch, a pilot was out cold on the bathroom floor and one Helo pilot was last seen crawling down the hallway in his under-shorts. Later that day a few of us got into a cab and said, "Hyatt" the driver answered excitedly, "Hyatt!" and nodded and we repeated "Hyatt." He said it more loudly and we said it again just as loud. Finally, we used the Japanese *Hayaku* (meaning fast) and he answered "Hayaku!" He did a big screeching U turn and parked in front of the Hyatt right across the street! We then went up to the Polaris lounge on top of the Hyatt–a great place with a fantastic view and made it to bed by 0500 and were up at 0800.

Donna's parents really took me in. Her father was an eye doctor from Naples, Florida, in Hong Kong for a symposium. The following night they treated me to dinner at the Eagle's Nest restaurant at the top of the Hilton –good onion soup and a great Italian opera singer, Romano Dragoni. He sat with us and went on to tell us how, during World War II in Italy, a hungry New Zealand soldier who was starving and had no money, took some eggs and paid the angry farmer, who was his father, by singing *Come Back to Sorrento*. That's when he decided he was going to be a singer. We danced and laughed all night.

When we told Donna's folks that we were going up to the top of Victoria Peak, her mother, who was the first twirler at the University of Miami (the license on her car read "Twirler One") said, "*Give me your hand.*" This was a line from the very romantic "Love is a Many Splendid Thing" with William Holden and Jennifer Jones, which took place there (*We have been blessed with love–a many splendor thing*). Donna and I took a cab up and just sat there for a few hours enjoying the spectacular view overlooking the skyline of Hong Kong and off into China.

On Sunday, we went out on the "Wan Fu" (Ten Thousand Felicitations) a 110-foot brigantine owned by the Hilton which catered the whole thing. A retired British sea captain was in charge, but was half in the bag before we even left the harbor, at which point his crew took over. We sailed to a small island where we ate, drank, swam and drank some more. Everyone jumped off the 20-foot bowsprit; Ken Knapp jumped in with a beer bottle in his hand and came up drinking from it. Some went higher and higher up the mast, depending on the amount of alcohol they had consumed.

A few pilots from CIA-operated Air America joined us and kept us entertained with tons of stories! Their apartment in Saigon had gotten robbed. Knowing that bandits always came back for more, they rigged the apartment with grenades. They got two of them but one escaped on a bicycle going down a small hill. One of the Air America pilots was a Native American who carried a bow and arrow. He hit the guy in the back as he fled–the bike with the dead bandit hunched over the handlebars with the arrow in his back just continued going down the street. Another Air America pilot had his 12-year-old son visiting from the States. When the kid froze up on the mast his father said, "Jump. All it can do is kill you!" A Vietnamese pilot, Nguyen, Nguyen (pronounced win, win) said that if he got shot down, his name would be *"No Win"*.

Two businessmen from San Francisco said that they'd rent the boat for another whole day, stock it, and put a map up and throw darts at it to see where we'll stop–only if we'd be their guests. I actually had a hard time back at the hotel trying to convince the married couples to join us. Nobody believed me. Eventually Bob and Linda Dunn, Bob Chisholm, Ken Knapp, Ron and Loretta Lankford, the Quack, John Horan and a few others decided to come. I had to laugh at a patch Loretta had on the back pocket of her jeans that read, "Kiss my patch." The next day we began another Wan Fu cruise with the group sailing with all kinds of drinks and food, exotic lunch and hot dinner. Mark and Al who rented the boat had a great hatred of communism–Al had fought in Korea so they really appreciated what we were doing. There were fifteen of us with a crew of ten. We anchored and swam in Repulse Bay; we had a blast! We visited Chung Chin and other islands, small fishing villages where everyone was busy working. On one such island, men, women and children intently worked, making small toy trucks destined for Philadelphia. Women would carry large, heavy pigs wrapped in wire at the end of along pole they carried across their shoulders. We anchored and swam and dived off the mast again. The view was great as we came back into the harbor with the city in lights.

The Star Ferry that sailed back and forth to Kowloon from Hong Kong charged ten cents for second-class, 25 cents for first-class. It left every five minutes and was a great ride. One night I rode second-class with Donna, who was wearing a formal dress, with chickens all around on the deck. When I went to the airport to see her family off, it was like watching an old "I Love Lucy" movie. They were wearing all their new jewelry to avoid customs. I told them the plane would be overweight and not get airborne.

The food in Hong Kong was great and the city itself was very clean. A city of contrasts–yachts, junks and sampans. Bamboo scaffolds were used alongside new skyscraper buildings with laborers who worked barefooted. At one point they tried making them wear shoes and use metal scaffolds but so many workers fell off that they went back to bamboo and bare feet. The Sara was painted by "Bloody Mary" and her crew of women–you could see the wavy waterline where they had painted down to. The locals were very nice and industrious. Since the U.S. dollar equaled $5.65 in Hong Kong, there were great deals to be had! Of course there was always an "American" type bar. I mentioned to the manager of one that I really didn't want to see pictures of Cleveland in a restaurant in Hong Kong. He took them down. It reminded me of the "Brooklyn" bar in Cannes on the Riviera during our first cruise. All the young sailors would head straight for it and never leave the place, homesick I guess.

The Chinese will not let their picture be taken since they believe that when they die, their whole body will not go to heaven. One of our pilots was sending back pictures of fellow air wing pilots. When a few were shot down, it caused the wives to write him and ask that he not take any pictures of their husbands. This replicated an episode in WWI where fellow pilots of the leading German Ace Wilfred Von Richt often refused to have their pictures taken before a mission. The Barron's picture had been taken prior to the mission when he was shot down and killed.

The last night in Hong Kong we ate at an Irish restaurant where the special was of course "Irish stew." There was a favorite feral cat hanging around the place the whole time. I asked the waiter the cat's name.

"*Stew*eyII."

I ordered something else. Didn't want to know what happened to Stewey number One!

As fantastic as it was, in the back of my mind I always knew I had to return to the war. Sure there was some rest but no real relaxation because my brain was always busy keeping a vigil, anticipating more combat that was to come. But I had a really great time, which gave me a new outlook on life. I hadn't laughed that much in five years! I returned to the Sara at 0400 on the 27th and was back in combat on the 28th–one minute I was having a ball and the next I was back in combat. What an artificial life, or perhaps a very real life indeed?

It was during this time that a note was slipped under Sandy "Ratman" Sanford's door on the ship." We have kidnapped your stuffed rat. If you don't pay the ransom of 24 cases of beer you will never see it again. It has already been dropped from the 10th floor of the Hong Kong Hilton." Rat wouldn't fly a mission until he got his rat back. He paid part of the ransom and when he got it back, noticed that one side of it was flat from being dropped. The helo guys had kidnapped it. Boot always referred to Rat as the "battle rodent."

"Rat" leading the pack. L-R Paul "Hvids" Hvidding, John "JP" Pieno, Don "Low Drag" Petersen, Steve "Hermes" Bryant, Sandy "Rat" Sanford.

CHAPTER THIRTY-ONE

MY SOUL IS OVERWHELMED

As we left Hong Kong, word came through that a B/N off the Midway was killed on a night low-level mission when one round went up through the canopy hitting him in the head. I knew immediately that it was Ray Donnelly, my friend from college.

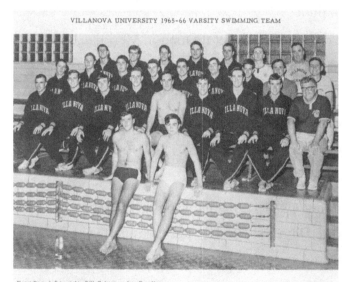

VILLANOVA UNIVERSITY 1965-66 VARSITY SWIMMING TEAM

Front Row, left to right: Bill Bohrman, Lee Capellaro.
Second Row: Ken Herr, Rich Lamb, Tim Turvey, Joe Parell, Captain Ray Donnelly, Frank Conlin, Greg Doyle, Don West, Head Coach Ed, Geisz.
Third Row: John Hoffman, Frank Musico, Tom Brennan, Bob Frey, Al Fischer, Bob Brenker, Tom Brady, Managers Peter Alter, Ray Curran.
Top Row: Mike Fitzmaurice, John Doherty, Bill Livingood, Chip Friday, Ed Ritti, Manager Tim Wahl, Assistant Coach Jack Lumsden.
Missing from Photo: Bob Biese, Gerry Gears, Paul Horneleth.

Author directly behind left shoulder of shirtless Ray Donnelly in middle of team picture. Within six years he was KIA.

Sadly it was! Ray and I swam together at Villanova, where he was All-American and captain of the team. He graduated two years ahead of me and went on to Yale Medical School. I, of course, was flying in the Navy. One weekend back in the States, I took my plane and flew a weekend cross-country trip to NAS Whidbey Island north of Seattle. While standing in front of the chapel waiting to go to Sunday Mass, I noticed someone coming down a small hill and across a field from the BOQ. I said to myself, *if I didn't know better, I'd swear it was Ray Donnelly*. He had very characteristically square shoulders and no waist. When he got closer I saw it was Ray. "Ray, what are you doing here?"

"I'm in the Navy."

"What are you, a Navy Doc?"

"Nope, didn't like Med School. I remembered you went through AOCS so I did too."

"Are you a pilot?"

"I wish. We were in basic jet training in Meridian, Mississippi. One day they herded us into the auditorium and said all those on the left-hand side are still in pilot training–all those on the right can either get out or come back as an NFO. I was on the right side, so now I'm an A-6 B/N." That's how Ray ended up as a B/N in VA-115 on the USS Midway.

Ray was flying a mission with pilot Mike "Mondo" McCormick, a Notre Dame boy. Soon after crossing the beach into the highly defended area of the Red River of North Vietnam, intense gunfire erupted. One round went through the canopy and hit Ray in the side of his head as he looked into the radarscope. He didn't move, didn't say a word. Mike headed back to the ship and noticed that he had a hard time seeing the instruments–everything was red. They were covered with Ray's blood. He just wanted to get back aboard ship to get Ray help. LT Raymond P. Donnelly never knew what hit him. Just like Larry Kilpatrick, Ray died in darkness so far away from home. I am sure that stars passed through his soul.

After he landed, Mike locked himself in his room for three days, not wanting to fly anymore. His father, a Navy Captain, got word back to the ship, "Get him back on the flight schedule–no son of mine is not going to fly anymore!" Their Skipper took LTJG Alan "Arlo" Clark, and made him Mike's new B/N.

Years later, a squadronmate of Ray's, Steve Coonts, wrote the book "Flight of the Intruder," the story being based on a B/N getting hit in the head. I was walking by a bookstore in 1986 and saw the book in the window. I went inside and just happened to open it up to the page telling about the B/N getting hit–knowing it was Ray I couldn't pick up the book for another three years. The original title of the book was "For Each Other" which spoke of how squadron members truly cared for one another.

These SOBs were taking my friends one by one. Seems like war always takes the very best. Bit by bit, you can be overcome by the death of your friends, which actually produces a lifelong sadness for those lost. This sorrow can weigh you down, and if dwelt upon, can make you useless for further endeavors. I recalled a reading from Mark in the Bible where he quoted Christ,

"My soul is overwhelmed with sorrow to the point of death."

When you see your friends die, it somehow makes the prospect of dying easier. I felt if it was good enough for Larry or Ray, it was good enough for me. I would love to make it back so that people didn't forget those who didn't make it back. It was a good feeling to know that someone was willing to die for you, and that you would do the same.

I learned to pray in a hurry. That's the same thing Pop told me he did during a bombing mission to Berchtesgaden, Hitler's mountain hideaway. It was a dangerous daytime single plane low-level mission. They were shooting the hell out of Pop with pieces of his plane flying off like potato peels. In between prayers he thought, *I'd go through this now so that perhaps if I have a son someday he won't have to do this.*

I was sure the guys who were shot down prayed just as much as I did.

*

29 July 1972–We covered Hancock's stand-down day and flew strikes around the town of Quang Tri in South Vietnam trying to lift the siege. They were in serious danger of being overrun. The gunner in the area had the ZSU-23-2 sending clusters of flaming golf balls at the others and me. Ronny Dean Lankford leveled the site. As usual, it was terrible weather.

The call would come down from the Air Boss in Pri-fly for the pilots to man up for a mission. Initially, the responses were formal. All eight Ready Rooms would answer, "Ready One, Roger; Ready Two, Roger; etc." Later on starting with our squadron, each ready room had its own type of reply. Ours was, Don, "Low Drag" Peterson giving the Tarzan yell. One had a bell, another a whistle, etc. The responses sounded like a midway sideshow. Leaving our Ready Room to man up, the last thing we saw was a sign on the door:

Smile you're gonna be on radar.

As I was manning up, my plane captain AO3 Bolena said, "Mr. Fischer, I don't know what I'd do if something ever happened to you." That touched me and really felt good. "Don't worry Bolena, I'll take care" and at the same time wondering if I would survive. He was a good kid and spent about 20 hours a day with the planes, keeping them fit to fly. I was astonished by how hard these young sailors worked, day in and day out–especially up on the hot, dangerous flight deck. Their average age was 19, just young kids.

A typical Air Wing Alpha strike consisted of four A-6s, six A-7s, seven F-4s, one A-5, and one E-2. All joined up in formation overhead the ship before heading toward the enemy. One time we were to go "feet dry" (go ashore) just south of the hourglass area and "surprise" the enemy. We got close to the coast without being "painted" by radar; however, the F-4s were lagging because they were flying slower to conserve fuel. The whole Air wing did a huge 360 while they joined up. As we approached the coast for the second time, multiple radar sites lit us up. So much for a big surprise! Coasting ashore at the Hour Glass area, we proceeded northwest along the karst ridges. These are ancient rock formations that seem to have come up straight out of the ground. Reaching as high as 4,000 feet in some areas, they look like solid black mud piles. They were especially dangerous for our night low-level missions. We used a 2200' hill as a turn point toward the north near Nui Con Thua. AAA fire always started the minute we went across the beach. Bursts were going off all around, over and under the plane. I was waiting for one to come up through the seat. The gunfire was joined by SAM launches, which intensified the closer we got to the Hanoi region. This was a brutal area to get in and out of. It was so heavily defended that in some spots there were AAA sites every 1/4-mile as well as a bunch of SAM sites. MiGs joined in the fray, some coming down from China. *Pick your poison!*

*

Orbiting off the coast was an Air Force C-121, the military version of the Lockheed Constellation. With the call sign of "Deep Sea", it was used to monitor enemy radar and radio transmissions.

The controller would broadcast anytime there was a threat. With a deep, very slow southern drawl, it seemed like it took forever for the message to be transmitted. This guy could win the "Slow Talkers of America" contest!

Slowly (so very slowly) he would transmit, "This- is - Deep-

Phu Ly Army barracks/warehouses

238

Sea - on -guard; Blue- bandits (MiG-21s) - 30 miles south - of - Bullseye (Hanoi) - heading - 180 degrees. Blue - Bandits - 15 miles, Blue - bandits - engaging."

"Oh really?!" came a grunting reply as a pilot was pulling 5G's trying to outmaneuver the MiGs.

Good hits!

Once again, Ramsey Clark and a few other Americans came over to see if we were bombing dikes. No one was going to go over the beach to get the hell shot out of them just to bomb a piece of dirt! While they were there, they should have checked out the towns where the VC rolled

Results of precision visual dive bombing

in with their tanks, killing the people. The senior military commander of the North Vietnamese, General Vo Nguyen Giap, and his troops committed horrific atrocities against their own people. A West German correspondent came across evidence of

Viet Cong butchers torturing to death a pro-Saigon village chief along with his wife and 12 children. According to *Reader's Digest* (November 1968), at least 100,000 acts of terror against the South Vietnamese people were recorded by the end of 1967. And what about the wholesale killing of refugees during the Easter Offensive of 1972, or the shooting at our downed aviators in the water? Didn't they realize Americans still died over here each day? Communists are just plain subhuman!

As many as 800,000 people fled China into the north of Vietnam when Mao Zedong and the communists took over in1949. Those who left China fled further south when the communists took over North Vietnam in 1954. During this original evacuation of North Vietnam, Navy Doctor Tom Dooley called North Vietnam "The rim of hell." In 1965, Chinese activist Lin Zhao referred to 'Mao Zedong Thought' as "blackened marrow of totalitarian politics." Democratic rights are God-given, she insisted: "Nobody has the right to tell me: In order to live, you must have chains on your neck and endure the humiliation of slavery." She was executed three years later. Anna Chennault, the wife of Claire Chennault leader of the Flying Tigers, called the Mao regime "masters of Chinese slavery." Over one million people fled the oppression of communism. These same people then had to fight them from taking over South Vietnam. Sadly, they eventually had to flee South Vietnam. They couldn't catch a break. They always referred to the enemy they were fighting as the communists, not North Vietnamese.

CHAPTER THIRTY-TWO

BUT ONE STEP

I found out that the "adage" about having "your life pass before your eyes" is true. Mine didn't happen during a mission, though. I was sitting at my desk in my stateroom writing a letter. All of a sudden, out of nowhere, I saw my life in a black and white comic strip. There I was as a young boy having a catch in the backyard with my mother (she would play ball with me while Dad was gone on a trip). Then there was little league, high school, college and dating. It left as fast as it came. Things that always seemed so important just went by the wayside while others became almost sacred. My past life was condensed while everything now was magnified in my perception (letters from home, family pictures, etc.). The return addresses on letters meant *home*. I would include my every thought in letters because I didn't want anything left unsaid. Life was accelerated in a big way and since it's been so long since I've been home I really I understood what true *yearning* meant.

I recalled reading a poem by Alice Duer Miller who was related to Irving Berlin. Her husband had died in WWI after they had been married only a short time.

She wrote in *The White Cliffs*:

Lovers in peacetime

With fifty years to live,

Have time to tease and quarrel

And question what to give;

But lovers in wartime

Better understand

The fullness of living,

With death close at hand.

We had reason to believe that MiGs were going to come out after a carrier during the night.

Commander Earnest stood up in front of the ready room and told us, "OK, you realize now that you aren't going to get killed every time you go over the beach. Concentrate on what you're doing and *we'll all go home together.*" If only that were to be true.

*

31 July 1972—We flew the STARM on an Alpha strike off Haiphong—Joint Chiefs of Staff had opened up a lot of new targets, especially near Haiphong. I fired two STARMS and a Shrike. The second STARM went crazy and blew up two hundred feet below us. Others went as advertised, taking out a few SAM sites. Later on we flew a night tanker hop. It was super dark with a low overcast. The fury of sea storms added to the night fear I had. VA-105 lost an A-7 off the CAT—the pilot was okay

3 August 1972–I was sick in quarters (S.I.Q.). It seemed like the real Hong Kong flu literally went through the whole ship–something like 3,500 sailors were sick. I crawled down to Doc Randolph's stateroom. "Bob, I have a sore throat, headache and I'm throwing up. What do you think it is?"

"I don't know, but I got it too. Take some of that medicine on the shelf."

A Navy pilot told writer Art Buchwald that a CAT shot was like being shot out of a cannon while someone pounded you in the stomach and tried to break your neck at the same time. For us there were other consequences as well. You could end up in the water right in front of the ship and get run over or get the hell shot out of you over the beach. This would make for a very long mission and was enough to scare you to death. If you got shot down you would spend a very long time being tortured as a POW. Or you could be launched into Eternity. In the words of David from Scripture, *"there is but one step between me and death."* Your very last footsteps on earth could be on the carrier. Options weren't very good. You could have no intention of death, but had come to anticipate it.

CHAPTER THIRTY-THREE

A LOST JOY

4 August 1972–Still S. I. Q. "Mail call, mail call," came over the One MC.

"OK, Boot, let's flip to see who goes for the mail."

"I'll go, Al; you went last time."

"Boy, Boot, you got back fast. It sure didn't take you too long."

"Well it seems the mail plane only had seven letters on it."

"You're kidding."

"Nope, and guess what? Four of them are yours. All the married guys are mad at their wives and YOU."

"As you know, Boot, my Mom writes almost everyday. In fact, here's one from Mom, my sister, the kids at the Cedar Grove pool and a bill. I'll open my sister's letter first. I wonder what she means 'I'm sorry about Gail'?"

While in college, Gail Clymer had spent the summers with her grandparents up the street from us. Her father was an executive with Chrysler and had been posted in such places as Beirut (when it was called the Paris of the Middle East), Hong Kong, and Australia. During the summers, Gail would visit so she could get to know her grandparents. They were wonderful people and were related to George Clymer, a signer of the Declaration of

244

Independence. Her grandfather used to call me his "flattop pilot" and always offered me a glass of Scotch. Both *his* grandfathers had fought in the Civil War. He told me that his grandfather would have a bunch of his cronies over to the house where they told their stories of the war. After they left his grandfather would say, "They were all liars, after the shooting started we all hid behind trees. It's the only reason we survived." One grandfather had a commission in both the Army and the Navy during the civil war. He used to tell me, "Never loan money to a friend–you'll lose both." During the presidential election of 1972, George McGovern said he was going to make a clean sweep. Mr. Clymer was fond of saying, "He's still sweeping" after losing 49 states to President Nixon!"

During college, Gail and I dated a bit and corresponded now and then. She was always concerned about my welfare. She was beautiful inside and out and I looked forward to getting to know her better when I got back. Her parents and sisters were class acts as well. Her sister Linda was dating a guy named Colin. Not caring for him, Grandfather Clymer "accidently on purpose" used to call him *colon* instead. I opened my mother's letter next. She said Gail was traveling with a friend in Mexico. Unfortunately their VW bug went out of control and flipped over, throwing her out and rolling over her.

"Gail is dead. I can't believe it I just can't believe it. Man this is terrible."

"Sorry Al. Anything I can do?"

"Thanks, Boot, but there's nothing anyone can do."

She was so full of life. When I spoke to Gail she was totally interested in what I had to say. She listened as if I was the only one she'd ever heard speak, even though she had gone around the world four times and hosted her own TV show in South Australia. Her sincere concern and constant smile made me feel good all over. Gail was lovely, a real delight, who was radiant and bubbled with life. She was only 24. However; the Navy didn't send one home for the funeral of a friend. The heartache caused my whole body to hurt physically.

A few days later, I received a letter from Gail! She told me how excited she was over the prospect of a vacation in Mexico. Her letter closed with, *"If God answers my prayers you are many times blessed. Think of me sometimes. Love, Gail."* Just knowing her enriched my life and although this tore my heart apart I had to carry this unhappiness in my heart alone. God, I wonder? I recalled a line from the song *Try to remember*–"without a hurt the heart is hollow." My heart was just fine before. Life happens, even as a war goes on.

Years later, I was at her sister Linda's, wedding. Suddenly, a cold wind came in from the back of the church as if someone had opened the door to the frosty air outside. The draft went up the right side–across the front and then down and back the left side. You could actually follow it as everyone murmured when the chilly breeze went by. Afterwards everyone said they really believed it was Gail visiting.

CHAPTER THIRTY-FOUR

MEDALS AND A CANDLE

We UNREP from supply ships about every three days taking on food, fuel, ammunition and supplies. While hoses and lines are attached between ships there is also a vertical UNREP going on as well. This is where large banana shaped CH-46 helicopters ferry crates of bombs and supplies between ships without landing by hooking up to the crates with cables hung below the copter. During one such operation I heard gunshots from the other ship. Seems the Skipper liked to shoot at flying fish with an M16 from the bridge of the ship—never hit any. It is tradition that during the UNREP, each ship serenades the other with their little dance band. When the USS Wabash broke away her band would play the "Wabash Cannon Ball!"

About this time, there was an article in a military newspaper about how an Air Force Crew had 'heroically" completed their mission, thus receiving the Distinguished Flying Cross. On the takeoff roll, the pilot of an Air Force C-141 Tanker lost his air speed indicator. Regardless, he completed the mission of refueling other aircraft while his wingman relayed the airspeed. So Boot in his "complimentary" fashion devised criteria for receiving such awards:

"AIR MEDAL: Awarded for correctly identifying your squadron type aircraft in an airwing lineup."

"DISTINGUISHED FLYING CROSS: Awarded for the ability to get airborne."

"PURPLE HEART: Awarded for the inability to get airborne, e.g., downing aircraft on deck for dirty canopy. Also awarded for hurt feelings anytime the squadron CO yells at you."

"SILVER STAR: Awarded for the ability to land. Air Force only: awarded for skill displayed in *not* using final 200 feet of a 14,000-foot runway."

"NAVY CROSS: Awarded for viewing WWII movie on VCR tape in back of P-3 while on extended patrol."

"MEDAL OF HONOR: Awarded for telling good war stories at Happy Hour without use of hand gestures. (With hand gestures, this award is downgraded to Sailor of the Month.)"

*

5 August 1972–We flew STARM on Alpha to Hanoi. Previously, the squadron policy prohibited bringing the A-6B over the beach since we only had two of them. The usual strategy called for us to hold offshore outside the SAM envelope. Since this strike went so far inland we held 20 miles southwest of Hanoi to protect the strike force and fired one STARM. Bandits were up as soon as we departed the ship. I felt like I was overland forever flying a holding pattern. The Air Wing struck factory work facilities two and a half miles south of the city. Again hot, salty sweat burned my eyes.

Coming back from a night mission we'd check in with RED CROWN which was a destroyer steaming in the Gulf of Tonkin off North Vietnam. One morning, just about sunrise, they asked if we'd come by for a 'helmet check' to see what color our helmets were. In order to give them a good look you have to be low and close into the ship. We obliged by making two screaming passes close in below their deck and then pulling up while doing a few rolls. Some hands were on deck and were really thrilled. They radioed, "one has a green helmet and one white and you just woke up 325 guys and WOW, thanks!!"

Boot and I agreed that our biggest fear was getting captured. We remembered seeing newsreel movies of trains with blacked out windows traveling through Prague around 1953. Someone who was able to get a sneak look in, and saw dozens of American POWs from Korea bound for the Soviet Union. We figured that if we were captured, there was a good chance of never being let go. We all knew the stories of the torture of the POWs. The treatment was animalistic. LT Dieter Dingler had done an amazing escape from Laos. At one point, his captors put honey on his face and hung him from a tree face down into a massive anthill. This was one of the nicer things they did to him. During this time Pop's favorite TV show was "Hogan's Heroes," a comedy series built around allied POWs in Germany. He stopped watching it while I was overseas, afraid that I might end up as a POW.

*

On one mission, LT "Fast Eddie" Bishop was flying the Iron Hand (an A-7 with anti radiation missiles) when all of a sudden he frantically called "SAM lifting at 3 o'clock, SAM lifting at 12 o'clock." I immediately started turning, jinking desperately straining to see where the SAMs were. Not seeing any, I wondered where he was. It turned out that he had gone too far ahead and set up his holding pattern over downtown Hanoi! He fired a Shrike missile, but its exhaust flamed out his only engine. "I've flamed out, I've flamed out!" Squadronmate George "Animal" Duskin whose nametag also included "Custom Strafing" nonchalantly said, "Well relight it!"

Calmly, Eddie answered, "OK, but I'll fire another Shrike first." On the way out, they locked him up again. He said, "I wish I had another Shrike. I'd make 'em eat it!"

A few years earlier, George Duskin had been flying A-1 Spads during a RESCAP. An A5 crew had been shot down and captured right along the beach. Each time a SPAD made a pass, the gooks would duck under the water. When they came up, the RAN (backseater) killed them with a 22 pistol he kept hidden in his boot and left unseen by the captors. He was rescued by the helo. He went on to become an A-7 pilot. His pilot was listed as MIA and never seen again. Unfortunately, in 2013, George Duskin's son was killed in action in Afghanistan on his 11th tour with the Army Special Forces. I always figured my number was up after one tour— there is no way I could have survived another combat tour!

*

I was touched by the story of Mrs. Davies, one of the Moms. She always kept a lit candle in the front window of her farmhouse in Moscow, Idaho. A beacon in the night, a sign of hospitality and safety, which could lead the way home for her two Naval Aviator sons, Bruce and Doug, should they get "lost." Years later it continued for her grandson, also a Naval Aviator.

Just for fun and in the form of harassment, we used to ask our squadron LSO, Steve "Hermes" Bryant, where his seeing-eye dog was who helped him bring aboard pilots. He was known as an FNG (freekin new guy) even though he had joined us when we first arrived overseas. Someone could join the squadron ten minutes after leaving the States and he'd still be considered an FNG. Bob Graustein took a few hits. They might be getting his number.

It was always comforting to hear our airborne controllers in the E-2 "roger" us when we radioed *feet wet* (back over water). They did a fantastic job of keeping track of everyone's location.

*

6 August 1972–Air Wing Three was very lucky today. We went back to Hanoi again. There was a huge thunderstorm directly over the target. Thirty-three SAMs were fired. Jim Kiffer had 13 fired at his Vigilante alone and had 30 holes in the plane. Afterwards, since it was Sunday, Jim went to Mass with me even though he wasn't Catholic. The Padre said, "Kif, it's good to see you here."

"I'm happy to be anyplace, Padre."

A few days later I was getting more inoculations along with Jim. I noticed his dog tags and said, "Jim, you're not Catholic?"

"Yeah, but when I signed up I couldn't spell Presbyterian."

During the cruise he did convert to Catholicism since his wife Janeen was Catholic. One Sunday he was doing the readings at Mass and said, "This is St. Paul's letter to the Filipinos" (Philippians) that was okay until the day he mixed up the word *Gentiles.* He is still a good Christian-based Catholic.

CHAPTER THIRTY-FIVE

FOR THE LOVE OF ZEKE

We had nicknames as opposed to flamboyant call signs. It could depend on your name (I was Fish) or something stupid or outlandish you had done that earned you amoniker for keeps. There was always a "Crash" a "Burner" or a "Warmth", because he wasn't. A pilot who always played pranks was "High School" or just plain "School." An officer who would constantly show up at a party even if it were across the country with suitcase in hand was "Suitcase Simpson." One of the best was Kent Clark–"Man Super." Others included Scott "Not so" Swift, Paul "Worm" Ringwood, Mike "Beef" Wellington, Vivan "Noodles" Ragusa (who unfortunately died while a test pilot), and Chris "Boomer" Wilson. Chris appropriately earned his nickname when he boomed the Cubi Point O' Club by going supersonic in his F8 cracking a plate glass window. Years later another fighter pilot did the same thing during an Air Show at Miramar NAS in San Diego. His sonic boom broke some windows at a local Mall. He had mentioned earlier that he was going to make a pass that would "suck the beer right out of your cup." He blamed a malfunction in his Mach meter/airspeed indicator as well as his rapt attention on his altimeter as he flew the pass at 50 feet.

When Jim Lloyd first showed up at his A-7 squadron, he was driving a lime green 1971 half-ton Dodge pickup with a white roof. He reminded the guys of "Zeke", the farmer. Of course it stuck.

6 August 1972–Tonight LT Jim "Zeke" Lloyd of VA-105 was shot down by a SAM deep in North Vietnam. We flew the night tanker during the RESCAP mission. All the guys flying RESCAP really hung it out, especially the 'Big Mother' rescue helo pilots.

Earlier that night, Jim's briefing told him to find a target of opportunity in the North and hit it. He was in the process of dropping a flare near My Nygoc about 20 miles northwest of Vinh when he received a strong warble of a Surface to Air missile tracking his plane. He broke left, then right and down trying to evade the missile. At night it was almost impossible to get an angle off the missile. Its rocket glow lit up the whole sky and you couldn't tell what direction it was actually coming from. At 6,000 feet, just as he broke left, the missile hit, blowing off his left wing. Jim frantically tried to fly the plane to get feet wet, out over the Gulf of Tonkin, where he could eject and be rescued. He struggled desperately, but the controls were frozen. The plane was spinning, pointed straight down. At 2,000 ft he punched out and found himself in-between two whirling circles of flame that used to be his plane. Jim later told me that he could hear the dying moan of the plane. Jim had gone from the warm comfort of his jet cockpit to an arena of flame, noise and wind. He anxiously tried climbing up the risers, not really wanting to land on the ground so deep in North Vietnam, very far beyond enemy lines. He was so low when he ejected that he swung only once in the chute before hitting the ground, cracking a vertebra and his left arm. To top it off, he almost landed in the plane's fireball.

In combat, Jim always felt that we were between life and heaven, and that the work we were doing could put you in either place. Your thoughts were such that you could fly up and join those friends who had gone before or return to the ship. This was his state of mind. Now it was his time to decide.

Jim knew that he had friends he could count on. He recalled a meeting he had with an F-4 pilot at the Cubi point O' Club. He was harassing Jim for being an "Attack pilot" and not a "Fighter pilot." He flippantly said to Jim, "A controller looked at his radar and said, 'can't be an A-7, it's too fast.'"

Jim replied, "Can't be an F-4 its night and it's over the beach."

Hitting the ground, Jim felt like a deer in headlights —*which way to go, where to hide?* He saw a dim shadow and decided that it was a karst ridge. These uneven formations of black limestone can go up to a couple of hundred feet. He figured he could climb it and hide out for days until a rescue helo could get in. He got up running toward what he thought was the rock ridge. Instead, he bounced off the side of a hooch, a farmer's house. People came out running, yelling and screaming. Jim took off in the other direction. Running, stumbling, falling, he managed to take out his PRC-25 survival radio and call. All he could say was, "I'll call back in 20 minutes. I have to hide; there are too many troops around." He crawled for 20 minutes, went to take out his radios and found he had lost both! His only choice was to vector himself back toward the soldiers' voices he had just attempted to get away from! He did just that and found his radios. About the same time, two soldiers came along the dike he was on. Jim lay still as they slowly approached. He played dead while they poked a rifle in his back. They got in an argument, probably about how to carry him away since Jim was so big. Just as Jim was going to jump up and make his "play" with his 38 pistol, they turned and ran to get help to cart him away. Jim ran the other way.

Jim's hiding place ended up being a bush in the middle of a field in a small depression. Just a few days earlier, he had received a green T-shirt from his brother to wear under his flight suit. It took the place of his white shirt he normally would have been wearing.

Unbeknownst to him, the largest rescue effort of the war was put into place. It involved 30 ships and over 90 airplanes proving that the United States will do anything to rescue one downed airman. That was right up there with the shepherd who leaves his flock of ninety-nine sheep in order to find the one that is lost! But this was no mere parable. Our Skipper, CDR Charlie Earnest, was the on-scene commander and did a phenomenal job. He and his gallant counterparts really get it!

One of our planes would fly over and drop a bomb a little bit to the north to try and lead the enemy troops in another direction. Blast and light, great noise. Besides destroying his hearing, Jim could see about 200 troops get up and look to the north. Jim also knew that there were just as many behind him looking to the north as well. He would hear the enemy troops calling his name. "Jim, Jim! Over here, we'll help you." As usual they had been monitoring our radio frequencies.

Jim said he had two feelings—comfort, due to the calmness of the very dark night—and jealously because he wasn't in one of the planes overhead. During the time Jim was down, his brother John, Jim's mirror twin, was deathly ill back in the States, knowing that Jim was in trouble.

Pilots were air to air refueling two and three times and then going back over the beach. Many were airborne four or five hours. LCDR Bernie Smith, a fellow squadronmate of Jim's, was told to go back to the ship after being aloft for some six hours. Bernie replied, "I ain't going home leaving Jim."

"This is Jehovah (Admiral Rasmussen, CTF-77– Commander of the Task Force 77) RTB" (return to base). Bernie reluctantly complied. The Admiral wasn't at all sure about trying to rescue Jim. Finally, CDR David McCracken, skipper of HC-7, the helo squadron, told him they could do it. He had complete confidence in the capabilities and courage of his crews. Finally it came over the air "This is Jehovah–get him!"

Back at the ship, the Chaplain's evening prayer over the One MC included a P.S. "Please dear Lord help save LT Lloyd."

A helo from DaNang got airborne and asked how far inland he was.

"Twenty two miles."

"We didn't know he was that far. We don't have enough fuel." They went to a destroyer to refuel and the refueling didn't work. Another helo went down on the deck of the USS Cleveland when the electric power cable blew out the entire electrical system of the helo. On board was frustrated rescue diver, John Wilson, who had previously rescued Larry Kuntz and Smokey Tolbert. He wanted to rescue Jim.

Finally a helo from HC-7 "Big Mother 401"–a huge lumbering SH3 Sea King from the USS England flown by LT Harry Zinser and LT Bill Young–arrived on scene. Heading over the beach, they put on their landing lights. They had never flown that low at night and didn't want to hit a tree. Jim said it looked like a movie theater coming in. With their lights on they were one big easy target. But they still couldn't find Jim. In the meantime, the gooks sent up pencil flares and light strobes that we carried to falsely attract rescue forces to their gunsites.

The North Vietnamese had moved in a 37 mm gunsite right next to Jim to use as a flak trap. They were so close that when they opened up on the helo the rescap aircraft couldn't bomb it. The helo dropped the cable with the hook, but Jim missed it. Pulling up, they came around again and landed! Landed deep in North

Vietnam! This would be tantamount to landing in Tokyo during the Second World War. Just then there was a huge explosion and bright flash right over the helo. *My God, they got the helo!* I thought while we were holding off shore flying the tanker.

Since the helo had landed in a depression, the enemy gunners couldn't ratchet the gun barrel down low enough for a shot at the helo. They let go a round that exploded directly over the helo. Their soldiers, thinking the helo had crashed, came storming up over the hill. The door gunner, Matt Szymanski, later said he was stacking them like cordwood. Jim ran and dove in the helo, getting pulled in by AT3 Ankney. All this time the helo was being fired on at point blank range by anti-aircraft guns.

During the egress, the helo was hit several times and also had two missiles fly by either side. The bravery of the helo crew revealed what I was taught about selfless love, which is the most difficult type of love since there is nothing in it for the one who demonstrates it. It is the result of a choice made by the free will. This decision to help others resulted in their exceptional act of heroism. Since such action flows from the heart I could see the infinite in the finite.

No sooner was Jim back aboard ship that we had him in the wardroom. He still had mud behind his ear. The banter was so typically non-sympathetic, gallows humor. "So, Jim, how do they log that? One launch- no landing - by the way, where's your plane?" Although we teased him, there wasn't a dry eye in the place. It amazed me how all the stops were pulled out to rescue one

259

person. I was very proud of all the guys. Although it was among the most harrowing rescue missions of the war, it was a great victory in that Jim was rescued with no losses. This was a most gratifying mission because it made a valiant statement on how much value we place on freedom and what would be done to rescue one man. It was complete self-giving, which proved that in such unflinching courage, that there is strength in the love of those around us. Jim said he could see every one of us flying overhead, even with our lights off.

Commander Zipperer, Jim's CO, brought him into his stateroom and showed him a piece of paper. It began, "Tonight VA-105 lost LT Jim Lloyd…" It was the obituary he had prepared. Jim read it and tore it up with a smile. Jim was flown into the P.I. to debrief the Admiral and call his wife. He was telling her the story but she didn't believe him it sounded too outlandish. She said, "Sure - who is this for real?"

"It's Jim!"

"Sure, OK, then where is that mark only your wife would know about?"

He told her and she agreed it was Jim. The Admiral said, "You can go home now, son, with honor. They know who you are since they have your helmet and ID. If they get you again, they'll execute you. You talk to your CO and decide." Jim flew back to the ship in the right seat of an A-6 with Ken Pyle. They heard calls of "Beeper, beeper come up voice." That plaintiff plea for a downed airman–"Come on, Joe, answer-answer." Joe had been in on Jim's rescue. Jim also thought about Bill Moyer's pregnant wife who was four days overdue. *If he's here, so am I.*

His CO also said, "Jim, you can go home with honor or get new gear." Jim had promised God that if he got out he'd never drop another bomb. But he felt he owed his fellow brothers-in-arms. With great determination and angst he stayed. From then on he said he always had a "gut wrenching fear" each time he launched off the ship. His first mission was to the same place where he had been shot down. On that mission, Bill Moyer's plane got hit and it was the one with Jim's name on it! Later in the cruise, Jim's collateral job in the squadron was verifying the logbooks. Going through Bernie Smith's logbook he noticed the entry showing he had logged six hours of flight time aiding in Jim's rescue. This was an extraordinary amount of time for a single piloted aircraft. In the remarks section it merely said, *"For the love of Zeke."*

"Give me another horse! Bind up my wounds!
Shakespeare

Jim "Zeke" Lloyd

CHAPTER THIRTY-SIX

BY A FACTOR OF TEN

The early morning launches with sunrise over the gulf were stunning, yet although the South China Sea was beautiful; it became just another enemy when the weather turned bad. The haunting feeling of possible death poisoned the magnificent gifts of the natural beauty of Southeast Asia with its aura of paradise.

I was beginning to realize that time, whatever I had left of it, was to be treasured. There developed an unspoken bond among men who had suffered and endured. It was a time when I personally felt most productive and useful.

My squadronmates were talented, loyal and faithful with a dedication that was enormously stimulating. The respect for each other was so strong that you could reach out and touch it. Basically they were a good group of guys—real men—genuine people with no airs about them and a fun bunch as well. Many of the pilots and B/Ns were powerful teams.

I was bewildered and amazed by the spirit and courage of my squadronmates. We knew nothing of the realities of war and probably were reluctant to even be there. But we had signed up and taken an oath. We did what our country asked us to do. Inherent character traits and virtues came alive. All the abstract ideals I was raised with became real, concrete and clearly visible. These were not mere theological concepts but actual experiences, a felt sense. Not myths but authentic reality of spiritual dimensions. Scripture tells us to "live not in word or speech but in deed and truth." These were not a mere passing of words, but a great fact, a mighty and persistence presence. The virtue of fortitude–the strength of mind and courage to persevere in the face of adversity, stood out the most. I saw this day after day and night after night in the actions of my shipmates.

We really cared for one another. Love and integrity seemed to be the common denominator. Karl Rahner said that when a human being expresses "genuine, personal love for another human being, it always has a validity, an eternal significance." There was great comfort in this. Instead of thinking *should* I help rescue the other guy; there was an automatic feeling that I *must* help him. It proved the fact that although the mind thinks, the heart knows. There developed a sense of well being just being around these guys. We made deep, lifetime friendships.

I understood what St. Thomas meant when he said, *"Love is to will the good of others."* To a man, this was a stalwart breed for the most part. Their caring came about, not from a role or obligation, but from their true nature. These guys were truly unique. There was an ample supply of spirit and courage, which was never marred by bravado. The whole air wing had a send-me attitude. They were an inspiration and were true Warriors but not in the sense of some yahoo charging into a battle. The Greek poet Menander said "Let bravery be thy choice but not bravado."

Instead, they fit the very best definition of a *Warrior,* written by a squadronmate of Major Duane "Duffy' Dively who was lost returning from a U-2 mission during Operation Enduring Freedom years later. Part of it reads:

The "warrior" accepts sacrifice so others don't have to. He doesn't fight solely for ideals but also for the people who treasure those ideals. Often his sacrifices are for those he will never know and sometimes for those he does not like. The warrior does not distinguish on behalf of which citizens for whom he will fight. Everyone is worthy of his sacrifice. And while the warrior is sometimes misunderstood or even hated by the public he serves, he still serves. Warriors never die. Memories will fade, but their spirit endures; perpetuated through the impact of life on the lives that follow. No single person could ever purposely influence the lives of nearly so many as the rippling effect of the life of a warrior.

I got to know men who not only had a depth of experiences, but also a capacity for compassion. I realized that their courage was the outcome of an inner love. It has been shown that men fight not for their country or for a cause, but out of love for their buddies. Although I believed in the cause of helping South Vietnam, another motive was to survive. Deep down I think the guys fit the adage; "Fate whispers to the warrior, 'You cannot withstand the storm.' The warrior whispers back, 'I am the storm' (Unknown author)." We may have been some sort of warriors, but we were not warlike—we just wanted to do our job and get home. We were the storm—we just didn't know it.

The young enlisted men who serviced our planes, loaded the ordnance, kept the planes running and taxied us safely around on the flight deck would also fit this description. They worked on a flight deck that was acknowledged as "the most dangerous 4 ½ acres on the face of the planet!" They deserve as much praise as the pilots and B/Ns. They worked day and night in brutal conditions and were professionals in every sense of the word. Not words, but deeds. In the last analysis it was action not talk; true virtues made visible.

These guys were great by a factor of ten and they enhanced my life. When and where could there not be thanks? Those who stayed in the Navy went on to cruise with other squadrons. Their feelings were always the same. They'd mention that they

Attack Squadron 75 - the very best!

remembered everything that happened with VA-75, but couldn't recall what went on with the other squadrons they had joined. It had been something very special to have been a Sunday Puncher. I pay homage to all the talent in the squadron that was manned with the best bunch of guys you could find.

CHAPTER THIRTY-SEVEN

THINGS YOU DIDN'T DO

7 August 1972–Night ARREC in RP-2 "Happy Valley" trucks-six Mark 82's, eight Mark 20s. Once again, there was that dangerous and impenetrable darkness. They were shooting so much that I was praying to just stay alive. How could anyone ever possibly know these feelings? I was scared to death! It was a world of gunfire and fear. Almost all my squadronmates were flying the same daring low-level raids night after night. Night should be a sacred time but it wasn't.

It would reach 140 degrees on the flight deck some days! With thick, soaking humidity it was like being on a griddle in a greenhouse of boiling water. The heat was sweltering. Days and nights were just blending together, collapsing in on themselves – mission after mission. Nothing seemed real, just a constant go-go and fear, real fear. The cruise was moving along like a glacier on molasses. It was turning out to be the longest time of my life. I was losing track of time simply realizing that today was just the day after yesterday. Once a week I knew that it was Thursday only because it was the day that the corpsman handed out the malaria pills. Now and then we got a pseudo-day off. Basically, we stopped flying at 0200 and started briefs at 2300. So now we were on the 2300 to 1400 schedule.

The next day we hit a bridge with 14 Mark 82s. I thought my head would burst from pulling so many G's coming off target, and then jinking to avoid a SAM and AAA. There were times over the radio when you'd hear "Yankee air pirates die" which harkened back to WWII and the Japanese with their 'tonight you die Yankee." Therefore, according to the gooks I am officially now a "Yankee Air Pirate," and I am proud of it. Naturally, we had a patch made to reflect our new status. With all these patches, my flight jacket was beginning to make me look like the south end of a Winnebago camper going northbound!

The USS America for some reason didn't show up on the line; therefore, we had to take over their Barcap, etc. During one mission LCDR Dick "Dirty Ernie" Earnest noticed another F-4 in his mirrors behind him weaving back and forth. All of a sudden his RIO (Radar Intercept Officer) yelled, "Break left." As a sparrow missile zoomed by him he saw another and broke right. Seems the infamous "Ginhead" thought Ernie was a MiG, once again proving there was no irony in his call sign! Back at the ship the CO of the ship as well as the XOs of both squadrons were standing outside of Ginhead's ready room to prevent Dick from killing him. This was a double whammy–first he shot at the wrong guy and second he missed. Thank God!

About a week later, pilot LT Harry Zinser and his helo crew, who saved Jim Lloyd, rescued the crew of an Air Force F-4 while under heavy gunfire right in the mouth of Haiphong Harbor. As they got the first airman and the swimmer half way up to the helicopter, a shell from the shore batteries exploded exactly where the man had just been, blowing his orange raft 200 feet into the air. Then a shell landed within 50 yards of the second man. As soon as they rescued him they flew at maximum speed 40 feet above the water while being followed by artillery explosions out to about ten miles. Another daring rescue by a courageous airman and his crew.

*

Many times on the way back to the ship after a mission, Commander Earnest would signal for the three of us to join up in formation. He would then proceed to do all kinds of maneuvers, including steep turns and rolls. I was still shaking and soaked through from the mission causing me to think, *who does he think we are - the Blue Angels?* Actually, what he was doing was making us more skillful in handling the plane, and it paid off in the long run. He was a good role model in all aspects of leadership and airmanship.

11 August 1972–During the night, we launched the duty five-minute alert combat air patrol F-4 to intercept an inbound MiG. He fought with the MiG for some 15 minutes. We listened to the radio transmissions in our Ready Room. All we heard was; "He's behind him."

"Who's behind him?"

"He's fired once."

"Who fired once?"

"He's fired twice."

"Who fired twice?"

We thought they got him. The MiG had been sent out on a suicide attack on the carrier. Gene Tucker and Bruce Eden of VF-103 did in fact bag the MiG 21, which was the only MiG bagged at night by the Navy during the war.

*

The wife of an A-6 pilot off another ship was waiting to surprise him in Hong Kong during his upcoming R&R. She wanted to make up for the argument they had had the night before he shipped out. It had gotten so bad that he left their home and spent the night in the BOQ before joining the ship, neither ever saying good-bye. Unbeknownst to her, he had been killed in action two days earlier.

Later someone wrote:

"Remember the day I borrowed your brand new car
and I dented it?
I thought you'd kill me - - - but you didn't - - -
...And remember the time I dragged you to the
beach and you said it would rain and it did?
I thought you'd say I told you so - - - but you didn't

- - -

Do you remember the time I flirted with all the guys
To make you jealous and you were?
I thought you'd leave me - - - but you didn't- - -
... And remember the time I spilled blueberry pie on
your brand new rug?
I thought you'd yell at me - - - but you didn't

... Remember the time I forgot to tell you the dance
was formal and you showed up in jeans?
I thought you'd drop me - - - but you didn't - - -
Yes, there were lots of things you didn't do - - - but
you put up with me, loved me. And protected me - - -
And there were lots of things I wanted to make up to
you when you returned from Vietnam - - - but you
didn't - - -

CHAPTER THIRTY-EIGHT

A SWEATER OF HIS OWN

August 12th was a gorgeous day in the Tonkin Gulf. Pure white billowing clouds floated above a stunning blue sparkling sea. It was hard to believe that just over the horizon was such violence. This was the first day back on the Line after five days in port resting up and getting ready for more combat. While in port, I had a young Filipino girl arrange a wreath at the Exchange. She could make flowers sing with her delightful floral arrangements. A navy-blue and gold ribbon was draped over the flowers. I took the wreath and went up to the catwalk along the edge of the flight deck.

With a solemn, silent prayer of homage, I tossed the wreath over the side in respectful tribute to LT John McDonough who had been lost in this area some six years earlier. At the same time, I was hoping that I would survive. I wasn't so much afraid of dying as I was of not getting a chance at life.

I never knew John, but had become friends with his family back in New Jersey. Years earlier I had sat next to his widow Joan and their six-month-old daughter Louise on a fight to San Francisco. I was telling her how I had graduated from St. Benedict's Prep and was a senior at Villanova after which I was going into the Navy to fly. Joan just looked at me in tender warm silence and for a few seconds time stood still. She sat there very quiet until she said "my husband John went to those very same schools. He was a Navy flyer and unfortunately died last summer flying EA-1 Spads off the USS Hancock. He was half way home from his second cruise when the ship was ordered back to Vietnam. He had been hired by Pan American Airlines and would get out of the Navy, start a new job and be a father all around the same time."

As it turned out, on the catapult shot, the bridle attaching the plane to the catapult shuttle broke. This prevented them from getting airborne and instead sent the plane careening violently sideways off the ship. John was able to push his two crewmembers out who were rescued by the ship's helo. All they found of John was his helmet.

She went on to tell me all about John. "He was a tall, good looking Irishman. His sandy-colored hair topped off blue–green eyes that peered out over freckles that gently flowed over his nose and cheeks. His shoulders shifted lightly as he walked with an air of friendliness. John would light up a room just by saying a few words, which always included an easy laugh. The soft sparkle in his eyes began in *his* heart and ended in *yours*. He was a man of good courage as well. At our wedding the soloist sang the song 'I Was Born in Love with You.' And I know I was.

"Alan, I know that he will stay with me in the mists of forever."

Because of this chance meeting, I had the good fortune to become friends with the McDonough family and even dated John's sister Roseann. I always felt bad entering her parent's home wondering if it would evoke sad memories. Instead Mr. 'McD' greeted me at the door with a genuine, deep smile and that warm Irish twinkle in his eyes. With the enthusiasm and interest of a best friend, he'd say, "Alan, how are you? Great to see you–come on in and sit down. Roseann isn't ready yet." His words and strong handshake would settle in my heart with the sincerity of an Irish blessing.

When I dropped the wreath from the catwalk, the soft tropical air held it suspended. Like a falling sugar maple leaf, it floated back and forth in a rocking motion toward the sea. It hesitated just before hitting the water. Caressed by small ocean swells, it floated in a soft revolving motion. The wreath slipped under a small wave, came up once and sank. Like John, it too vanished–alone.

I wrote his brother Chris, telling him what I had done. Someone had to know in case I didn't make it back to tell him in person. As usual I didn't want anything left unknown or unsaid. His reply letter started with, *"I am in an emotional whirl…"*

A few years later, John's mother, Rosemary McDonough, was part of a church group from Our Lady of All Sorrows that traveled to Ireland with the Pastor Father Tom Groggin. They stopped for a late lunch at a pub in a small seafaring town on the mystical western shore of Ireland. In front of a huge log fire, a meal was washed down by a pint of Stout beer. Evening came early in the winter there. O'Neill's pub was well over 450 years old and had sent the sons of the town off on many a fishing expedition. The Innkeeper told how young many of these boys were as they went down to the sea with their fathers and brothers. The area had never recovered from the potato famine of the 1880s. The only way to survive was to fish with boats being passed down through the families. The mothers would knit sweaters for their fishing sons with a unique design on each. It would serve the purpose of providing warmth during their North Sea trips. Oil from the wool also kept them dry. Of equal importance was the particular pattern–if a boat went down and a body was found, they would know who it was by the distinguishing design.

Father Groggin saw Mrs. McDonough sitting all alone on the thick rock windowsill overlooking a fog shrouded inlet with small fishing boats riding at anchor. She was looking out at the sea through the rain and gray mist. As Father approached he noticed she was crying. "Rosemary, what's wrong, dear?"

She looked up at him. "Johnny didn't have a sweater of his own."

CHAPTER THIRTY-NINE

THE DEATH MIST

The last time in port, I ran into Captain Ray Seymour, an Air Force F-4 pilot from DaNang. He told me if I got to DaNang to eat at a local gedunk (Navy jargon for a shack with tables) known as the Bucket of Blood Saloon. He said they named the lone Vietnamese waiter *No Hob*. Each time Ray went there for breakfast, he asked for eggs since the eggs at the base were powdered.

"No hob eggs."

"How about pancakes?"

"No hob pancakes."

"French toast?"

"No hob French toast."

Ray settled for cold cereal and named him "No Hob."

This went on for two or three times. Then one day, "Good morning, sir. Butt bould you like for beckfist?"

"Eggs."

"How would you like them?"

"Hey, they got eggs!" Ray mentioned to the other guys.

"Over easy," he answered.

No hob came out with two runny eggs over easy on a paper napkin dripping over the edge. "No hob plates."

Ray said he would have shot him if he had had his gun.

13 August 1972–we flew a night STARM and night tank. I was totally and utterly exhausted, completely battle weary. I was so drained I could barely stand and still couldn't sleep well at all. I can never get used to the schedule and sleeping only two to three hours at a time.

America's A-5 went "Waterloo White" means it over flew part of China. The very next day one of their A-6's went "Waterloo Red," mistakenly flying even deeper into China. So now their CAG and Captains were on our ship talking to the Commander of Task Force 77. As a result, we now had to cover their missions while America stood-down while they figured things out! Today a few of us made double Centurion with 200 traps on the Saratoga.

When this whole thing started, I memorized the Morse code for SOS just in case I got shot down. Hopefully I wouldn't have to use it.

Pop would send me Snoopy cartoons and write a note or two on them. He always signed it *"A proud father."* That meant the world to me. I thought the world of him, too. Jerry Lewis once said, "When a man is his son's hero, it's about the best thing that God gave us on this planet." I tried to let him know. In one of Pop's letters he asked, "Please don't send any more pictures of the sky, planes or water." *That's all there is out here Pop!* That's right up there with the Navy wardroom-protocol: no discussions about women, politics or religion–what's left?

During one briefing, we were told about a place named Tchepone, which was the most dangerous target along the Ho Chi Minh Trail in Laos. Since it was pronounced *Cha poon ee* it sounded Italian causing someone to chime in "I don't want to bomb no Italian village!"

There were numerous foes out there–fear, the pang of loneliness, the longing for home and the weather (not to mention those who shot at us). The bad weather, being just as deadly as the gunfire, was way up there on the hit list. There is nothing routine out here. I'd give anything to hear birds chirping or light rain falling on a roof at night, see green leaf maple trees or a round-eyed girl. No one really talked about being homesick but we were. If you started to think about home too much, the loneliness increased to a point where you developed *"channel fever."* You became consumed by the longing to be in the channel leading into the homeport. The yearning for home could play havoc with you until it was totally devastating. You just couldn't eat and were unable to sleep. Guys would spend all their off time, whether it is day or night, just watching movies in the Ready Room. This could go on for days at a time. You had to surrender your personal feelings in order to focus on the essential things namely to fly and fight.

*

14 August 1972, 0200–another single plane night low level strike deep into North Vietnam. Our target was a railroad bridge at Tho Kai northwest of Hanoi and not far from the Chinese border

deep inside enemy territory. The rail line was being used to bring arms and supplies from China. Although it had never been attacked, the North Vietnamese knew it was just a matter of time. Accordingly, they had built up substantial defenses. Boot and I were flying below a heavy overcast at 200 hundred feet and 420 knots - seven miles a minute - making sure to avoid the karst ridges that went up to 4200 feet. Any inattention and we would become a fireball. The night was tight and solid. The driving rain pummeled the aircraft, which was ladened with 14 MK 82 (500 pound) bombs. We almost flew into the ground while dodging two SAMS and were also alerted to MiGs in the area. Enemy radar sites had us dead in their crosshairs, and there was a good chance of getting killed.

Boot's head was embedded in the hood that covered the radarscope. He was intent on finding the target while navigating me away from higher obstacles. I was on the gauges following his commands while trying to stay "above ground."

The only thing visible through the intense black rain was gunfire. Tracers from quad mounted 23-millimeter radar controlled guns sprayed the sky. It was as if someone had cut the nozzle off a huge fire hose and was soaking the sky back and forth with bullets—every fifth one lit up with fire. Arching tracers filled the sky. Huge bright colored balls of flame totally engulfed the plane getting closer and closer. This stuff was savage! It was said that flying over North Vietnam without getting hit was like walking in the rain without getting wet. I felt I was running through quicksand trying to get to the target. More 23mm cannon shells are headed toward us. I could see them all. This must be what mortality looks like!

I know how I got here, but how do I get out?

We hit the target and spent what seemed liked the longest night of my life trying to evade the furious gunfire on the way out.

It was suggested that the Saxon name derives from the Latin saxa (stone) reflecting what their natures were–harder than stones. We'd say they were as tough as nails. However they called the darkness of the night the *Death Mist.* Now I know why! These marauding Germanic tribes were mean characters, yet they were in fear of the night. Now I was, too. I guess it's OK to be afraid of the dark–especially in this case.

CHAPTER FORTY

THE RITCHIE MYSTIQUE AND THE GRUNT PADRE

On my next mission, I pulled off a target near Hanoi. With bursts going off all around, I was jinking and sweatin' and praying. Just then, the A-5 Vigilante from our ship went smokin' by and I heard, "Is that you, Ritchie?" I was so scared with my mouth as dry as cotton that I couldn't even speak and had to *roger* by quickly clicking the mike twice to acknowledge. It was BD (Brian Dempsey) from Heavy One. Although others had heard "Ritchie," no one really truly knew who he was except perhaps for the guys from Heavy One, the A-5 squadron. LT Brian "BD" Dempsey was from Highlands, New Jersey and we became lifelong friends. He told me that his barber was Johnny (Gianni) Kizadich (something like Cosadiche in Italian means "what did he say?"). Since he didn't know a word of English every time the authorities at Ellis Island asked his last name he responded in Italian, Cosadiche? They wrote it down how it sounded to them namely Kizadich.

I had some close friends, but it was nice that I had many friends within the Air Wing. Some I had gone through AOCS, while others were in flight training with me. I could literally go to any Ready Room and feel welcomed. This was particularly good during movie time - our only real entertainment on the ship. If the one in our Ready Room wasn't any good, I'd go from Ready Room to Ready Room until I found a better one. While it took 28 days to get to the P.I., we had the time but no good movies. The best one was with William Powell and Myrna Loy. There also were a lot of "Spaghetti Westerns," which were cowboy movies made in Italy and dubbed in English. When we got into combat we started getting good flicks like *The Godfather* and *The Summer of '42,* but didn't have time to watch them. When a movie was bad, we'd tell the yeoman, "Trade with the destroyer alongside and tell them it's a good one." The next day, the ship came with her guns trained on us saying it wasn't any good! It reminded me of the Russian destroyer, DLG 557, who dogged us all through our Med cruise. As we left the straits of Gibraltar, he flashed a Morse code light message; *Pilots of your attack aircraft carrier are very good.* Saratoga replied, *Thank you.*

One movie that I watched when I was in the Heavy One Ready Room was called "Lovers and Other Strangers." Throughout the movie, the big Italian father from Brooklyn would say to his oldest son, "So what's the story, Richie?" After that, anytime someone from Heavy One would see me they'd ask the same question. Being from the East Coast, I became Ritchie. The "t" was added for sophistication.

Ritchie's last name came about in an almost "to be expected" way. We were at a party at the Nurses' quarters. On the way in, we were asked to fill out a nametag with our squadron on it as well. Since I was with the guys from Heavy One, I used their squadron as mine. It was written RVAH-1 for Reconnaissance (V) fixed wing Attack Heavy One. The three of us were standing next to each other when a well-fortified tipsy nurse came up to us. A bit wobbly and blurry eyed she moved her whole head from nametag to nametag. Seeing the *RVAH-1* she glanced up at us and quickly said, "Oh the *Rivachi* brothers." From then on I was Ritchie Rivachi.

When it was our squadron's turn to pick the movie I was banned from getting it because I would always show up with Disney flicks. The guys wanted something with skin and ordnance while I just needed to laugh. The squadron policy was that a movie couldn't be shown until the last recovery was over–which in our case could be about four in the morning. Invariably, the last guy aboard had some problems. In some cases he may have been shot up or had to land in horrible weather. He'd come through the hatch in the front of the Ready Room, usually soaking wet. Immediately the lights would go out and someone would say, "Roll the flick, hey down in front!" The pilot stood there transfixed while the movie was being shown on his body.

"Hey, guys, didn't you see? It was rough, real rough; they shot the crap out of me."

"Yeah, sure, down in front, focus!"

We all knew what he had been through but there was no slack given.

*

The North Vietnamese would listen to the news at 0900 to follow the growth of the anti-war movement. Continued visits by Jane Fonda and Ramsey Clark gave them confidence that they should hold on in the face of battlefield reverses. Their leaders said they were "elated" when Jane Fonda, wearing a red Vietnamese dress, stated at a press confidence that "she was ashamed of American actions in the war" and that she would "struggle along with us." Although Jane Fonda and Ramsey Clark visited Hanoi and assailed us, they never went to AnLoc or Kontum to see the North Vietnamese killing innocent civilians on the road. They called us destructors and wrongdoers! How about Communist Imperialists? Didn't anyone understand their stated goal of world dominance? Chairman Mao of China said, "Political power grows out of the barrel of a gun."

We heard an Air Force pilot who was shot down radio, "They are 15 feet away and now they've got me." Such a terrible, helpless feeling.

*

We all were going through a pretty rough period. I'd completed 81 missions and felt as if we'd been gone forever. Hadn't we? We had been gone a long time and still had far to go but didn't even know it. It's amazing that humor can be found in the most unlikely places–like in a war. Jokes, nicknames, etc. were one way to ease the tension. One day while on the flight deck, I had to laugh. Painted on the side of the XO's aircraft of RVAH-1 was *Commander Rub E. Begonia.* By his back seater's cockpit was painted *Ruby's RAN* (Radar Attack Navigator). On another A-5 was "BDT" which stood for Big Dumb Texan, referring to Larry Kuntz.

LCDR Dale Raebel of VA-37 was hit near Nam Dinh. He made it to within six miles of feet wet but had to get out. He was surrounded and probably was a POW. The emotional impact of losing friends was enormous; it just tore your heart apart. The shadow of death was ever present. Sadness and loneliness was yet another seemingly unwinnable war that waged deep within. Did it matter that one sacrificed for his country? Did anyone back home know or even care? Boot and I were an audience of two as to what was going on over the beach. When I started thinking about how rough it was I would think of the young GIs and Marines who held out for so long at places like Khe Sanh, etc. It was then that I knew I didn't have it so rough.

18 August 1972–We were scheduled for a strike in the Hanoi area, but plans were cancelled because of the weather. We went on an armed recce into Happy Valley in Route Package Two, deep in the back country of North Vietnam carrying 14 Mark 82's. Tracers went so close by the cockpit that I could have reached out and touched them. And those were the ones I could see, which every fifth one was. They put up so much I could also actually see the regular 23mm rounds go by! I rolled in on a bridge but pulled off because I felt that if my bombs went long, they'd hit a village to the north. I remembered Pop telling me about one of his

missions over Germany. As he made his first low-level run on a factory, he could see people running to a bomb shelter. He knew they were just poor workers forced into labor by the Nazis. He told his bombardier to hold off and went around for another run so the people could be safe. Of course he was a prime target for the gunners as he was staying in the area longer. It is interesting to note that he was attacking an area his Grandfather had emigrated from years earlier. Perhaps some of those workers were his cousins? As I pulled off the target, without dropping my bombs for fear of hitting the village, massive gunfire erupted out of the "village." We went elsewhere.

*

During most missions at night, while holding over the Tonkin Gulf, waiting our turn to go ashore on a mission, you could see the first A6 in getting shot at. You could follow him all the way up to the Chinese border and back, just by watching the bright colored tracers of AAA attacking him. It was sad because the lovely, soft composition of night was being destroyed. Night should be a calm time meant for rest.

That night on the way back to the ship, there was some unexpected compensation. For some strange reason Navy Chaplain Father Vincent Capodonno popped up in my mind. It's funny how the mind works. I had known his story for some years and greatly admired him. Affectionately known as the "Grunt Padre," he was deeply loved by the Marines because he was always there for them. In September 1967 he had already extended his tour so he could stay with "his" Marines. One night at 0430, a North Vietnamese battalion that outnumbered them five to one ambushed them. Father could be seen moving from foxhole to foxhole giving Last Rites and offering encouragement; *"Stay calm, Marine. There will be someone here to help us. God is with us all today."* Although severely wounded, he refused to be medevacked out by helicopter and continued to comfort and minister to the wounded and dying. He gave his gas mask to a Marine and dragged a wounded Marine and literally threw him into a foxhole thus saving his life. When he saw a corpsman trying to aid a young lance corporal out in the open, Father ran out and gathered the corporal in his arms and used his own body to shield the wounded man from enemy fire. Father was shot 27 times in his back with a 50-caliber machine gun. Because of the fierce fighting they couldn't recover his body for two days. He sacrificed his life for his Marines, his country and his God. He died faithfully performing his final act as a good and faithful servant of God. In 1969 he was awarded posthumously The Congressional Medal of Honor, part of the citation read "he gallantly gave his life in the cause of freedom." Later on, I became friends with Navy Doc Jim Grimes, a friend of the Father who was also stationed with the same Marines. Unfortunately, he was the one who had to declare him killed in action. A few days later, Doc Grimes shipped back to "the world." He said he spent his last night sitting on the beach at Chu Lai drinking and literally crying all night. On May 19, 2002 the Cause for Canonization was officially opened and he is now referred to as a Servant of God–one of the steps on the way to Sainthood. Years later I attributed my reprieve from a terminal disease to his intercession from the prayer requests I had sent his way. He's still watching out for his troops.

Servant of God
Father Vincent R. Capodanno, MM
February 13, 1929-September 4, 1967

Chaplain Capodanno, a Saint among men

CHAPTER FORTY-ONE

WHERE YOU GOING?

On one alpha strike to Hanoi, we took a circuitous route to the target. Instead of flying right up the Hour Glass area over land, we flew parallel to the coast with the idea of coming ashore just northeast of Haiphong. Brian Dempsey was in the A-5 flying Tail-End-Charlie in order to take post-strike pictures. They were waffling along at 320kts, the same cruising speed of the A-7s at 20,000 feet. Brian kept hearing a little twerp in his headset but didn't see anything on his ALR25 scope that denoted enemy radar activity. This went on a few times until Brian saw a little strobe on the scope generated by the enemy radar. He told his pilot, Gordie Kuehn that they were pinging them with AAA radar at the 10 o'clock position. He could look out and see Hon Gai island. All of a sudden he saw in his rear view mirrors huge black bursts going off just behind and above the aircraft. He said, "Gordie, look in your mirrors."

"Oh Shit! They're getting our altitude and will set the charges for the correct height and then unleash a barrage of heavy 85 or 100 mm cannon fire." Gordie broke left and low and then up to throw them off. This was before they even got over land! The whole air wing started more jinking. Continuing north, we then turned westward and flew along the Chinese border before heading south to hit the Hanoi area target.

*

On most nights, heavy rain was thrown out of the obscurity of the sky. Together with the great fury of the sea, it seemed like the weather, sea and enemy were all one and we had to fight them constantly in order to survive.

Many times we launched right into a thunderstorm. On one CAT shot my entire instrument lights went out. Paul always held his flashlight on my instrument panel. A popped circuit breaker was the problem and we were able to reset it. We checked out the aircraft and computer systems and then dropped down to 200 ft to begin our ingress at our "coast-in-point" near Haiphong. As we headed in about 10 miles off shore, there was a powerful, loud explosion together with a violent jarring of the aircraft, throwing the right wing up 90 degrees even with the weight of eight one thousand pound bombs.

"Wow! What was that? Let's do a quick 180 and check things out, Boot. Maybe a North Vietnamese gunboat or fishing vessel opened up on us." Because of our speed, the turn radius was larger than I had wanted. We didn't actually go over the beach but the turn put the upturned belly of the aircraft just tangent to it. That's when the whole shore area opened up with barrage fire. It was a wall of deadly flame that looked like a stage curtain on fire, burning from the bottom up. Lead flew everywhere. In a skidding turn, we avoided the gunfire, but barely.

"That was too close–they really knew we were coming." After checking things out, we crossed the beach in a different location a little farther south. As always, we initially planned to fly the mission at 200ft above the ground and 360 knots that would give us a precise six miles per minute. This allowed Paul to match up radar checkpoints on the ground for timing and help in finding the target on his scope. We hit a warehouse and supply dump. Usually by the end of the mission I had the throttles bent over the stops flying at 50 feet as fast as the plane would go.

USS America had another stand down day for a total of 11 days and would be in port two days after us! They really coddled that ship!

*

23 August 1972–We worked in MR-4 with a forward air controller using 14 Mark 82s to strike a village that the VC had taken. Our hits resulted in good sustained fires. Flew with CAG 35 miles southwest of DaNang - beautiful mountains. This area along with the beaches would probably make a fine resort some day. *Just don't ask me to visit unless I'm carrying a 500-pound bomb.*

Before we left our room one night, I mentioned to Boot, "Look, if we get shot down tonight I want you to surrender and tell them you're the pilot of an A-7. That way they won't look for me and I'll go for help. But if they get me and don't get you I'm going to help them find you."

"Oh good. Knowing my luck they'll probably throw us in the same cell!"

Behind this light hearted-banter was a deep respect for each other. I never had to worry about what Paul was doing on his side of the cockpit. He knew it backwards and forwards. In my heart, I knew that if Paul were hit on a mission and the plane was unflyable, I'd have to ride it in because I couldn't let Boot die alone. On the way to the flight deck we had to cross a small catwalk bridge that went over a large empty space or void. The ship decided that this would be a good place to store coffins! After a few crewmembers mentioned it, they were moved.

During one night low-level mission deep into North Vietnam, we were looking for trucks. We were only at about 200 feet when I spotted a row of trucks running with the lights on. I said, "Okay, Boot, let's go get them." Substantial antiaircraft fire opened up on us immediately. As I turned, the headlights of the trucks turned with me! Basically, St. Elmo's fire had built up on the leading edge of my bombs and resembled truck headlights. It must've been pure joy for the gunners as they watched this dumb plane flying a circle overhead. They were using me for target practice.

I was still extremely tired–my back was killing me. I was exhausted and totally drained again–still. Day and night flip flopped and just all merged together. The next night was another mission at 100 feet. As we ran the target, three different gunsites opened up on us–one on either side of the warehouse and one on the far side. Caught in a three-way crossfire, I felt I was in a street fight right in the middle of all kinds of violence. The far site kept tracking us even after we dropped our 500 pounders and pulled off to the right. It remained locked up on us, hosing us down something fierce. I couldn't break the radar lock. Figuring I didn't have much of a choice and against the policy of not making a second run up North, I did a 180 and decided to run the gunsite with rockeye. He was shooting straight at us with bullets going down either side of the aircraft, as well as over the canopy. I have no idea how he missed. We headed directly to where the gunfire was coming from and ran right down their throat, pickling our rockeyes on top of them and finishing the gunsite. I did another turn and rolled out with my eyes locked on my Vertical Display Indicator (VDI) to make sure I didn't fly into the ground.

Boot asked, "Where are you going?"

"What do you mean 'where am I going?'"

"You're still heading north."

I had done a complete 360! A big circle right over the target!

"You're the bombardier slash NAVIGATOR–you're supposed to say–come right to heading 120 degrees! Is that the gulf? I see water reflection." I was really getting more scared, if that was possible.

"No, it's the Red river–just keep it coming," he said as calmly as a Boy Scout leader.

CHAPTER FORTY-TWO

A FATHER'S PRAYER

Most nights it was so dark on the flight deck that you could hold your hand up in front of your face and not see it. I told Paul, "We could be parked in the middle of an Iowa cornfield and not know it. We're going to launch off the ship on a night like this, into a thunderstorm, go over the beach and get shot at. Then we're going to come back here and land in this storm with the heavy rains and pitching deck… we're not playing with a full deck!"

Even during the 0200 launch, it was still hot and humid. As usual, I had to go through my emergency water even before I launched off the ship. Once again on the CAT shot, all the sweat from my forehead flew into my eyes, burning the heck out of them. *This is not fun,* I thought.

Each time I'd trap aboard ship, Boot would reach over and pat me on the shoulder and say "nice shot Al." I'm thinking, *man if you only knew how bad I had vertigo!*

I prayed constantly for we were living dangerous lives. At times in my room, I would put my head back, close my eyes and actually smell the incense that mingled with the rich, deep Gregorian Latin choir chant of *o salutarus* when I was in church as a little boy. I realized that so many events that affected me growing up produced ideals that influenced my life.

Although dimly lit, Holy Angels Catholic church warded off the cold, dank winter night outside. For as long as I could remember, as a young boy my mother would take me to Church each Monday evening. She was making a "Novena," (Nine visits of distinctive prayer and devotion as a way of petitioning God for a special favor). She never mentioned what she was seeking and I never felt I should ask. I learned about the perseverance of prayer. The church was filled mostly with women and their small children. The men were either away on trips as Pop was, or they were just getting home from a very long day at work. Being taught by Franciscan Nuns in addition to these weekly devotions provided me with a good solid framework for my love of my Catholic faith. I found that it was OK to ask God for favors and, just as importantly, for help. Toward the end of sixteen years of Catholic education, I came to a wonderful realization. As my classes of theology became more sophisticated and discerning, I discovered what my religion was based on. As the studies became more advanced, my faith reverted back totally to the faith of a child. I also developed a deep reverence for the Blessed Mother, always asking her to protect me.

Of course I did learn the formal prayers such as the "Our Father" and "Hail Mary", both of which I still revere. But in retrospect, there was one special, profound sincere prayer I learned from Pop. He didn't sit down and teach it to me, yet to this day I can repeat it over and over. It is as natural as breathing or seeing and as solemn as a benediction. Any time Pop saw someone who was limping or in a wheelchair or had any kind of malady he would say, "God bless 'em." The sincerity in his voice reflected the deep genuineness of his heart, a true blessing. He not only felt deep compassion, but also at the same time thanked God for his good health with a prayer that it may continue. His faith, like his kindness, was constant. His words and thoughts were also put into daily action. Pop was also my little league manager. Each year the managers would hold a players draft to fill out their teams. Ward Strafford was born with one leg shorter than the other which made running difficult. Pop would pick him first, knowing that no one else would. Ward played on our team for three years as our catcher and in that time only got to base once. But that never mattered to Pop.

So to this day, although I still like going to services with all the trappings and traditions of the church, my favorite, best prayer is, "God bless 'em." Now I always add, "God bless us all and keep us safe."

Along the same lines I had to laugh when I thought about our Jewish swim coach, Marty Greenfield at Catholic St. Benedict's. Before one big swim meet he was nervous and really wanted to win. He got us together in a circle and said, "You pray to your God and I'll pray to mine."

"Marty, I think it's the same guy."

As time went by I went from praying to stay alive to thinking, *if this is it, I hope that I am in good stead with the Man upstairs.* I wanted to be right with God. Many times I would man-up, look out over the ocean and up at the sky and think *this is a good day to die.* At times I felt I needed to stay alive just a little while longer so I could gather my thoughts. On one mission, I actually prayed to stay alive one minute more. I had to determine in what disposition my soul was. The combat missions were beating me up physically, mentally and emotionally. Close calls were on a daily basis. It also seemed the experiences of my lifetime were condensed and at the same time I had a certain clarity into my life giving it purpose and meaning. Life was instantaneous. I could not remember a more awakening feeling within me. Time had no meaning; I was totally unaware of the past or future, the present was all I had–what was happening now. I was totally immersed in the present. The essence of the moment loomed large.

Loaded for bear!

CHAPTER FORTY-THREE

CAPTAIN AMERICA

We were due to head off the line the next day. I was relieved to end another line period. There was a Double Centurion party in the Ready Room with cake. CAG said that the A-6s flew the toughest mission and to get 200 landings on the same boat was really special and to do it in such a combat environment was really something. Later there was a candlelight dinner and music provided by the stewards. We had our end of the line meeting in the Ready Room and passed around the ration of "medicinal spirits" from the Doc!

24 August 1972–We flew on CAG's wing on an early fly-off to Cubi. The three-hour hop was extended because the A5 clobbered the runway and then the field went below weather minimums with heavy rain. The skipper of the A-5 squadron could not get his flaps down, causing him to land faster than normal. In trying to stop the airplane on the runway, he blew two tires, which resulted in aloud "boom boom." From then on he was known as Commander "Boom Boom–Captain America." He had a cape made with those words on it and a leather helmet to match. When we finally landed, I was totally exhausted. Later on "Captain America" was seen riding the cockpit in the CAT room with nothing but his cape and leather helmet on.

*

25 August 1972–While in port at Cubi Point I called home. Afterwards I ran into Pete Degnan, my classmate at St. Benedict's, sitting at the bar in the O' Club. He was a Marine Captain back-seater in an F-4 out of "Rose Garden" Thailand. The real name was Nam Phong. It got its nickname from a Marine Drill instructor telling a terrified recruit, "We never promised you a rose garden." They had no running water or electricity and slept in tents that were floating on a lake of mud due to the constant rain. It was a real garden spot. He was having one drink after another. I said, "Man, it must be really tough over there in Thailand."

He said, "Yeah, but I just found out that they're closing Benedict's!" After the race riots, parents in the suburbs wouldn't send their kids to Newark for school. They felt it was just too dangerous."

"What? The school has been in existence for 104 years!" I couldn't believe the school was closing! "Give me a drink too."

Later on I ran into LT Jim McMurray, with whom I had spent Feedback Duty in Atlanta. He was flying A-7s off the America. We had some good laughs over that set of orders. It was really great to see all these guys.

It rained hard every day–very hard. Cubi Point got six feet of rain in July–the resort town of Baguio got 15 feet–feet! In port it was great to have real milk and real ice cream and hear real world music. Jokingly guys said they wouldn't order a salad at the O'

Club because the lettuce was green whereas at the ship after a few days it was brown! Bands and singers at the club, although they usually can't speak English, are great. They can mimic anyone.

Things, as usual, got a bit rowdy at the O'Club. One night the Base Officer of the Day (OOD) came to the Club with the XO of the Base and a Shore Patrol Officer to shut the place down. When I last saw them, they were duct taped to bar stools! I got out of there real fast. Later on in the BOQ I was walking down the passageway and literally ran into Jack Keegan from AOCS days and Meridian. He was flying A-6s off U.S.S. Midway. Jack had just returned from R&R in Hawaii with his wife Johann. We all had been writing each other. A few seconds either way and we would have missed each other.

Rourkie told me that she and the other nurses had spent round the clock watches over a young, wounded Marine who was comatose. All at once he blurted out, "I made it, I made it!" and died. It was his eternal moment—he had made it to the other side.

*

My good friend, LT Buck Jameson, a supply officer (referred to as a "pork chop" due to their insignia) told me that when big generators were brought in to be fixed they were left out in a field for a week. The Vietnamese wouldn't work on them until the "evil spirits" left them. He had traded his 45 pistol with the Marines for a 38. He decided to go out a ways from the base for some target practice. He was driving his truck along a dirt road when he saw a rock fly over the cab and land next to his door.

300

When the "rock" exploded he realized it was a grenade and high-tailed it back to the base. A few days later he was leaving DaNang for orders in Saigon. The night before they had thrown a going away party and Buck had a bit too much to drink. He got on a C-47 piloted by a Lieutenant who had been passed over for LCDR two times—probably because he lacked the common sense gene. Buck, still green around the gills, sat in the copilot's seat with the window open and got to fly a bit, not really knowing what he was doing. The pilot said, "Watch this—I'm going to make a perfect three point landing." Buck said, "OK" not having a clue as to exactly what that meant. On approach, Buck could see that the pilot was lined up right of course. When the plane landed, it went off into the grass, kicking up stones and dirt and rattling back and forth as the pilot tried to get it back on the runway. Throughout all of this, Buck was throwing up out the window. When it was all over the pilot said, "That didn't go quite the way it was planned."

CHAPTER FORTY-FOUR

AUTHENTICATE!

1 September 1972–we entered the Gulf of Tonkin only to exit due to Typhoon Elsie. The next day we tried to launch in the middle of the Typhoon–we almost did, but it was cancelled. The waves were so big that green water was coming over the bow of the ship. There was always a competition between the Air Force and Navy as to who flies the most sorties–just more politics. Once again half of ship's company and half the Air Wing were down with the flu! We spent the next few days riding out the typhoon.

Racing back from a night low level, we broadcasted, "Ace 505 feet wet" as we departed North Vietnam for the relative safety of the Tonkin Gulf. In reply, the E-2 Radar plane radioed: "Authenticate!"

"Ok, Boot, give them the code."

"I don't have the mission card for today with the codes on it. Don't you have it?"

"No."

"What!?"

"No, I thought you had it."

"Oh good, Boot!"

"Authenticate!" the controller in the E-2 Radar plane (Screwtop) was getting impatient, a little bit nervous and perhaps trigger-happy. The MiGs had come out and actually bombed some of the picket ships up on the north line. There had been intelligence rumors that they would come out at night and attack a carrier. We had just flown a low-level over North Vietnam–probably one of the toughest. It didn't seem like it would have been that hard when we planned it. We had hit a warehouse about 80 miles inland.

"Now what? We don't have the mission cards with the codes."

The radio call went out "Missiles free"–meaning the picket ships would shoot down anything that came out of North Vietnam.

"Oh great, now we're going to get shot down by our own guys after dodging all that garbage the gooks put up!"

Commander Jim Grey in back of the E-2 radioed, "Say DOG".

In my best rendition of a Jersey dialect twang, which would have made Vito, the patron saint of broken-legs proud, I answered "DAWG."

"OK, it's Jersey. Let him out."

Wonderful, here we had a five million dollar airplane and I had to say dog–whatever happened to asking what team Mickey Mantle played for?

*

The following night after our launch off the ship, we heard our radar plane broadcast, "Screwtop on guard–Blue bandits (MiG 21s) over coordinates 21.20 N 108.02 E." "Wait a minute, Boot, that's the bridge at Duc Thang exactly where we are going! How did they know? Let's hold off until they run low on fuel and return to China"–which they did. Turned out John Walker, a Navy Warrant Officer had become a turncoat in the late 60s and for 18 years spied for the Russians and eventually sold our secret Crypto cards to the Russians. The Russians had gotten the top-secret Crypto machines when the North Koreans captured the surveillance ship USS Pueblo in 1968 while it was in international waters. They were unusable until Walker sold them the cards for the computers. Targets in Vietnam were selected by the Joint Chiefs of Staff and the President–far from the front lines and probably over lunch. The bad guys, in turn, intercepted the targets sent from DC to the ship. That's how they knew. Also, years later, a book came out detailing how the State Department gave our targets to the Swiss Embassy in Washington who sent it to their people in Hanoi and then to the Communist government. Secretary of State Dean Rusk was asked point blank if there was any truth to the rumor that the United States provided the North Vietnamese government the names of the targets that would be bombed the next day. He responded "yes." This was to prove that we weren't after civilians! So naturally they moved in more defenses in anticipation of the attack. It sure made it easier for them to get us! Our government just hung us out to dry! Secretary of Defense McNamara and perhaps President Johnson himself intentionally betrayed us.

Enroute to the target we could see small rockets fired ahead of us to give the gunners our relative heading. JJ Miller had been in ahead of us and, as always, we could follow his route all the way to the China border and back by the intense illuminated gunfire. "Bombs gone once," JJ would broadcast over the air, echoing the words from WWII British Bomb Aimers (Bombardiers). I'd think, *Gee JJ, you can bomb them; just don't tempt the gunners by rubbing it in!*

One particular night our approach to the target brought us up a valley and below the ridgelines. A low overcast hid the peaks of the hills on either side. Gunners were actually shooting *down* at us as we got lower and lower. The fire became so concentrated around our aircraft that I figured it was just a matter of a few seconds before we were knocked down. *Oh great!* We barely got out of there after hitting the target.

Back aboard ship word came through that terrorists at the Olympics killed a bunch of Israeli athletes. How could there be a

My plane and Pop's

killing zone at the Olympics? It's hard to comprehend that such deeds could take place at sporting events that are supposed to be non-political as well as safe. We're the ones in a war–not them. What's going on in this world?

CHAPTER FORTY-FIVE

WOULD JOHN WAYNE SCREAM?

6 September 1972–we flew a day tanker on Haiphong alpha strike. LCDR Don Lindland and LT Roger Lerseth were in their dive-bombing run when they were hit by two surface-to-air missiles that had been fired right down their throat. An A-7 pilot called out, "Ace Lead, get out you're on fire!" Don was about the best pilot in our squadron and he gets shot down! *I realized then that it didn't matter how good you were; if they're gonna get you, they're gonna get you.* Since the radios were dead, Roger never heard Don telling him to punch out. All of a sudden there was a huge rush of wind, leaving Roger all alone looking at a big void where the pilot used to be. He punched out in a 50-degree dive going 500 knots. Don was seen on the ground rolling up his parachute and running. He was never heard of again. The violence of the ejection tore off Roger's boots, helmet and pistol, broke his left leg (which was just flopping around in the wind) and fractured and dislocated both elbows. Once on the ground, he couldn't move and noticed his leg went off in three different directions. He was splattered with mud from bullets hitting around him. The first person to reach Roger was a teenage boy whose weapon of choice was a broken bottle. He started to repeatedly bash his head and face with the bottle and then switched to kicking his broken leg. North Vietnamese soldiers

showed up, cut off his flight suit and did a six man carry. The gooks carried him above their heads across the field with his arms and legs just flopping all around. The pain was excruciating and although he really wanted to scream, he said to himself, "Would John Wayne scream?" And he didn't. Later on he didn't have the option.

When he was first brought into the prison camp, the other POWs sang, "New POW, who are you, who are you?" They wanted to get his name in the system to help guarantee his release someday.

He sang back, "I am Lerseth, Lerseth."

Again they asked since they couldn't understand him due to his injuries.

He sang, I spell, "Lima echo Romeo ah S ah E ah T ah H." Once again he had forgotten the phonetic spelling!

The first person he saw in camp was Gull Randall from the ship who had been shot down a few months earlier. "Hey we all thought you were dead." One of the other POWs got into his cell and was trying to tell him the code for communicating, but was caught and dragged out. They asked him what he was doing in Rog's cell. He said he heard him cry out for help. When they asked Roger that question, Roger gave the exact same answer. This gave them both a little reprieve–which didn't last long. He was told he would not be given any aid until he told them his CO's and XO's names, as well as what the turn-around time was for the A-6. They said, "You either tell us what we want to know or you'll never go back–we still have Frenchmen they don't know about." (The French Indochina War had ended in 1954!). This was the exact thing told to other POWS.

Navy Captain Red McDaniel, another POW, would later write: "Later in my imprisonment there was a young Navy flyer named Roger Lerseth whom we could hear screaming in the Quiz Room from the torture. With his broken leg and both arms dislocated, he was in great pain." In *American Patriot*: Robert Coram on Medal of Honor recipient and POW Bud Day wrote: "The heart of a fighter pilot is too big for his chest. It must be big to accommodate his fighting spirit, his patriotism, his sense of duty and his willingness to sacrifice. But it is not big enough to contain his anguish when he hears the cries of brother pilots who are being tortured and he can do nothing." After his release, POW Admiral Jim Stockdale spoke of honor and sacrifice and the sanctity of promises kept. Verse eight of chapter six of Isaiah reads, "Also I heard the voice of the Lord saying whom shall I send, and who will go for us? Then said I, "Here am I." Once again enormous offerings-of-self existed, although no one back home knew of them.

For the longest time they denied Roger any medical treatment. They finally did an "operation" on his leg and implanted a metal rod. After the surgery, they literally just threw him back in the cell, bending the rod in his leg, causing continuous pain. The way the POWs were treated was horrific and barbaric with hellacious torture! For them, life became a lingering death; it was an early stint in hell. Besides being brave, Roger was a man of sterling character. His wife, Nini, was one of the wives who had moved to the Philippines for a few months to be near their husbands. She was sitting around the hotel pool in Manila about noon when she felt sick to her stomach. That night she was awake all night tossing and turning with great anxiety. The next day she received a call from her mother in the States telling her Roger had been shot down. She screamed and everything went dark. Squadronmate John "Warmth" Fuller escorted her back to the states, turned around and came right back. George "Duck" Hyduck and Bob Miller were also hit on the same mission but made it to DaNang safely. Later, before a mission, we would tell George, "Be careful. The "Duck" hunters are out!"

The very next day it was business as usual with a day RECCE where we hit a railroad bridge south of Than Hoa. When CAG was making his second run by trucks I heard someone say, "CAG, push it up." He got hit with 23 mm and I saw him punch out three miles from the ship. He was okay but hurt one leg. He got back on flying status by showing Doc how he could jump up and down on the leg. Of course this was his good leg but he didn't tell the doctor.

Knowing full well they were off limits, Hanoi, Haiphong and Vinh were lit up like Broadway at night. Not having to fear our bombs enabled them to avoid any hardships! We should put their lights out. The same was true for third country shipping in Haiphong harbor being totally off limits as well. The gooks set up anti-aircraft sites close in to the ships at the docks knowing they couldn't be attacked. During this latest mission, we took off and landed back on ship in pouring rain with lightning flashes all around us.

On one recovery, Bill Moyer, "The Offender," called in and in as low monotone easy going Southern drawl said, "Well, I think I have a little battle damage."

"Do you want priority landing?"

Quietly and slowly he answered, "Ah, well no, it's nothing serious." When he landed, there was a hole in the wing of his A-7 that a man could stand up in!

Quite correctly, one Navy pilot had mentioned that the Big Show happens at sea i.e. all the air battles occur far away from spectators and no one sees the life and death maneuvers of modern air combat or the tough exertion launching and recovering aboard ship. Heroism existed even if it wasn't seen or recorded. One night an A-7 radioed his wingman, "There's someone else up here with us" and was then shot down by a MiG. After I flew my 101st mission deep into the North I had heard that the Air Force guys got to go home after 100 missions!

September 12 and 13, 1972–sick in quarters. Greg Everett of VA-37 was shot down but made it out to sea OK and was rescued.

15 September 1972–we had an awards ceremony. I received a Medal from Vice Admiral Michael is COMNAVAIRLANT (Chief of Naval Air Forces Atlantic). One

pilot in ranks spoke up. "Admiral, instead of an Air Medal can I get a day off?" The Admiral coughed and said, "We'd like to son but there's a war on and we're very busy." I'm very proud of my medal and feel close to those who have received them before me, including Pop. In high school I found his medals in a drawer of an old desk in a spare bedroom that my mother used as a sewing room. It was the only way I even knew that he had received any medals. The Admiral said he told the "Wives club" we'd be home by October. *I thought there's no way we'll be back by then. Man, I'd hate to get the wrath of the wives down on me.*

It was always a comfort to look up from the flight deck and see the huge American flag flying high up on the mast of the ship. It meant HOME and a country that embodied much dignity with a commitment to democracy and liberty.

17 September 1972–CO of VA-35, Commander Verne Donnelly and B/N Ken Buel off USS America failed to return from a night mission. They were both really nice guys. I had just talked to the mat the O'Club the last time we were in Port. They too were never heard from again.

Alpha strikes were going to Kep airfield and Hanoi and the Kep Yen Vien railroad yard–all very highly defended areas. I thought, *this war has been going on for so many years, and they've never been hit before? Who's running the show?*

CHAPTER FORTY-SIX

BUG AND ART

20 September 1972–At Cubi Point I ran into LT John "Bug" Roach, a CAG LSO who was an authentic super-legend. He contradicted the fact that if you "can't be good, be colorful"–he was both. Like other LSOs, he saved many a pilot by helping him come aboard ship. They could tell you were making a mistake long before you realized it and helped you correct it. Bug's especially calm voice, expertise and demeanor added to his professionalism. He was worth his weight in gold. His "uniform of the day" when he was out on the platform waving consisted of Oshkosh bib coveralls, T-shirt and cowboy boots with fancy metal toes. One time he wore a bow tie because he felt a gentleman should dress for dinner and he was on his way for a slider in the wardroom. He was also very literate. He wrote a piece called *"We are the Nation."* In it he said:

> *The bloodlines of the world run in our veins*
> *because we offer freedom and liberty to all whom*
> *are oppressed. When freedom calls we answer. We*
> *left our heroic dead at Belleau Wood, on the rock of*
> *Corregidor, on the bleak slopes of Korea, in the*
> *Steaming jungles of Vietnam and under the rubble*
> *of Beirut. We are the nation."*

Unfortunately, in 2002 while flying an A-4 out of Miramar, his plane flamed out over the ocean. He unsuccessfully tried relighting it a few times. Right before he punched out, he told his wingman, "This just isn't my day." The ejection seat malfunctioned causing Bug to hit his head on the tail, killing him instantly.

*

Whenever we pulled into the Philippines, I went straight to the base library and checked out as many books as I could on humor, cartoons, and comedy, including books by Art Buchwald. I desperately needed some humorous relief, something to lighten my mind. Other guys headed directly to the O'Club to have a "few" drinks. Years later, I had Art Buchwald on one of my airline flights. I told him that I read one of his books in the P.I. in order to ease my mind. There was a line in it about him flying off the USS Independence in the Mediterranean where he said, *"We launched off the ship and before I knew it we were up to 10,000 feet. Then before I knew it we were down to 150 feet and then back up to 10,000 feet and down to 150 feet. Then before I knew it we were flying over Corsica, then before I knew it we were flying over the Independence, then before I knew it we were flying over the cup of coffee they gave me before we had taken off."*

I wanted to know what the name of the book was. He told me it was *"Is it Safe to Drink the Water"* and sent me an autographed copy.

At times I would go on the rounds at the hospital with Rourkie. I had become friends with a young wounded Marine and wanted to see how he was doing. I didn't see him, and asked another Marine, "Where's Private Eddie?"

"He's in heaven sir."

Man does this ever end?

CHAPTER FORTY-SEVEN

HAFA ADAI

21 September 1972–The ship was going to be in Cubi Point for a week so pilots Jack Ludwick and Bob Dunn of HS-7, our helo squadron, took me to Clark Air Force Base to catch a MAC charter flight to Guam for some leave and a visit with Joanie, my little Navy Nurse who was now based there.

Bob and Jack had previously served in HAL-3, a highly-decorated light attack helicopter squadron. Light Helicopter Attack Squadron Three was known as the Seawolves and flew the navalized version of the Bell UH-1 gunship. They had successfully operated in the Mekong Delta Region of the Republic of South Vietnam. Although their operations were of a covert nature, their citations spoke loudly of what they did. They read: "*…through his tenacious and courageous attacks, composure under fire and great personal valor in the face of almost overwhelming odds.*" They all had volunteered to be in that squadron.

Their job was flying the SH-3 with HS-7, providing plane guard for all launch and recoveries as well as other duties such as flying the "Holy Helo" bringing our Chaplain to some of the small boy tin cans of our task force. The destroyers referred to our carrier as "Birdfarm."

"Hey, Jack, any chance of you flying me over to Clark Air Force base so I can catch a hop to Guam to see Joanie?"

"Sure, Fish. No problem."

Although the distance was only about 60 miles, driving took about eight hours because the roads were so bad. Also, the local Communist party, the Huks, was very active in the area, and dangerous. Jack had flown me there on other occasions so that we could all have the Mongolian cookout that Clark AFB O' Club offered.

I felt like someone super special as I boarded the helo on the flight deck while we were in port at Cubi Point. I noticed Bob Dunne was the co-pilot on this run. "Gotta get some supplies at the Clark O' Club for Dunners Bar and Grill," Bob exclaimed over the roar of the chopper blades. His room had been voted the "Best Bar in the Western Pacific." Later, the XO of the ship actually closed it down on Christmas Eve. An enlisted guy had written his congressman, wanting to know why the officers could drink and they couldn't. Bob opened "Dunner's Annex" down the passageway.

Jack took a scenic route to Clark. We went down toward Manila Bay where the bright blue water was disturbed only by the World War II island fortress of Corregidor. A sweeping left turn brought us right to the spine of the Bataan Peninsula where great human courage somehow overcame the inhumane torture of our troops by the Japanese troops. During the 65-mile forced march, most of the American and Filipino troops died. Those who

317

survived spent the next four and a half years in a prison camp that equaled the harsh brutality of the concentration camps of Nazi Germany. The lush jungle spread out below us like a green carpet. We flew over the resort area of Baguio where in 1911 the heaviest rainfall for a single day in history was recorded when 46 inches of rain fell in 24 hours. Volcano Mt. Peniputo, 8,000 feet high, loomed over Clark Air base as we made our approach. Jack placed the helo down right next to the Chartered Pan Am 707. "That'll give those airline guys something to talk about," Jack called out over the strong downdraft of the helo blades as I departed the craft on the tarmac of Clark AFB. "Have a good trip!" Years later on a Friday I asked about the whereabouts of Jack Ludwig. I was told he was a test pilot for Hughes Helicopters at Palomar airport. I mentioned that it was right near my home and that I'd call him on Monday. That Saturday, while on a test hop, Jack was hit by the T-28 chase plane that was taking movies of the flight. His body washed up on our local Ponto beach two days later. I didn't go back to that beach for two years. He was such a kind man.

After spending the night at Clark, I caught a chartered Pan Am Boeing 707 MAC flight. They closed the door and then opened it to put two sailors on as a priority because of emergency leave. This happened three times removing passengers to use their seats. I got to stay on as the last "standby" passenger. Believe it or not, I ended up sitting next to Bob Knoph, a classmate of mine at both St. Benedict's and Villanova. He was on his way home after being an Air Force sergeant in the airbase tower at DaNang. He said, "Why don't you just stay on the flight since it is going all the way home to the States?"

"I'd love to, Bob, but I have to get back to the ship. The Navy frowns on 'Missing Movement.'"

It was a three-hour flight to Guam where we landed at Anderson Air Force Base. I asked where my bag was, and was told that I'd have to get it myself in the cargo compartment. I had to climb over duffel bags and parachute bags with M-16s, and I'm sure some grenades as well. I found my bag and was met in operations by Joanie. We went into the Officer's club to have a drink. Suddenly, a bell rang at the bar with the announcement, "Combat crews arriving."

"I want to meet these guys, Joanie. They're probably F105 drivers or FAC drivers.

They're the best." I introduced myself and asked them what they were flying. Turns out they were B-52 pilots! "How far north have you been?" I asked.

"Quang Tri." Which happens to be in South Vietnam.

"We sure could use you up North."

"I know we'd sure like to help you out." Talk is cheap.

They eventually did come up North but a handful of them turned in their Wings, never wanting to fly combat over North Vietnam. Once again I thought how some Marine or Army Private in South Vietnam didn't have the option of leaving the combat zone.

I stayed at the Dai Ichi hotel, which means "number one" in Japanese. That night on TV while watching *Victory at Sea,* I saw Japanese troops storming ashore on Dec 8, 1941 at the same beach that my hotel was on. They completely overran the US Territory of Guam. The next day we visited the Hilton where the B-52 crews stayed with their wives revealing yet another tough duty station for the Air Force!

*

On Sunday, Joanie and I went to mass at the Cathedral where the women all wore flowing colorful muumuu dresses. Their golden-tanned skin glistened as they sang the hymns in their native Chamorro language, a Malayo-Polynesian language (Austronesian) mingled with Spanish influence. It was absolutely enchanting. The priest mentioned that *Guam* means "have" orexpanded "we have." Those who live there have always felt that they *have* it all ... food, fish, water and a beautiful island. I also learned that *Hafa Adai* means, "Have a good day" in Chamorro and pigeon English. Guam license plates say, "America's day begins in Guam" because it is an American protectorate and located near the International dateline.

Driving around the island on Sunday night, we listened to a radio program, *Hawaii Calls.* This is how they used to start all radio broadcasts in the old days. For example, "This is Hong Kong calling, this is Hawaii calling, this is Manila calling..." The show was originally broadcast from the courtyard of the Moana hotel in Waikiki and was quite fitting. It was like stepping back into the

1930s. The sunsets were unbelievable with brilliant reds beginning on the horizon out in front of you, up in the sky over you and then all the way to the end of the earth behind you. Pleasant and cute, Joanie was the real U.S. Navy Nurse Nellie Forbush from Oscar and Hammerstein's South Pacific. It was a meaningful, fantastic respite from war but always that nagging; *I have to go back into combat, back to war!*

*

While I was gone, the Huks blew up the terminal at Manila International Airport. Pan-American kept calling me to know if I cancel my return trip. I told them, "I don't have a choice." A few days later and after a sincere good-bye to Joanie, I took a 0500 Pan Am 747 to Manila. On the flight back I sat next to José Gordo, a Portuguese/ English/Japanese businessman working with the UnitedStates Navy. Since the terminal at Manila had been burned out, there was only a small room for the 275 people from our 747 to go through customs. It was areal hassle. That night Jose treated me to a great steak dinner at the Manila Hilton where I got a room. I called home and while I was on the phone I heard some commotion out in the hallway. I looked out to see a sand bagged machine gun emplacement, manned by two Philippine army troops at the end of the hallway due to the Martial Law. I told my parents, "You won't believe this!" I thought *I am not leaving this room for ice. I hope they're there to protect me!*

26 September 1972–I was up at 0400 to ride back to Cubi Point with José. He paid the $55 for me, and also hired a well-armed Colonel Daniel Estrada to come along as a bodyguard to prevent any funny business because of the Huks and martial law. The Colonel had been on the Bataan Death March and had also had fought with NATO in Korea. He said they were sent to Korea with summer uniforms just in time for winter to set in. Now that was rough! It took four and a half hours to drive 60 miles. We passed thatched huts and water buffaloes, which are considered part of the family, in the river alongside women who were washing their clothes. I felt like I was in the Middle Ages.

CHAPTER FORTY-EIGHT

RIPPED OFF THE FRONT GATE OF HELL

I learned a lot from my Italian relatives. For example, it doesn't matter how good the food is at a meal; if the bread isn't any good, it's a failure. Or if there isn't enough left over for two weeks, the meal is definitely a failure. When I asked why they didn't learn Italian from their parents they had been told, "you're in America now–speak American!" There was also a great deal of discrimination so they wanted to fit in as much as possible.

In addition to my survival gear and the Browning 9mm automatic that Pop gave me, I also carried a small compass that he had carried in WWII. This would come in handy in trying to evade in the event of being shot down. Also in the pocket of my flight suit over my heart, I carried a small catholic medal wrapped in a little handkerchief. My great grandmother, Loretta Caputo, left the small family farmhouse in Caserta, Italy in 1898, and emigrated to America. In one hand was a small suitcase, while the other hand clasped the hand of her little daughter Vincenza. In her pocket she had a Catholic medal that was a gift from her mother, Rose, for her voyage to la Amerika to join her husband Guiseppe. He had left four years earlier to earn enough money as a tailor in order to bring his wife and their daughter Vincenza to America. Although they had heard that the streets were lined with gold, Giuseppe soon found out this not to be true and had to work day and night to accumulate the money needed. The golden copper religious medal was perfectly round with a small blue ribbon through the metal loop on top with a pin to hold it to her blouse. The front had a relief of the Holy Family. The infant Jesus sat on the lap of the Blessed Mother who balanced him gently with her arms. Saint Joseph's left hand rested on the shoulder of his beloved family as he gazed upon his little family with loving pride. While crossing the North Atlantic, my great grandmother could feel the scene with her fingers bringing her comfort during nights that were as dark and cold as the cave where they had stored their milk on the farm. The medal was wrapped in a small soft white handkerchief made from some material left over from a pillow her mother had made. Delicate white double stitching bordered the handkerchief around the edges and on each corner she had embroidered little green leaves that surrounded a small pink rose to remind Loretta of her mother Rose. They knew they would never see each other again. Two years after they arrived in America, my grandmother, Anna was born, and on her 16th birthday she received the handkerchief and medal from her mother. A few years later, on the day she married Charles Falco, Anna pinned the medal to her wedding dress and carried the handkerchief in her purse. The medal was carried by her husband while he was a Merchant Marine sailor on convoy duty in the North Atlantic during WW I.

She eventually gave the medal and handkerchief to her daughter

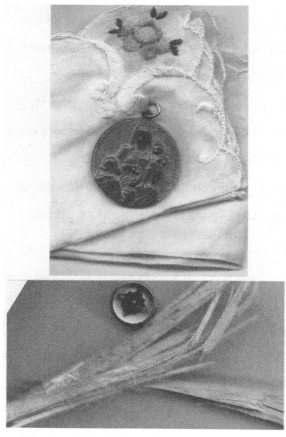

What I carried and pieces of tree that Mike Schuster brought back from North Vietnam

Loretta, my mother. She carried the handkerchief to her high school prom at the Meadowbrook Inn a swing-era ballroom in Cedar Grove, New Jersey where she danced to music played by Glen Miller. Pop's radio operator in WWII would notify the crew on the way back from a mission over Germany that they were getting close to England because he could pick up Glen Miller music being broadcasted from the armed forces radio station. Years later, I called my mother from a hotel in New York. She said, "give me the phone number, I'll call you right back." It was Pennsylvania 6-5000, which was the name of a popular Glen Miller song–I was staying at the Pennsylvania Hotel! All this, past and present, just blended together. Mom carried both the medal and the handkerchief when she married my Dad. He carried it during combat missions in WW II as the pilot of a B-24. Now the gentle family medal again went to war, this time with me on the rough night missions deep into North Vietnam, wrapped in the soft handkerchief. My wife Nancy carried it as "something borrowed" during our wedding as did our daughters-in-law. In 2003, Nancy's cousin, LCDR Don Mendler, arrived back at North Island NAS in San Diego after a very dangerous combat tour flying Navy Helos during Iraqi Freedom. In a little leather pouch he handed me back the medal. "Thanks, Alan. It got me through a lot of rough missions."

*

September 28 1972–We pulled out of Cubi. No next port– no home date. It was said that if you wanted to know when you were going home, you just needed to ask the wives club or the taxi drivers in the P.I., but no one seemed to know. Since it would take 30 days to get home, if we left right away, we wouldn't be home until November.

September 30, 1972–We flew a day tanker and I had a gut feeling we wouldn't get back until February! The Beaufort Scale of Wind Force was developed in 1805 by Admiral Sir Francis Beaufort as a means for sailors to gauge wind speeds through visual observations of the sea state. This night it was officially classified as a sea state of 10, defined as having very high waves with long overhanging crests. The ship was pitching and rolling like a piece of driftwood that was trying to get out of the waves along a beach, only to get thrown back into the maelstrom of the churning shore-break. With thunderstorms right down to the deck, there was no horizon and no stars. The only light was from jagged green lightning bolts that struck the water around the ship as well as an antenna aboard the ship. The large aircraft carrier was now reduced to a bobbing cork. The catapult shot was like being launched into a void where everything stood still in a violent sort of way. Right after launch, our plane was buffeted by strong updrafts and downdrafts from the thunderstorms with heavy rain and wind. As soon as we crossed the beach, the North Vietnamese and Russian gunners responded with their version of a sound and light show. The whole sky around us was filled with colorful, yet deadly, flak. Although we were in a cocoon of a cockpit and wearing helmets with sound mollifying headsets, we could still hear the explosions of the flak. At the same time, the plane would jolt violently while I tried to follow the steering commands on my instruments that Boot was feeding me via his computer and radar returns. As always, he would lock up the target and as we made our run he would continually "sweeten" up the target lock-up by refining his radar picture. The anti-aircraft fire was brutal, intense and accurate. That area was defended with three times the force and vigor that protected Berlin during WWII. *I can't believe they can put up so much so fast.* Quad mounted 37-millimeter radar controlled guns unleashed volley after volley with red balls of death. Deadly streams of bullets were sprayed all over the sky and directed accurately at us–all different colors. Red, blue, white. I definitely know that *there's no way I'll be able to watch the*

Fourth of July fireworks show again. Some bullets would seem to get caught in the wind stream and come up over the nose of the plane and over the canopy. *How can they miss?* It was heavier and more accurate than normal. I could see the newspaper headlines "killed in action." But how would anyone know it was by a hail of gunfire since Boot and I were the only ones seeing it.

In his book, *American Patriot,* Robert Coram correctly stated, "In 1967, North Vietnam was the most heavily defended real estate on earth, a place where pilots could walk on flak and play tag with SAMs. So when a Vietnam-era fighter pilot says he flew up north that means that he ripped off the front gate of hell and flew into the deadliest air-defense system ever devised."

I don't think it was by accident that I recalled a passage from the bible *"Tonight your soul will be asked of you."*

Some squadronmates would mention that I was lucky that I had no one to worry about back home. I knew it had to be rough having a family to be concerned about. Actually for me the opposite was true. If something happened to me, I had left nothing behind–especially a child. *At this rate it may never happen.* I didn't even have someone really special waiting for me or to share this experience with.

CHAPTER FORTY-NINE

MY ETERNAL MOMENT?

October 3, 1972–We were still caught in a typhoon with 90 mile per hour winds, but they wanted to launch a night go, but it didn't happen because the weather was so bad. If I hadn't known better, I would have thought that we were in a race for the most sorties.

I heard that Father McElroy of the USS Newport News was injured when an 8-inch gun exploded while the ship was engaged in naval gunfire support. The explosion permanently damaged the gunmount killing 20 sailors and injuring 37.

No *"go home"* date.

Fresh water on the ship is a precious commodity. Salt water is distilled and heated into steam to power the catapults while the leftover is used for drinking and showers. When water ran low, we were placed on water hours allowing us to take showers only at certain times. There was also to be a "Navy shower." You'd get wet, turn off the water, soap up and then rinse off. Many times they'd turn the water off just as you tried to rinse off, and you'd end up tapping the shower head to try and get a few drops out to help get the soap off. They also stored water in the ship's empty fuel tanks so now the water tastes like gas. You'd have to wipe the oil slick from around the inside of your coffee cup and one CO told the guys not to smoke in the shower.

*

7 October 1972–We flew another mining mission in Haiphong Harbor South of Ill DeCatBa with the CO. I was at 420 knots and 200 feet and the Skipper was below me! I could see water splashing around his aircraft from heavy gunfire from the beach. All of a sudden my windscreen was soaked and water was running off the wings. The shells were getting bigger and closer! The mines prevented the enemy from resupplying from the sea.

9 October 1972–0100 go–Night ARREC. We lost our radar but were able to hit trucks south of Vinh with the help of A7s dropping flares. Dropping bombs under flares was like flying in some kind of mythical arena. You go from complete black to blazing light and of course the gooks can see you under the lights. It was like being hung by your ankles on a Broadway stage with the spotlight on you and you couldn't tell what was up or what was down. I had to use whatever strength I had. I felt suspended in time. Perhaps this was my *eternal moment*.

*

One of our crews had diverted into DaNang (Marine Corps air base in South Vietnam) with some battle damage. They were sitting out in front of base ops when a Marine F-8 driver pulled up to "hot refuel and rearm." While new bombs were loaded and more fuel was put in, they had a coke with the pilot. Before manning up, he said, "Watch this takeoff." They knew he was planning on doing a "hot shit" takeoff. Basically, the pilot would take the runway and put the landing gear handle up before even starting his takeoff roll. This way, as soon as there was weight off the wheels, the gear would come up. He'd keep the plane low and close to the ground as he built up airspeed and then zoom straight up and out of sight. They watched as the plane accelerated down the runway and saw the gear retract while he was still close to the ground. The heavy, fully loaded plane settled back onto the runway in a ball of flame. The pilot ejected. The seat went one way and the pilot went the other–he had failed to strap in.

*

CAG Bordone, together with John "Warmth" Fuller and CO Earnest, flying with Grady "Silver Fox" Jackson, volunteered to fly a low-level *daytime* strike to Bai Thuong Air Field to protect the B-52 strikes. One rule was that in North Vietnam you didn't go below 3500 feet in the daytime or they got you. They went in at 200 feet! For their action they received much-deserved Silver Stars. The B-52s never came in! The whole thing was getting really grueling. I was constantly exhausted and the heat remained oppressive. We still had that Russian trawler near us all the time sending info to the enemy each time we launch. During World War II, we would have sunk the bastard by now.

14 October 1972–Returning to the ship from a night tanker hop the sunrise was spectacular. We then flew an armed recce with Dick Engeleach carrying 14 mark 82s in route pack three. We rolled in on a bridge and the whole world opened up on us.

Muzzle flashes covered the ground and tracers went up and over the canopy. Dick rolled in on an AAA site and the whole sky opened up; 37, 57, and 85 mm. It was the most AAA since Vinh Sohn. Dick got one of the sites and we went onto hit another bridge to the north. We had to weave in and out of the bad weather just to find the target.

I just learned that we'd been extended on the line! Great!

There is a lot of good-natured kidding going on. We told B/N Dave "Poppin' Fresh" Warren he could be set up at Abercrombie and Fitch's in NYC for Christmas. Anyone who kisses his stomach will automatically become a Shellback without crossing the equator. Or he could eat a three-year supply of food and become a Buddha.

*

16 October 1972–We flew another night armed recce into route package six where we hit a row of warehouses. The AAA site right at the target opened up when we had two miles to go. There were tracers right in front of us that came up and over the cockpit–again; I didn't know how they missed. We flew directly overhead, dropped rockeye on him and silenced the gun. It was a real YGBSM (You Gotta Be Shitting Me) mission. The patch for this was originally made by the Air Force guys who flew hairy "wild weasel" missions out of Thailand.

It seemed the B-52s received all the publicity and did nothing–they turned back each night for fear of SAMs, and now they cancelled all B-52 flying up North because they said the

332

gooks knew they were coming. But hell they *always* knew we were coming! A guided missile frigate, known as Positive radar advising zone (PIRAZ) ship in the gulf of Tonkin, stood "Red Crown" duties off NorthVietnam. MiGs came out and bombed the picket ships.

17 October 1972–Due to recent political developments, our three carriers are limited to 76 sorties in the North and 74 strikes in the South. Targets within a 20 nautical mile radius around Hanoi are off limits. A big political game! What nonsense.

One of the cooks on our ship wore a T-shirt that read *Death from within.*

CHAPTER FIFTY

LONG LIVE VIETNAM

20 October 1972–Dixie station. Pleiku Province in South Vietnam was under seize and declared a "TAC-E" (tactical emergency) since things had gotten critical. A radio call of "Broken Arrow" went out, which meant any and all assets in the area had to show up to help. Our troops were greatly outnumbered and in danger of being overrun. They would pull out all the stops to help the troops on the ground. Eight of our crews had already gone ahead to Singapore to meet their wives, so we were very shorthanded, which was very shortsighted. Boot and I flew a close air support mission with the CO, worked with FAC, Covey 116. We dropped 14 Mark 82s hitting troops in the tree line located 25 miles southeast of Pleiku. The Air Wing had to add sorties. Since we were short crews, I flew six missions in one day even though I had a terrible sinus block. On one dive-bombing run I thought I took a hit in my forehead as the pain in my sinuses was so sharp and intense it threw my head straight back. The FAC radioed, "100% on target–good hits, shit hot!!!!" We were able to lift the siege, which really felt good. About a week later, the Air Wing received a large brass bell from the Senior American Advisor, bearing a plaque.

The inscription read:

"To the brave pilots of USS Saratoga, in deepest respect and most sincere appreciation for their valiant support of the Territorial Forces of Pleiku Province, Vietnam, in their desperate defense of the Village of My Thach 19 and 20 October 1972. The significant victory achieved against the 320ᵗʰ NVA (North Vietnamese Army) is directly attributable to the precision and persistence of the pilots of SARATOGA. 'VIET NAM CONG HOA MUON NAM' (Long live Vietnam).Cords, Advisory Team 36, Pleiku."

You will also be receiving from the Province Chief of Pleiku a certificate of appreciation for your support, which, in simple fact, saved the lives of more than 250 Vietnamese RF Officers and men, as well as two American advisors. Please accept, along with these inadequate tokens, our trust and profound gratitude. You were our only hope and our trust was abundantly upheld. Both the Vietnamese and we thank you most sincerely.

My warmest personal regard to each of you.

Sincerely yours,

Lamar M. Prossen

FSR3 Province Senior Advisor

*

21 October 1972, Dixie station–I was still unable to sleep at night since I had become used to the all-night schedule and now were on days. As usual I got two hours of sleep at any one time at best. Boiling black rain clouds sent torrents of water onto the flight deck –and us. The stress of combat and the horrendous

weather brought us to places we never thought we could go emotionally and physically. I was a riot of emotions. My God was I exhausted! It really began to feel that it's been so long since I was home.

22 October 1972–Enroute to Cubi we went to general quarters twice. It seemed there was a racial issue going on in the Mess deck. This made it even harder to catch up on sleep. We pulled in at 1900 and went directly to the Subic O' club for a big birthday celebration since so many of us had October birthdays. "Black Bart" Wade, who was in charge, got up and said that he was "The what am in charge and the mudder better work." As a birthday present I was given a piece of the number one wire from the ship since that was the only one I seemed to catch. Boot got it for me. *Hey, if they didn't want me to catch the number one wire, they wouldn't have put it there! Besides, I wanted to get aboard as soon as possible.*

23 October 1972–I was thrilled to turn 26 especially since I didn't think I was going to make it past 25! Hopefully I get another year of life? Shopped, then got a haircut and the works i.e. message. Rourkie took me out to dinner. Seeing her always gave me a sense of well-being. We ate escargot, drank Harvey Wallbangers, and wine. Chuck Smith and Larry Kuntz (the A-5 guys whose rescue I covered) sent over Champagne, Irish coffee, Kahlua and Creams, etc. We met an Aussie pilot–who turned out to be a great guy. It seemed only fitting that I should be over here with these people, the pilots, nurses, etc. during my birthday. They

meant so much to me. We'd "all go home together," just as Commander Earnest said.

Once again, politics stopped us bombing north of 20 degrees. This gave the gooks time to rearm and resupply. More brainless policies! There was absolutely no strategy involved to win this war. The military could win this war but the State Department could very well lose it.

We had been gone so long that our immunization shots ran out. I asked the corpsman if he could just write in my logbook that I had gotten the shots. "No, sir. The Commanding Officer will not let you go ashore in Singapore if you do not have the updated shots." I got the shots–along with big time hurts!

CHAPTER FIFTY-ONE

SINGAPORE

27 October 1972–Singapore for R&R. Since we anchored off shore, we had to take boats to the dock. I hitched a ride on our ship's U (Utility) Boat, a 50-foot motor launch whaleboat that held about a hundred enlisted personnel. The coxswain asked if I wanted to drive and told me to keep an eye on a spot on shore a few miles ahead. I kept over-correcting–going left, then right, and then left again. This elicited calls of, "Hey, get that zero (O or zero being short for officer) outta there. Get him down–we're getting seasick."

Singapore is a beautiful city, all spread out with lots of trees and flowers, a city within a jungle. There was a Chinatown area, an English area, Malaysian area and Indian area complete with a multitude of religions and variety of foods. The high degree of harmony was amazing. The city was immaculate due to strict discipline and high fines for littering or for spitting gum on the ground with caning being the punishment of choice for most crimes. There was a lot of building going on and many beautiful hotels such as The Mandarin, the Hyatt and the Hilton. Of course I had to have a Singapore Sling where it was invented in 1915 at the Long Bar of the Raffles Hotel. Beautiful Burmese and Chinese jade jewelry was reasonable but not cheap. Locally made Pewter was good as well. Terrible taxi drivers who saw a red light as a signal to step on the gas tended to run the place because of the hustling, which was worse than in Naples. I attended Mass at an orphanage with a children's choir and where the Priest preached in English and Malay. On a street corner I asked a man who was squatted next to a basket what was in it. When he took off the top I jumped back horrified to see a cobra shoot straight up!

On the walls of restaurants there were pictures explaining that men who had long hair would be served last. Even at fleet landing, where we came ashore, there was a picture showing how short your hair had to be before you were allowed to come ashore. In all the big department stores, the sales people used an abacus to work the sale. The Chinese have used the abacus for generations. Their fingers flew over the beads to come up with the correct result. They were faster than I ever was with a calculator. Ken Knapp did, in fact, buy the brand new small hand held calculator for $60 and thought that was a good deal. By the time we got back to the States they were selling it for $12.

A group of us ate at the Pavilion Steakhouse on Orchard Road that had very good Chinese and Malay food. It had an Old English dining room with whitewashed walls and crisp white tablecloths. Trying to order reminded me of giving a tour to a bunch of Italians while we were in port in Naples during our first cruise. No one understood anything. The southern boys referred to them as 'It lee ans'. The cooks and waiters were watching through a porthole in the door to the kitchen to see if we liked the food. We gave them the thumbs up and, with huge smiles, they all jabbered happily in a language that was gibberish to us.

Later that night, we were all sitting around in the lobby of the Hilton. One of the A5 navigators was fiddling around with the tie of his wife's wraparound skirt who was sitting crossways on his lap. When she got up and walked away, her skirt fell away. All I said was, "You look good in pink (her undies) Sue." With a little wiggle she just kept walking.

The next day I went for a walk and literally stumbled into a Hindu religious ceremony by walking through an open archway into a temple. Inside men were walking on hot coals and had strings with fishhooks embedded into their chests with limes at the end of the string for weight. Different strokes for different folks. The following evening a bunch of us had dinner at Gino's–good Italian food–although everything here was cooked with Indian spices. A kid growing up here thinks Italian food has Curry in it. Chinatown was a place of many odors where the market area and restaurants had uncooked, featherless chickens and ducks hanging upside down out front. It was a bustling area with old men digging ditches and women carrying huge bundles. I later ate at Fatty's restaurant on Albert Street where the food was great. When we left, we noticed the waiters washing the dishes at a faucet in an alley.

*

After the fall of Singapore in WWII, the Japs went on to murder some 4,000 civilians in the city. There was a hotel built near where the massacre took place. Crews from Japan Airlines who stayed there had to leave after being harassed by "spirits of the dead" at night. I actually thought we might be going home soon when Henry Kissinger mentioned at the peace conference in Paris that "peace is at hand."

Unfortunately, on October 29th we had a fire in the number two-machine room of the ship that killed three men and injured 12. Chaplain Father Witt had to crawl through the smoke to survive. Neither of these events delayed us one bit from going back into combat!

CHAPTER FIFTY-TWO

A SOUNDLESS SORRROW

Back home in the States, it was a typical late October day in the Pacific Northwest–steel gray, cold and damp with continuous light rain. It produced a harsh sensation that went right through a person–much like the ceremony being held at Naval Air Station Whidbey Island in Puget Sound. Along with the Navy personnel, the wives of the men who were still on deployment with VA-115 on the USS Midway were paying their respects at this Memorial Service. The solemnity of a Navy service was always so meaningful and reverent. LT Ray Donnelly, a Bombardier Navigator, was one of their own.

They had gotten to know Ray over the past few years. He was a wonderful man. Ray always wanted to be in the sky while serving his country. He had come to Whidbey Island full of enthusiasm and dedication. Ray was much involved in the local church, including attending Mass daily, which was a ritual he continued on cruise. He was to wed his girlfriend Mary Lou upon return from cruise.

Tonya Clark sat transfixed, watching, listening, but not really hearing. Her mind and heart were many miles away with her husband Alan–a Bombardier Navigator in the same squadron. Tonya had met Alan the very first Monday morning in the very first class in college. They sat next to each other in Music 101 at Cal Poly San Luis Obispo, California. Within a few years they were married. She was nineteen and he was twenty. Right after graduation, Alan went off to get his Navy Commission through the Aviation Officer Candidate program in Pensacola. To his great disappointment, he was turned down for pilot training because the day of his physical his eyesight wasn't exactly 20/20. The flight surgeon would not sign it off. Although disillusioned, he decided to step up to serve his country and opted for the Naval Flight Officer (NFO) training. As soon as he finished B/N training at Whidbey Island, he was sent to Westpac to join VA-115. Everything happened so fast. He already had the call sign "Arlo" from his love of the music of Arlo Guthrie–someone he tried to emulate by learning the guitar and even writing a song or two. Tonya, like many of the other wives, was experiencing a soundless sorrow. Ernie Pyle, the WWII correspondent once wrote, *They are a strange corporation of loneliness and close kinship, the women of aviation who sit at home and hear that their husbands are dead. Death comes to other women's husbands too. But nowhere in the world are so closely linked together as the people of aviation, and it is the long and very real shadow of death that links them. ...that won't happen to my man; he can handle any emergency.*

Only the mournful sound of taps brought her back to the moment. She recalled the words the trumpet spoke, *Thanks and praise for our days 'neath the sun, 'neath the stars, 'neath the sky. As we go this we know, God is nigh.* Her love was with Arlo and

343

his child that she was now carrying. *Please, God, stay with Arlo.* A few weeks later Tonya gave birth to their son, Tad David Clark.

*

A few days after Ray's death, Arlo's CO told him, "You will take the place of Ray Donnelly and be Mike (Mondo) McCormick's new B/N. We need all the crews we can get." It was always hard for a new B/N and pilot to crew up, especially part way through a cruise. This case was doubly hard–Mike really did not want to fly anymore and was more than petrified each time he went up. To make it more difficult, every so often he would call Alan by Ray's name, unable to get over his deep loss. As the next few months went by, it seemed that this pair up was a good one. They worked as a close team. On the night low levels, Alan was able to pick out the correct targets on the radar. Together with Mondo, he played havoc on the North Vietnamese defense sites and military installations. They hit what they went after.

*

3-4 November 1972–Despite the statement of, "Peace is at hand" from Henry Kissinger, we were enroute to Yankee Station. While we were in Singapore, there had been much talk of a cease-fire and peace, etc. which turned out to be very far from true–talk about highs and lows! There were many more restrictions on us now–no mines or DSTs, which were explosives we were to lay as a corridor across the country; no offshore wiblics to be hit; no Alpha strikes; no going north of 20° which meant no strikes into North Vietnam. Lucrative targets like Vinh and Than Hoa were all of a sudden off limits, once again giving the enemy time to rearm and resupply. The North responded to this goodwill gesture by moving in more SAMS and AAA sites south of 20° north. Who's in charge here? More abysmal politics! On top of that, we were riding out Typhoon Pamela with a peak intensity of 125 miles per hour and very heavy seas.

5 November 1972–Since it took 30 days to sail back, once we hit September, I realized we were not going to be home for that "scheduled" October yard date. Then when we hit October, I realized we wouldn't be home for Thanksgiving. Now that we were still here in November there is no way we could make it home by Christmas.

Prior to one mission while I was on the flight deck, I felt really lousy, practically sick to my stomach. It wasn't until we got airborne that I realized that I had been a bit sea sick from the rolling of the ship! As we climbed up to a high altitude over the Tonkin Gulf, the plane stopped flying – we had stalled out! Looking out on the wings I saw about two feet of snow! Diving down I was able to burn off the snow. One minute I'm seasick from tropical waves and the next snowed in–this is wild!

Day after day I got "care packages" from home with notes saying, "Do not open until Christmas." Now I was wondering if I was even going to be alive at Christmas–but I did wait.

8 November 1972–President Nixon won 49 states.

We lost LCDR Fred Wright from our CAG Staff today just north of the DMZ. He was in an A-7 from VA-37. Since he was on the Staff; he really didn't have to fly, but wanted to do his part. He was another good guy.

Only time will tell where this will lead, how it will end.

CHAPTER FIFTY-THREE

TO DREAM PERCHANCE TO SLEEP

Yesterday's mission was especially rough. I don't know how we got out of there in one piece. I can still see it, feel it–fear it. The strain of combat was unrelenting. My whole being was just filled with fear. Earlier, since we had about four hours before starting to plan for the next night low-level mission, Boot and I decided to turn in. Like so many other times before, I couldn't get to sleep at all tossing and turning, still remembering that last mission and, in a cold sweat, thinking of the next one. Of course Boot easily fell off into a sound sleep. I told him he could sleep on a clothesline and he said, "You could hear someone knitting on the fantail of the ship and it'd keep you awake." I needed to get some rest and there was only one way to do it. I had to try to dream myself to sleep. Think of things, happy times in my past to make them become a dream and possibly fall off to sleep. To try and dream away the violence and fear. *To dream, perchance hopefully to sleep.*

The only real way I could get to sleep was to remember bedtime stories Pop told me when I was a little boy, and the good times at the Cedar Grove pool. All of a sudden, I was a young boy in my small bed in our little family house in Little Falls, N.J. Pop would tell me bedtime stories about how rustlers had stolen cattle and that the cowboys had followed the tracks to a small log cabin.

During the night they put flour from the chuck wagon on the ground by the back door and waited until the bad guys left. Walking through the flour left a track of white footprints leading right to where the horses were hidden. That's how simple it was to catch them. If only life was so simple now. The bedtime stories from Pop so long ago played such an important role.

The other good recollections were of the Mitchell manor pool in Cedar Grove, New Jersey. Owned by the Mitchell and MacAvoy families, it was a private pool opened from Memorial Day until Labor Day. Pop would save the whole year to pay the $125 family membership fee. Situated back in the woods, it was a lovely location. It was where I learned to swim. This was after Pop had to save me from drowning. I jumped into an area that was over my head—right in front of two women who were too busy talking to notice me going down for the third time. Pop swam as fast as he could across the pool to save me. I eventually ended up on the swimming team like all the other kids at the pool.

The summers during High school were the greatest, actually magical. Since there was no local high school in town, the kids from Cedar Grove and the surrounding towns went to a myriad of local high schools: Bloomfield, Montclair, Passaic Valley, St. Benedicts, East Orange Catholic, Seton Hall and Essex Catholic. At times we competed against each other in school sports, but other than that we actually didn't see each other until the following summer. Some guys told us that their football coach at Passaic Valley asked them to "line up in alphabetical order according to height." They were bumping into each other trying to do just that!

One such friend, Mike Faltraco, swam butterfly for rival Seton Hall. He'd come to a meet whistling and twirling his tank suit on his finger. I was one of those superstitious athletes who always packed my sports bag the same way. I'd have an extra suit, then a towel, my sweat suit, another towel and my meet suit. Mike would always say, "Hey, Fish, can I borrow a towel?"

One meet he came and asked "hey can I borrow a suit?'

"You come to a swimming meet and don't bring a suit?"

He'd go in, win his events setting a few records, give back the suit and leave whistling. Anytime I'd get too cerebral about things I'd say to myself, "Just be a Faltraco." This was long before Nike's slogan of "Just Do It."

*

Summer at the pool was a great impetus for getting good grades so I wouldn't have to go to summer school–it would just ruin the fun. We'd get dropped off in the morning for swim team practice and spend the whole day. We teenagers commandeered the grassy area by the deep end that remained "ours" each summer. At lunchtime we'd go into the clubhouse and play the latest 45 records. Some of the guys would bring their guitars and a set of drums and play for us. We'd dance and dance and dance. It was Happy Days but we didn't realize it. There was Beef Boyer, the original Fonzie, who had the record for drinking huge milkshakes known as Awful, Awfuls (awful big and awful good) at Bond's Ice

Cream shop. He was a tough guy with a heart of gold. My sister was dating a guy named Beansy, a name I thought was way too sophisticated for him. That lasted until Pop found out my sister was cutting class with him. Our Aunt Terry was the attendance secretary at her high school and called our Dad. The very next day Lory was in East Orange Catholic High School for girls! The pool was also where I met Marian. She was cute as a button with a figure, a real figure. Our parents had actually known each other since she was a year old.

Earlier that Spring, I was on the bus on the way to school, and I thought, *Man, they've written all the good rock and roll songs—there's not going to be anymore.* That very day at St. Benedict's, Father Ignatius, aka "Iggy," said, "The mind is infinite—it can think of anything" I thought, *Hey they can still write more songs!*—and of course they did. He was also fond of saying, "You don't want to study? See the Prudential building over there. You're just going to get a boring job where all you do all day is roll the pencil from one side of the desk to the other side of the desk. You want to get a good education so you can move out of the city into the suburbs away from people with garlic on their breath. That way you can have a nice big house and chase your wife around and no one can hear you." The facts of life at 15 years of age! He also mentioned that he was an authority on cats and asked the question "Do you know what kills cats the most?" Mike Bertelli answered "curiosity!" and paid for it. To Iggy, the parking lot was the "Valley of the tin gods."

350

But in real life, not everything ended in fun and games. It was during that time that John Flood, a boy that my sister had dated, died. He joined the Coast Guard and went up on the roof of a Coast Guard building to fix an antenna during a vicious storm and was electrocuted. Another friend, Bill Lentz, lost his hand in a meat grinder at the local deli where he worked after school.

*

The town of Cedar Grove built a Community pool in 1962. After being a lifeguard there for two years, I decided I needed to make more money and left to work in a Grand Union grocery warehouse. Although the pay was good, the work was brutal and showed me what I didn't want to do for a living. We unloaded boxcars of food where it was 120 degrees inside. Combined with working alongside some tough teamsters was not my idea of summer fun. One day I sat on a box and asked myself, *if I had a choice, what would I want to do? I'd like to coach the swimming team at the Cedar Grovepool.* The very next day I got a call from the pool manager wanting to know if I would like to coach the team. They fired the coach for sneaking in the pool after hours with his girlfriend. He didn't have to ask twice.

That was the beginning of a four-year run as coach. The team and families were a blast, plain and simple a lot of fun. St. Benedict's classmate Rich Mariani ran the snack bar that allotted me some really good, free food. Later on, after serving in the Army, he also became a very successful attorney as well as an accomplished private pilot. To this day he is one of the most proficient and conscientious pilots I know. It felt good passing along to the kids on the team what I knew about competitive swimming. This also included teaching them the Villanova fight songs and naming the team the Kahunas. Practice was like summer camp in the Catskills with some of the Jewish kids. Herbie Shapiro was as good as they got. With a Jewish accent I would say, "Heubee, I want you should swim." All the kids were polite, hard working and just plain fun and we won a lot of meets. Eight year old Mike Schmidt, who also was Jewish, would mirror the Catholic kids and bless himself–backwards–before he swam. The Dads said, "Don't tell him!" He set every record in the book.

Then there was the Gilligan family. They were a complete joy in every sense of the word. At any one time eight of the ten Gilligan children were on my team. Each one had a special nickname, including their mom whom we called Groovy. They were a delight, had real guts and were great swimmers. I would get a smile on my face just thinking of them. A local New York area newspaper did an article entitled "Cedar Grove Raises its own Gilligan's Island." In World War II, Mr. Gilligan, their Dad, was a 20-year-old Ensign on a supply ship in the South Pacific. Right before the war ended, they had lost their navigator. When the Captain asked if anyone knew how to navigate, Ensign Gilligan raised his hand although he didn't really, but somehow he got them to Pearl Harbor. At Pearl all the senior officers left to catch military flights back to the states since the war had ended. This left Ensign Gilligan as the senior officer on board and, hence, the commanding officer of the ship. Before arriving in Long Beach, he sent a message to the Navy asking what he should do with all the extra supplies on the ship. He was told to throw them over the side. Since it was a supply ship, it had everything from eating utensils to refrigerators. When he pulled into Long Beach he contacted all the hotels in the Los Angeles area and sold the goods to them, splitting the profit with the crew.

The pool manager, Mr. Tom Gallucci—Mr. Ga-luch to us— was the Athletic Director and football coach at Nutley High School. Each day his lovely Italian wife Catherine brought him lunch and dinner. It was an honor to be invited to have a lunch with him that was soup to nuts—usually Lasagna, meatballs and spaghetti. It was so heavy that you couldn't go back to work on the guard stand for two hours after eating. It was best to just lie on a towel on the grass until you could move.

"Al, it's time." Being on the top bunk, I groggily turned my head and came directly face to face with Paul who was standing up next to my top bunk. He had his red lens flashlight shining up on his face. Being the only light in the room, he looked ghoulish. It startled me so much I would have shot him if my gun hadn't been locked up in the safe on my desk. It always took forever to finally dream myself to sleep and now, at 0200, I had to get up and fly another mission. *If only I could step back into those dreams—and stay there. My God, I wish I were home!*

CHAPTER FIFTY-FOUR

GURU OF LIFE

When I flew with B/N "Black Bart" Wade, I told him that I didn't know whether I should go on a mission or rob a bank! He had been on shore duty and volunteered to join us. We flew up next to A-6s from VA-115, the A-rabs, his former squadron, off Midway. Bart asked, "How are CO Alibaba and his 40 thieves?"

Most days we are deluged by torrential rain–seemed the weather kept getting worse. It was always wet and raw. We had to man up and land in the rain, soaked to the bone. One night we launched our "Ready Alert" F-4 Phantom at 2300 to cover B-52s as a BARCAP (Barrier Combat air patrol). During the rendezvous his wingman called out, "Vinny, do you see that bright light–do you see it, do you see it?" Then a bright flash and an explosion.

"Vinny, Vinny?!"

Then, "Mayday, mayday!"

Once again "Ginhead" had aptly lived up to his name by letting the rendezvous circle get too big. This put them over downtown Haiphong instead of staying out over the water. Consequently, a SAM missile site opened up on him, knocking him down. Luckily they were able to get out over the water before punching out. "Ginhead" and his RIO, Don Cordes, punched out at 21,000 feet and were in a cloud down to 300 feet. On the way down they took out their survival radios. Vinny could hear Don but Don couldn't hear Vinny. Vinny finally put down the radio and yelled, "I hear you!" Don heard him since they were in the same cloud. Vinny said he yelled, "help" over the radio because he said he couldn't remember "Mayday." When picked up by the helicopter, Vinny was wearing his slippers that he wore while standing the alert five. Vinny was the one on our first cruise who flew an F-4 down the main runway at Athens International Airport and also the one who fired at Dick Earnest earlier in the cruise.

21 November 1972–Cancelled due to weather–Typhoon Pamela

23 November 1972, Thanksgiving–a welcomed day off. I decided to have a wisdom tooth pulled that had been bothering me, plus I figured it would give me some time off to rest. The Dentist with the apt call sign of "Pain Merchant" that was written across his jersey told me to eat late and then get it pulled since I wouldn't be able to eat for 24 hours afterwards. I went into the wardroom in the afternoon and saw five beautiful turkeys laid out on the tables. When I went back later that evening to eat there was only little scraps left and I could barely make up one sandwich. I had my tooth pulled and went back to my stateroom to lie down. Ten minutes later the phone rang, telling me I had to stand the Squadron Duty Officer (SDO) in the Ready Room. Consequently, I was up the whole night so I put myself back on the flight schedule, which once again was the night schedule.

*

At night on the way to the Ready Room from my stateroom, I'd walk through the hangar bay before beginning a mission. I'd look out and see waves hitting the elevator; wind blowing heavy rain horizontally through the area and ominous black waves crashing all around, and nothing but pitch-dark black. The horrendous weather, together with the bad guys who were trying to kill you, made for a terrifying existence.

Before manning up an aircraft I would make one last stop at the Head. I looked in the mirror, saying to myself, *Well, you did it last night. You can do it again tonight.*

I always remembered Dan Jones's mother telling me to say three Hail Mary's for safety before going on a trip, whether in a car or plane. I figured a mission fit the bill as a trip. I tried my best to say them and focus on the "perfect Hail Mary" which meant saying all the words of the prayer. Many times I couldn't do it as we were rushed to get the plane up and ready for the launch. I'd start with "Hail Mary full of grace" and skip right to the end "now and at the hour of our death, amen." Was that prophetic? Most times I couldn't get in all three prayers. However I did come to realize that I had to "pray" a prayer not just "say" it.

Mrs. Jones was my "Guru of life." When I'd come home from college, I'd visit her. We'd have a cup of tea and cookies and discuss everything from religion to politics to girlfriends. This continued during and after my service years. A young priest named Fulton Sheen, who eventually became Archbishop of New York, had performed her marriage. On Saturday, October 16, 1999 Mrs.

Ann Jones went to her eternal reward after a stunning 92 years on this earth. Her son Dan called the following Monday and said his Mom passed away at 11:00 a.m on Saturday. He told me that they now knew how long Purgatory lasts—namely four hours and thirteen minutes. Dan and his brother Paul both were Notre Dame Alumni and consequently big fans of the school. Dan went on to tell me that the storied rivalry Notre Dame - USC game started at 12:30 PM that Saturday. At the half, Notre Dame was losing 21-0. Notre Dame came back to win 25-24 (four hours and 13 minutes after Mrs. Jones left us). The boy who scored the winning touchdown for Notre Dame was Dan O'Leary. Both Mrs. Jones's father's name and brother's name was Dan O'Leary! During the TV interview following the game, Notre Dame Coach Bob Davie acknowledged that there was some kind of divine intervention. "Seems in the first half the wind was at our back and during the second half it was too." I always liked the plaque Mrs. Jones had in her kitchen: *May you be in heaven a half hour before the devil knows you're dead.*

*

26 November 1972–Peace Talks in Paris broke off after five days. Seemed the North Vietnamese were mad, something about the shape of the table! Our spirits went down somewhat. They're playing political games with us. This is a real roller coaster ride! With the weather still bad, we had to fly Paved Phantoms missions known as "sky spot." These were Air Force F-4 Phantoms (acting as a radar FAC) that had special radar which

helped show where the bad guys were. That way we could join up on them and bomb on their command through an overcast. This was done only in South Vietnam when the area was socked in with bad weather. Pilot Tom Connelly would come back from a mission and throw his flight gear in the corner of the Ready Room and leave it there. One time his B/N, Dick Schram, said, "Pick it up." Tom did just that to the surprise of everyone. A year after we were back, we had a squadron party and someone asked Dick how he got Tom to listen. Seemed Tom and Dick were on a sky-spot mission when Tom lost sight of the F-4 FAC. All of a sudden he heard, *"Stand by, stand by"* with the next callout being *"hack,"* indicating it was time to drop his bombs. Tom finally saw the plane in the distance, gave it full power and rejoined up just in time for the *"hack."*

"Don't tell anyone, Dick. This is embarrassing–what's it going to take for you not to tell anyone?"

"Obey me."

CHAPTER FIFTY-FIVE

ANGUISH IN MY HEART

28 November 1972—We were scheduled to be off until 1300, but at 0100 we got a call that airplanes from the America had seen 300 trucks heading south on the outskirts of Thanh Hoa. We briefed for the mission and sat in the Ready Room to wait for the call to man up. I was surprised to hear Skipper Earnest, tell his B/N, Grady Jackson, "I'm going to sleep 20 minutes; wake me when it's time to go." Here was a man who got by on four hours sleep a night. Yet here he was tired enough to want to take a "combat nap," hoping for a few minutes of shuteye.

On the flight deck, the skipper got in one plane and for some reason it was "down." He then got in another that had been worked on. It was a night with a low overcast and heavy rain. Initially everything looked normal on his catapult shot. At the end of the stroke, the plane abruptly pitched up violently to an unusually nose high attitude, causing the plane to stall out. The Skipper tried to "hold" the plane as it flipped brutally to the right and then whipped ferociously to the left. During the catapult shot, the small heavy radarscope that sits low and in front of the stick had come out, pinning it full aft. CDR Earnest struggled to keep the plane flying. Grady said when he saw the Skipper's hand push the stick full right and the plane went left it was time to get out.

There was a flash as Grady ejected successfully but the Skipper was never found. He had fought trying to save the plane, which gave Grady time to eject. It turned out that the sailor who had been working on the radar put the equipment back in using the wrong small bolts. He correctly used the bolts marked with the number three when in fact they were number four bolts. Someplace upstream they had been marked incorrectly. The 18-year-old sailor actually lost his mind over the Skipper being killed. We proceeded to hit the trucks.

Charlie Earnest was a good man. He had 371 combat missions over a period of a few cruises. The North Vietnamese even had a price on his head. I reflected on how he had said, *"We'll all go home together."* And now he was gone. This was very hard to take–more heartache. I know what Saint Paul meant in his letter to the Romans *".... I have great sorrow and anguish in my heart."* Besides his wife Minna, he left two young sons. Some eighteen years later, his son became a Special Forces soldier. On a training mission in North Carolina his whole squad was wiped out in the crash of their transport helicopter. As it turned out, a small bolt had shaken loose.

My mother had been on the way to her bowling club when she heard on the radio that an A-6 off the Saratoga had been lost. She turned around and went home to an empty house because Pop was gone on a three-day trip. She must have been terrified. There was nothing to ease the pain of not knowing. Later on when she wrote me about this I told her, "Don't worry, the Navy will contact you before it is on the radio"–which wasn't the least bit true. The newswires always got the information first.

*

1 December 1972–Memorial service for CDR Earnest was held in the hangar bay. The solemnity of the service was profound and most fitting for the skipper. It was an overcast day with heavy, restless, angry seas. After all the tributes and prayers, our XO, CDR Bill Green, placed a wreath over the side. It was a very heartrending moment that will stay with me forever, the sadness is impossible to put out of your mind. When the wreath hit the water, the sea suddenly became calm and although we were 200 miles out to sea, a white bird flew into the hangar bay and all around the overhead and back out again. As soon as the memorial service ended, following taps and the gun salute, the sea became very agitated again, tossing whitecaps into the hangar bay. It was noticeable that the sea was not its usual emerald green, but rather a turbulent black. We finished with the Navy hymn, which included:

> *Lord guard and guard the men who fly,*
> *Through the great spaces in the sky,*
> *Be with them always in the air,*
> *In darkening storms or sunlight fair.*
> *O hear us when we lift out prayer.*
> *For those in peril in the air.*

CHAPTER FIFTY-SIX

ONLY IN MY DREAMS

2 December 1972–We flew a day tank then went on an alpha strike to Bai Thoung Air Base. Gunfire was furious the whole mission. The Navy was then limited to 50 strikes a day into route packs two, three and four in South Vietnam–this among three carriers. We used to put out 80 to 100 a day on our carrier alone! With the decrease in missions, we certainly didn't need four carriers on the line. Why couldn't we just go home?

Politicians were still playing a bunch of games. Morale was really low as they continued to keep us here when they didn't need us. The Air Force said they couldn't handle all of us in the South. The North's weather was zero-zero and we were limited to 16 strikes a day into the North. The next day we flew for only four hours at night! We were the lone ship on the 0100 to 1300 schedule! Then changed to the 1300 - 0100 schedule. It continued to feel like we were being used and taken for a ride.

3 December 1972–I was up in our intelligence center known as IOIC (which we referred to as 101 Clowns) going over some maps for our next mission. Word came through that Army had defeated Navy in the BIG game. When I returned to the Ready Room, I noticed that the TV screen showed Navy ahead of Army

at half time. I went around and made bets with a few of our Boat School graduates and even gave them a few points. Later on the final score was posted and of course I won all bets. I collected my winnings nicely and never said a word. All's fair in love and war!

*

The weather was still bad and we were again on the night schedule. I was so tired that it ran right through my whole body, physically hurting me. My side along my ribs was tender to the touch and hurt so much that I could barely cinch up my torso harness the pain was so great. My nerve endings were frayed, terribly battered and inflamed due to the stress of months of combat. No one even knew what fibromyalgia was back then, but I guess I had it. Life is lived at full speed in war, concentrated and intense. This is the real stuff although combat is completely unimaginable. I received even more Christmas presents in the mail but still won't open them.

Later that night we flew a seeding mission where we dropped mines in a river bend south of Vinh. Total IFR at 400 feet made it super dark. Quad mounted 23mm guns and others opened up to our left, barely missing us. We seeded 12 Mark 36s mines. The night just swallowed us up. On the way back to the ship, we saw two huge green comets that helped calm me down a bit. Back aboard ship I had barely gotten to sleep when General Quarters sounded. Grabbing my flight gear, I headed for the Ready Room and could smell smoke enroute. As it turned out a fighter pilot had fallen asleep with a cigarette in his mouth catching his mattress on fire. He was able to get out of his room but not before it put out tons of smoke. He was given the call sign "Arson!"

4 December 1972–We had to man up at night in the wind and driving rain. Sometimes we would do a "hot turn." This entailed getting in a plane that just returned from a mission and was being refueled and rearmed as you climbed in. You strapped in and went. It was like being thrown into a football game at the last minute with no warm-up.

As it got closer to Christmas, I got even more scared–if that was possible. I figured if I got bagged around this time, my parents would never be able to enjoy Christmas again. My being in combat must have tormented my parents.

*

8 December 1972–I flew a damaged plane off to Cubi with Don "Low Drag" Peterson. We had to circumnavigate Typhoon Teresa by going north before heading east and south.
"Where are we Don? We should have picked up some land by now."

"Yeah I know but this storm is huge! Repeating a refrain from a Frank Sinatra song he said, "I think we are somewhere east of the sun and west of the moon"

"Just what I need a comedian who can't sing!"

We almost went too far north. Don picked up a little sliver of the Philippines on his radar behind us to the right. We had missed the Air Defense Identification Zone (ADIZ) by 200 miles! If Don hadn't picked up the Philippines on the radar, we'd still be out there with Amelia Earhardt. It's a very big ocean out there. We landed at Cubi Point—saved by a B/N again! The ship arrived the next day.

9 December 1972—A bunch of us went up to the nurses' quarters, which was decorated with Christmas lights on Palm trees and cards from other nurses stationed around the world—they were very dedicated people. Out there it felt that everything had purpose and meaning with every situation magnified. I'd look at Christmas stamps, especially those of the Blessed Mother and stared at the return address on a letter because that meant home. A Walt Disney stamp reminded me of the good times with my parents at Disneyland. As always I was very specific in writing letters since I didn't want anything left unsaid.

*

The Air Wing held a party for local orphans on the ship today. The children were very cute, well behaved, and very, very shy. Even though they didn't speak or understand English, they still laughed at the cartoons we showed them. I had one little boy, Benji; all of seven years old and weighing about 40 pounds—only three feet high! The little guy ate two hamburgers, one hot dog, ice cream, cake, and cookies. At one point, he dropped his hamburger on the floor and was picking it up to eat it when I got him another one. You should have seen their eyes when they saw Santa, the food and the gifts. They wouldn't open the presents until they returned to the orphanage because they wanted to use the wrappings to decorate the walls. Back at the orphanage they had hot water for only one hour a day and electricity for two hours. All of my so-called worries left me. Talk about misplaced and unwanted people—such poor kids who were on the fringe of society. Did anyone else even know these poor kids existed? My Dad had told me how the British kids during WWII would go through the garbage cans by the base or come by and ask, "Gum chum?"

The next day at Mass the Padre said we were raising funds for the orphanage. "I want donations—none of that little stuff more like tens and twenties." We eventually raised enough to build a whole new wing with running water and electricity. It was named the Air Wing Three building.

17 December 1972—I stayed behind in Cubi Point waiting for aircraft 521 to be repaired—this took until December 30!

18 December 1972—President Nixon started bombing the North with B-52s. During this time 15 B-52s and three F-111s were lost. 1085 Sam's were fired in ten days. The President told the Chinese and Russians that we were going to bomb the North and if they started anything, he'd bomb them too! As we know, they didn't do a thing; although, the Chinese already had thousands of troops fighting in Vietnam. The Russians and Chinese were also flying some MiGs as well as manning the SAM missile sites and anti-aircraft batteries. They also had Russian and Cuban interrogators in the POW camps.

An A-6 pilot from the Midway was blamed for hitting a Polish merchant ship. He had to go see the Admiral on the Enterprise. Whose side are these Admirals on? You put your life on the line and then get called in on the rug for it? They agreed that a SAM had probably fallen back on to the ship that caused the damage. Many years later there was a picture of that merchant ship in a Hanoi military museum with a bomb hole in the side– somebody did in fact get a good hit.

*

The CO of the Midway really pushed the A-6 squadron. So much so that the majority of the planes were down, broken or damaged. When a certain target came up, the CO of VA-115 said they couldn't possibly hit it due to lack of parts to fix the planes. The Captain of the ship removed him as well as the XO and Ops Officer because they all agreed. Jack Keegan was next in line to get canned. All of a sudden the ship picked up speed and made a big turn. The CO came up on the IMC and said they were heading to Singapore to have the Bob Hope show on the ship – so much for an important target!

Our squadron lost Bob Graustein and Black Bart Wade on 22 December during a night low-level mission. The only thing heard was "fire!" Bart didn't have to be there, he had volunteered off shore duty to come fly with us. He could have stayed safely at home. Bob's wife, Dudney, lived next door to the CO of the helicopter squadron that had rescued Jim Lloyd earlier in the cruise. When she was notified, she ran over and pleaded, "Jan,

367

have your husband save Bob, please." But they were gone. In my mind, I felt that anyone we lost after October should still be with us because originally we were supposed to have been home by now. This was getting real personal with more silent sorrow, creating a lifetime of sadness for the friends we lost.

While in Cubi, the Bob Hope Christmas show came through, which really brought home to those of us there. His wife, Dolores asked us, "What song do you want to hear—*On a Clear Day* or *White Christmas*?" We all sang *White Christmas* with teary eyes. A very nervous Cubi-based LTJG presented Bob Hope with a picture of the base and stated, "The *prescription* reads, To Bob Hope with best wishes."

Laughing Bob said, "The prescription?"

At the end of the show, none of us made through singing *Silent Night.*

I also got to see a touching USO Christmas show put on by students from Oklahoma City College, a small Christian school. It was very nice of them to give up their holiday time to entertain us. You could catch a movie on base for twenty-five cents, which always began with our national anthem. It really hit home with the lines, "Land of the free and the home of the brave." To this day I always get choked up when I hear the anthem and it feels good to know where the brave were! At the O'Club Filipino entertainers would say, "Although we neber seen snow before we'd like to sing *White Christmas.*" And they were very good.

*

On Christmas Eve I went to midnight Mass at Cubi. The old Quonset hut chapel didn't have any stained glass windows; hand carved statues or any other frills yet the Mass meant more to me than any I had ever attended in a Cathedral. It was a real treasure, powerful and inspirational–a real privilege. Christmas day was spent at the nurses' quarters, singing carols and drinking eggnog. It was all very moving. The girls were crying while opening presents, homesick like all of us. A few were playing guitars. I think this was one of the most memorable and meaningful Christmases I've ever had. I was with people who were really doing something, who were sacrificing and caring. Even with all the tumult and fear in my life I was truly happy. The carol *I'll be home for Christmas* actually meant "only in my dreams."

I reflected back on Christmas as a child, which my parents made very special. The tree didn't go up until we children went to bed on Christmas Eve. Santa would come, put up the tree and decorate it. In the morning we were allowed to open one present and check our stockings. We then had to go to Mass before we could open the rest of the presents. That felt like one of the longest masses on record. To this day I can recall every present I got because we would only get one or two–usually made by Pop.

Late one night a few days after Christmas, while still waiting for the plane to get repaired, I went out back alone on the deck at the O'Club with a drink. Out loud I prayed-pleaded, *"Knock this shit off, there are too many good men dying!"* I didn't even say, "Please." It was a real Jersey prayer. I threw my empty glass down the hill into the jungle and heard it break! I was physically and emotionally drained. The stress and anxiety were getting to me big time. Like Jeremiah *"I grow weary holding it in, I cannot endure it"* Three weeks later the war ended!

Of course there was a whole litany of Christmas carols made up by Don "Low Drag" Petersen. One such was the chorus sung to Jingle Bells:

OH JINGLE BELLS, TRIPLE-A SHELLS

SAM IS ON THE WAY

OH WHAT FUN IT IS TO RIDE

IN A GOOD OL'A-6A–Hey!

…

JINGLE BELLS, TRIPLE-A SHELLS

SAM IS ON THE WAY

AT TIMES LIKE THIS, I REALLY WISH

I FLEW A-5'S TODAY.

*

30 December 1972–The President stopped bombing north of 20 degrees trying to get the Communists to negotiate in good faith.

It didn't work.

Each day I would go out to Base Ops in Cubi to see what was going on with the plane. "Still working on it, sir." When we finally went to test fly it and spread the wings, the "over wing" locks and the control rods in the wings broke and the wings went completely down to the ground with the most excruciating sound! Although it looked like a wounded duck it was actually dead.

The next day at Operations they told me they received a message from our Commanding Officer saying he wanted me back at the ship.

"How do I get there?"

"That Air Force C-118 leaves for DaNang in 15 minutes."

I got my gear and climbed on the plane. I think it was one of the slowest planes I've ever been on—watching it climb at 200 feet a minute. When we landed at DaNang I asked, "Where's the helicopter for the ship?" They said it couldn't get here for two days. This was December 30th. I was terrified at being in country, especially since I didn't know who was who! B/N Doug Ahrens and I checked into the BOQ, an old splinterville building. I told Doug, "Your flak vest and helmet are under the bed."

He said, "Sure."

"No really, I just saw the sign on the wall that says, 'flak vest and helmet under bed'."

The whole area was kind of old and depressing. The base was known as Rocket City because the gooks fired Russian-made 122 mm rockets from Monkey Mountain some six miles away. The "Club" was the Red Dog Saloon, named after CDR "Dog" Davidson. It consisted of a few old chairs and tables, and a small FM radio. Plywood walls were painted red, white and blue with some girlie pics. There were two refrigerators, two barstools and a small metal box to put money in for the drinks. On the wall was written, *"You guys really have class"*–Laurie Lee Schaefer, Miss America 1972. At the water cooler there was part of an exploded 122 mm shell, on it was written:"Alarm clock 12/26/72."

An air raid siren called Big Boy would go off to warn of an attack. It sounded like Banshees wailing and the sound alone could freeze your blood! There was machinegun fire and rockets exploding all night long. The siren went off on New Year's Eve as the bad guys came through the perimeter, so we spent most of the night in the middle of the bedlam not knowing where the good guys and bad guys were. The most amazing thing was how very loud the sound of the explosions was. War movies don't even come close. I was thinking if *I get bagged here, no one would know for months–no one knows where I'm at. No orders, nothing.*

A little 6 cent stamp brought me a bit of happiness

1 January 1973–I went to Mass in a small chapel on the base. The service was stopped a few times by mortar and gunfire. The Chaplain would stop the Mass, listen and then say "outgoing." It all sounded the same to me! Later that day we caught the helicopter to the ship. It was great to be out of country. That place was terrifying.

CHAPTER FIFTY-SEVEN

SOMEBODY IN THERE DOESN'T LIKE YOU!

While I was gone, Boot decorated a little fake Christmas tree in our room and put the presents from my parents under it. I got to hear some of the stories of the action that took place the past few weeks. There had been four Russian-built Komar boats in the area. Basically these are PT boats armed with surface-to-surface missiles that could sink anything within 80 miles. They had been sent from Russia to China to the North Vietnamese. Some A-7s found them and sunk two; they damaged one and the other took off.

The maneuver for evading a missile in the daytime was to dogfight with it (i.e. out maneuver it by banking hard and pulling high G's one way and another). But at night, being so close to the ground on a low-level mission made this an impossible move for two reasons. One, the bright light from the exhaust of the missile would light up the whole sky, preventing you from being able to get a good angle off it—you couldn't tell exactly where it was coming from. Secondly, high G maneuvers with steep bank angles so close to the ground would most likely make you a part of the terrain. The only way to get a missile off your tail at night was to get lower and lower and have its radar lose you in the ground clutter. One night right before Christmas, Mike "Shu" Schuster and Jerry "Moon" Mullins were trying to evade a missile by doing just that. But as they got lower and lower, so did the missile. They just couldn't break the radar lock. All of a sudden, there was a deafening noise and a thud, and both Mike and Jerry prepared to eject. They had actually flown through a stand of trees and bounced off the side of a hill. In testimony to Grumman "Ironworks" and the crew coordination of Mike and Jerry, they miraculously made it back to the ship and somehow landed okay. The A-6 had lived up to its tough trait of "grit!" as did the crewmembers. In the hangar bay where the plane was parked, it smelled like a campfire because of the trees the engines had ingested and burned. There were pieces of trees embedded in the leading edge of the wing and dirt in the intakes. We told Mike that to become a River Rat you only had to fly OVER the Red River Valley, not land IN it! The Christmas Carol of choice that year was *"O Christmas tree, O Christmas tree, Mike Schuster bagged a Christmas tree."* Sailors thought the smell of the pine trees added to the Christmas season. That same plane actually went on to fly in Desert Storm. The tail of Mike's plane is now on the wall in the "O'Club at NAS Oceana.

*

The Executive Officer of VA- 196, the A-6 squadron off the USS Enterprise (CVN-65), Commander Gordon Nakagawa, was lost during this time. The last time I saw him was in port at the O'Club.

Pilots would come out of North Vietnam, broadcasting "Burn baby burn" and someone would reply, "Wait, I'm still in here!" Morale was high–we were finally hitting them. But why did it take so long? One of the main reasons B-52s were shot down was the fact that they would fly the exact route and pattern night after night. They flew the same speed, same altitude in cells of three about 15 minutes apart and coming ashore at the exact same place just north of Haiphong. The Air Force couldn't be accused of using their heads! You could see SAMs being fired and B-52s getting hit from the flight deck as you manned up. We stayed on the night schedule.

One night, the helo from our ship picked up a tail gunner from a B-52. They brought him into our Ready Room since our Flight Surgeon was hanging out there. He was still wet, wrapped in a blanket. He was a little Sergeant from South Carolina who kept "siring" me to death. I had to tell him to stop doing that! I asked him what had happened. He told me that enroute to the target he had bagged a MiG 21 that tried to sneak up on the big plane from behind. "I just put the radar crosshair on him, pressed a button on the quad mounted 20 mm guns and *vroom*–he's gone." Moments later, a near-miss SAM exploded by the plane, damaging the controls and starting a small fire. The pilot turned toward the Gulf of Tonkin to get away from enemy territory. Safely out over the water, he decided to try to make it to one of the allied airbases in South Vietnam. The middle part of the plane was burning and the tail gunner lost radio communication with the pilots. He pulled a handle that jettisoned his 20 mm guns, unstrapped his seat belt, stood up and took a big step-a leap of faith, into the black unknown. A few seconds later, the plane exploded. Pulling his D-ring on the parachute, he noticed the lights of a "moving runway"– our aircraft carrier. The Saratoga was completing a recovery and was respotting the planes for the next launch at 0200, hence the lights on the deck. Our ship had seen the plane explode and launched the rescue helicopter from HS-7. They were able to pick up his chute and pluck him out of the water a few minutes after he landed.

*

2 January 1973–We flew a day tank in the usual weather, BAD! In between flights I was up in Pre-flight watching flight operations when I saw Boot taxi by in a plane with Bruce Cook. When he returned, it was his 400th landing. I wrote on a piece of paper, "Oh good Boot–400–you're not playing with a full deck!"

Many times before a mission, we looked at the wall chart of North Vietnam and saw 'no bombs' lines, which were areas we were prohibited to hit. We always thought it was probably due to some politician or movie star peacenik visiting the area. After the war we found out that Navy Seals had been working in those areas trying to find downed airmen as well as gather intelligence. On one such mission, a Navy Seal was killed and his buddies carried him for days to get him out. They never left anyone behind.

When the ship left Cubi for the last line period, our belief was that we were to fly down South with an easy schedule. The next thing we knew, we were up in area 6B, deep in North Vietnam! We were finally getting good targets after all those years! However time is really dragging!

7 January 1973–I think Paul went off the deep end today with a wild, crazy, nutso idea. He said tonight when they locked us up with their radar; we should turn toward the strobe coming from the missile site and when we got right over it, pickle our bombs on the SAM site. I said, "What are you crazy? The SAM sites are ringed with antiaircraft guns not to mention the missiles themselves! I just want to find some easy target that we can get in and out from quickly." We found a trans-shipment point (TSP) at a location some 20 miles south of Vinh. All we had to do was coast in a few miles, make a right turn and run up a valley to hit the target, and another right turn to get back over the Gulf. Should be a piece of cake. It was super dark with a very low overcast, making it a total blackout underneath. The hills were very close in on both sides and the rain so heavy it was like flying up a tunnel in a carwash. We carried the usual load of 14 Mark 82s. They were shooting down on us from the hills as well as directly in front and beneath us. We'd get lower and the gunfire would follow us down. AAA was all over the place. I needed more that a rod and staff to comfort me in this valley. Then a SAM site locked us up. Ronny Dean and Dave Warren were sitting offshore in the STARM. Seeing all the gunfire, Dave sung out in a lilting, singsong voice over the radio. *"Somebody in there doesn't like you!"* No shit, Sherlock!

Officially known as "Linebacker II," this "Christmas Bombing" was a max effort to destroy major targets in North Vietnam instead of just interdiction raids of the past. The only ones over the beach at night from the ship were the A-6s. CAG Bordone told the Skippers of the other Squadrons that "VA-75 was carrying the load" and to "say something to them." Experts considered the Christmas bombing of North Vietnam as history's most surgically precise bombing campaign ever. Up to that point, when we hit a rail yard, we damaged about a quarter of it. Later that night there would be thousands of Chinese coolies in there repairing it. When the B-52s hit, it took out the complete rail yard without touching anything around it. Prior to and during B-52 strikes during Linebacker II; the A-6s were tasked with hitting Sam sites. This was very treacherous because they were non-radar significant targets and were surrounded by multiple anti-aircraft sites. During this time, the North Vietnamese with their Russian counter-parts fired 1293 missiles. The last three nights they fired only a few and the last night, none–they were out. I always felt we should have paved the place with bombs making it a parking lot so that all they had to do for the next 50 years was rebuild. But we stopped!

I wrote in my journal: *If I never work again–I'm even.* This past year it was 24/7, physically and psychologically–even when in port.

*

JJ Miller on his last mission broadcast over the air ala Walter Winchell saying, "Mr. and Mrs. America and all the ships at sea–goooodbyeeee, Vietnam!" My last landing on the ship was a night tanker, finally my last landing! When we left the states, I made up my mind that if I were alive the next-to-last day, I wouldn't fly on the last day. I had remembered stories from World War II and Vietnam about pilots who were killed on their very last mission. I'd been a nervous wreck all week waiting for the last day–couldn't sleep or eat. Some guys wore the same flight suit and same underwear the whole last week of ops. It was a tense time for everyone.

> *"Keep your fears with yourself but share your courage with others."*

8 January 1973–The last day of ops. It was just a shortened schedule with plenty of replacements who wanted to fly. Since I wasn't flying I went on the flight deck and took movies. All returned safely. I was glad it was over, yet I was really sad for the men left behind. At 1430, the Commanding Officer of the ship came up over the One MC and said, "Right 20° all ahead flank, steady on course one zero zero!" East to the Philippines, out of the war zone. We were heading out. We were done! God Bless us all!

> *"Stars may be seen from the bottom of a deep well, when they cannot be seen from the top of the mountain. So many things are learned in adversity which the prosperous man dreams not of."*
>
> (C.H. Spurgeon)

Later that day, a Thanksgiving service was held. It was great to sing our national anthem- I'll always know what "home of the brave" means.

Boot and I were straightening up our room and packing a few items for the homeward trip, when he asked, "Hey, Al, have you seen my pistol?"

"What do you mean, you weren't carrying it?!"

"Nope."

"Why not?"

"See I didn't need it."

I could have killed him right then and there!

CHAPTER FIFTY-EIGHT

THE WAR CONTINUED WITH MORE LOSSES

9 January 1973–A target at Ha Dong popped up in the Intelligence center on board USS Midway and was assigned to VA-115, the A-6 squadron. As always, the only planes that can attack at night in bad weather. As Mike "Mondo" McCormick and Alan "Arlo" Clark were planning the mission, their Skipper came in and told them, "You're not to go there. That target is a magnet for planes. Besides, the monsoon is making the weather terrible. No one should even be airborne on a night like this." He relayed his feelings to Admiral Christensen, Commander of the Task Force (CTF 77). His reply was curt and to the point. "That target will get attacked no matter what! We have to cover the B-52 strike that is coming back in tonight. President Nixon wants to put more pressure on the North Vietnamese to capitulate."

Anything to protect the Air Force, especially their B-52s. They finally come up North after eight years of war–"Where have they been up to now?" in toned Arlo as they planned the mission.

"OK, Arlo, let's man up. I'll buy you a beer when we get to port the day after tomorrow."

"Sure, Mondo, but it sure would be nice to stay home tonight. I'd settle for some chips and a coke."

Something just didn't feel right for either of them, yet they knew they had to go. Like so many times in the history of America it was the total effort of the few that kept others and us free. As they passed the F-4 Fighter Ready Room, the crews were eating popcorn and watching a movie–weather was too bad for them to fly; plus it was nighttime. Just manning the aircraft was a chore. Winds approaching 40 knots drove rain into every part of their flight suits and up and under their helmet. Arlo felt like he should be snorkeling rather than flying.

"A-rab 511 Feet dry." Alan transmitted in the blind as they crossed the beach into enemy territory. Back aboard the E-2 Hawkeye radar aircraft, the controller marked the fact that they were now headed toward the target. He sent it along via secure voice to the Combat Information Center (CIC) aboard the ship. They got pounded as soon as they crossed the beach with AAA that was intense and accurate. They planned to fly the mission at 360 knots but were now going 420 trying to outrun the gunfire and radar lockups. Mike had the throttles bent over the stops trying to get every last ounce of speed from the Intruder. Thoughts of Ray Donnelly flooded his mind and soul. Across the top of the instrument panel the ALR 45 was lit up like a Christmas tree, indicating all the radar threats that were locking up the aircraft. Mike had to descend below their original planned 200 feet in order to avoid missiles that were directed at their plane. Each time he'd have to get back on the original course toward the target. By now the gooks knew exactly what their target was and they aimed to thwart the attack. "Got the target, Arlo?"

"Just about; I'm sweeping the area. OK, now I've got a good lock on the target and I'm updating it. Steady, Mike. Steady, it's OK to follow steering." As the symbology on his Vertical Display Indicator (VDI) worked its way down, Mike got the required signal that the bombs were to be released automatically– as a back up he mashed down the red manual pickle button on his control stick with his thumb. They had to hit it this time since there was no way they'd ever want to come back to this place again. The plane leaped about 50 feet in the air as the 12,000-pound bomb load left the plane. At the same time they heard another plane calling "Missiles in the air, missiles in the air!"

There were huge fireballs and loud explosions followed by secondaries–they hit the target. The controllers in the E-2 waited for a call of "feet wet," indicating that 511 was back safely over the Gulf. Nothing but dead silence filled the airwaves. Finally, they called frantically asking, "A-rab 511 say your position, 511 acknowledge, are you feet wet, are you feet wet?

Acknowledge please!" Continued blank silence. Mondo and Arlo were in fact short *one feet wet* call. No one should have had to attack that highly defended target in such filthy weather that night.

Back home in Whidbey Island Tonya Clark was abruptly awakened early in the morning by a stern knock on the door. As soon as she saw the Chaplain, the Base CO and the Skipper's wife she knew something was wrong. Now she understood why she had not slept well during the night.

"Is it Alan, is he dead?"

"We don't know, they just didn't come back. They are classified as 'Missing in action. We are so sorry."

Ernie Pyle wrote during WWII, *"Missing"–that is aviation at its worst. Suddenness of death is like a knockout blow: it hurts and bewilders and then it gradually diminishes. But the missing - that is the torture screw, with each hour that passes giving the screw another turn. You can't resign yourself to grief; you must hang alone by the tips of your hope dangling, imaging, lying to yourself and waiting.*

Tonya picked up Tad and held him tightly–her tears soaked his baby blanket. The "missing" status would torment the families for many years to come. The very next day the USS Midway left the war zone for good. The war ended seventeen days later. They were so close–Mondo and Arlo almost made it.

*

Back in Cubi, it really was a very strange feeling realizing that I didn't have to go back to war. I thought I would be excited and happy, but I wasn't. Not exactly the way one would expect to feel–I had lived in turmoil for almost a year and having lived on the edge where the highs were high and the lows were low it was very strange just to stop. I wondered what home would be like. It just felt abnormal leaving with guys still POWs or missing and the war still on. It did not feel right and there was no real sense of relief. However I did know I didn't ever want to be scared again. I certainly didn't need any kind of excitement to make my life complete. Boot called such activities as bungee jumping and extreme sports "artificial danger." People were actually trying to get some sort of buzz by taking on self-produced risks.

11 January 1973–I received a medal from Rear Admiral Dick in the Captain's In-Port cabin. He said, "By all rights you should be dead now. Remember that when your birthday comes around." A few years later when I told this story to our friend Gayla she wrote a poem which ended with; "And the medals still remind me every birthday is a friend 'cause I lived to read that story, from beginning to its end." Again I felt great pride in receiving the same Medals Pop had been awarded.

I walked into my room for the last time. For some unexplained reason I made a fist and hit the ducting of the rumble

LT Fischers receiving the same medal 27 years apart "perhaps my son won't have to go."

machine with the side of my tightened hand. The noise stopped! All this time I had had to listen to that incessant noise.

*

We all hung around the pool that had an "Annex" O'Club complete with a bar. Naval tradition required that anyone entering a bar "covered" (i.e. with a hat on) had to buy the place. We had one hat. One by one we'd walk in wearing a bathing suit and the hat. The bartender would ring a bell indicating you owed the place. We'd say, "Oh no!" having to buy a round. This went on all day long. We were done–we loved it–we made it!

CHAPTER FIFTY-NINE

A SELLOUT

12 January 1973–Subic Bay. I watched as the ship pulled out with the crew lining the rails. The Saratoga was to go to Singapore for two days and then leave on the 17th to sail home. I stayed behind to catch the Early Bird, or Magic Carpet flight, home on the 19th with a World Airways charter. Traditionally, they sent home the married guys or boys who were wounded. As it turned out, Doug Ahren's wife, Linda, wasn't going on vacation until after the ship returned, so somehow I got Doug's seat. On the way over, everything was new and exciting but now I was done, finished. There was no way I wanted to ride the ship for another 28 days. I just wanted to get off the ship and go home. I never wanted to be Skipper of a squadron or a ship. I especially didn't want to be part of ship's company. I didn't mind being on a ship as long as I could fly off it. I joined on account of the war and went to it. For me there was nothing left to do in the Navy.

I was watching TV in the BOQ lounge January 14th when a live broadcast via satellite came on. It was Elvis doing the "Aloha from Hawaii" concert. Here I had seen him the night before this whole thing started, and now I'm on the verge of going home and I see him again!

19 January 1973–"Rourkie" came by to see me off. She said, "I can tell you this now–after your first line period you looked thirty years older to me." Believe me, I felt it too.

Every stress leaves an indelible scar, and the organism pays for its survival after a stressful situation by becoming a little older. (Hans Selye)

*

We were told to be out of the airfield at 0600. We kept waiting and waiting for a chartered World Airways 707. Someone started to complain until one of the sailors said, "I've been here almost a year, so a few more hours aren't going to make any difference." He was right. The plane arrived at two in the afternoon.

When we took off, it was 105 degrees. We flew and landed at Yakoto, Japan where it was 40 degrees and then Anchorage Alaska where it was minus 13 degrees. Of course, we were wearing our summer uniforms. I went into the gift shop at Anchorage and was looking at something and said, "I want to buy a gift, but I already filled out my customs form." The lady behind the counter said, "No you don't, you're in America now."

I said, "That's right. I'm in America!" Boy did that feel good.

It was a great flight but I couldn't sleep at all, just thinking about getting home. I sat next to Jim Lloyd and he went over his whole shoot down and rescue experience. He said it would be nice if the war ended now so we could feel that we had something to do with it. When we left the good guys were winning. Our biggest problem was trying to figure out how to set the day in English instead of Spanish on our new Seiko watches we had bought at the Exchange before leaving. After twenty hours of travel we landed in Norfolk at 0200. LCDR John (XYZ-cause no one could spell his name) Skrzypek and CDR "Barney" Boecker met me and someone handed me a bottle of champagne, which I never opened. The next day, January 20th, I flew home to Newark airport and was welcomed by my parents, brother and Roseanne McDonough.

Jim, too, arrived back on a flight to Florida in the middle of the night. His wife drove him home at about 0300. They got a little Boston terrier named Jigs just two months before Jim left. Jim was gone longer than he had known the dog. Walking in the door, the dog let out a yelp and jumped up into Jim's arms. Jim had a month's leave. The neighbors would say, "Hi, Jim, haven't seen you for a while," not having a clue as to what had gone on. Jim said his best friend was Jigs and he couldn't wait to get back to the squadron and his other friends.

*

There were no welcome home parades until twenty-five years later. Then with Operation Desert Storm and Iraqi Freedom, the returning troops were treated like heroes. To us it was like seeing your younger brother getting all the gifts at Christmas while you got none. Although you were happy for him, you couldn't help feeling bad for yourself. Perhaps people felt that it somehow made

389

up for our poor treatment, but it was too little too late. It was just plain hollow.

23 January 1973–The President announced a cease-fire to take effect on 27 January with the signing of the Paris Peace Accord. With this Accord it was agreed that the DMZ at the 17th Parallel would remain a provisional dividing line, with eventual reunification of the country through "peaceful means." The North Vietnamese said they would not initiate military movement across the DMZ and that there would be no use of military force to reunify the country. The only way President Nixon persuaded President Thieu of South Vietnam to sign it was to tell him, in writing, that if the agreement was broken the United States would return to help with full force. President Thieu took Nixon at this word.

On January 27th, CDR Harley Hall, former Leader of the Blue Angels and Executive Officer of Fighter Squadron 143 onboard USS Enterprise, flew a close air support mission in an F-4. He was working with FAC Covey 115 near the Cua Viet River just north of the DMZ. There were trucks moving along the road as the Communists were rushing to occupy as much of the area as possible. This was just a few hours before the Paris Peace Accords were to take effect. He came under intense fire while attacking trucks and took several hits, severely damaging his plane. He and his RIO both ejected safely. Harley was seen running on the ground. His backseater, RIO LCDR Phil Kientzler, was shot in the leg and captured, but there was no sign of Harley; however, a few days later the front page of "The Hanoi Times" told of "Leading a Big Blue Angel down their main street." He was never heard from again! Years later, classified material made available to the families proved that he had been interrogated by the Soviets! The original on-scene commander was the Forward Air Controller Harley had been working with. He, too, was shot down. He and his co-pilot were found–tied to a tree–decapitated.

When the prisoners were to be released in Hanoi, they noticed that a new shoot- down was kept isolated. They heard him whistle the "Streets of Laredo." They yelled and asked who he was.

"LCDR Phil Keintzler!"

His name had not been given to the American POWs and they had no intention of releasing him. Other POWs went on a hunger strike to embarrass the gooks, who eventually gave in.

With the signing of the Peace agreement, the War was finally over for the United States. As we were to see later, Secretary of State Henry Kissinger totally sold us out. It was a good feeling to know that we played some part in ending the war. But we could've hit them like we did years earlier and ended the war in the first six months. I think that's why many people became disenchanted with the war and protested. However for the South Vietnamese people the war continued. In 1973 alone they lost some 29,000 men trying to hold off the Communists. Major Khang of the ARVN said that he had a hatred of the Communists that ran soul deep.

CHAPTER SIXTY

THE HOMEFRONT

I was home only four days when Pop showed me a telegram from American Airlines that had been sent December 12th. It read, "Please call us collect at 212-426-8800 if interested in employment in consideration as flight crewmember." I had totally forgotten that I had applied to all the airlines the year before.

Pop said, "I think you ought to at least go see them."

"They're not going to give me a test are they? I haven't been able to even read a newspaper since I've been back." I was in a fog, not to mention 15 hours difference in body time.

I was more concerned with fitting back in. I was busy showing my appreciation to my family by giving them all one gift each day for two weeks. I received a framed crochet from one of the wives *"Today is the first day of the rest of your life."* My cousin Carla gave me a beautiful Catholic medal. Her accompanying letter said in part: "God Bless you Alan, for in our heart, despite all the ugliness of war, is the comfort and beauty in one's mind–in knowing that you have contributed to the Peace there is today." These were the only mementoes so to speak that I received for returning home. I just would have liked anything– something to remember my return. The only other gift was one I gave myself. It was a plaque with the quote that was attributed to one found on an empty ammo box during the battle of Khe Sanh, *"Life has a different flavor to those who have fought for it. Than it does to those who are protected."*

Pop drove me to LaGuardia Airport in New York to talk to folks at American. I heard him talking to a fellow pilot on the employee bus to the terminal.

"Well hell, he was dropping bombs just two weeks ago!"

Captain Dan Weatherbee was the New York Chief Pilot for American Airlines. He was one of the very few who had flown 25 missions in both B-17s and B-25s in WWII. He did most of the talking, telling me how his son had just been accepted in the Air Force ROTC program at Notre Dame.

He said, "I see you don't have a big watch like most fighter pilots."

"No, but I'll get one."

"No need."

He then sent me over to the personnel people who at that time were running the hiring show so much so that if a pilot recommended someone it almost always guaranteed him not getting hired.

The Personnel Director asked to see my flying license. I told him I had taken it out of my wallet to make it thin so my suit pants looked good.

"It's home on my bureau."

"How about your log book?"

"It's on the ship on the way back."

"What's an A-6? Is it like an A-4?"

"Yes, sir, I guess so."

"Do you have your DD-214?"

"A flight plan?' (That was a DD-215). My mind was in a whirl.

"No they're your discharge papers."

"I'm still in the Navy until August."

"What are we talking about?"

"I don't know, don't you hire for August?"

"No, we are hiring now."

My heart sank.

Then he said, "We're going to give you a test and if you get 98 or above, you won't have to come back Sunday and take the Stanine test (a nine hour test)." All I thought about was that Sunday was the day my mother was having the relatives over for a party. It was a timed test and here I was counting on my fingers during the math problems. My eyes were burning while trying to read and understand the questions. In the English part, one word stuck out, "Lieu." I recalled that was what an award said "Gold star in Lieu of a second medal." *Hey, it means "instead of."*

While I was taking the test, Pop was walking through the hangar saying the rosary to himself. I somehow got a 99 on the test.

Afterwards, the secretaries who knew Pop invited him for a piece of cake since it was Dan Weatherbee's birthday. Pop asked me how it went. I told him about the Personnel Director's questions. I saw Pop corner the gentleman and heard him say, "Well hell, it's as big as a B-24!"

A week later Pop said, "Maybe you ought to give them a call since you should have heard something by now."

"Naw, I don't want to make any waves."

Pop said, "Give them a call."

I did just that and they said, "Yes, you've been accepted. We sent a telegram to you in Essex Falls, New York."

"But I live in Essex Fells, New Jersey!"

"There's one opening for the March 2nd class, can you make it?"

I held the phone to my chest and told Pop.

"Tell them yes."

"Yes, I can make that." After I hung up I said, "Pop–I'm in the Navy until August, I can't be in two places at one time."

I called Navy Bupers (Bureau of Personnel) in D.C. They told me I needed a recommendation from my Commanding Officer. I had no idea what kind of empire CDR Bill Greene wanted to build once we were back. As XO, the second-in-command, he had taken over after our CO, CDR Charlie Earnest had been lost. He was still riding the ship back.

*

12 February 1973–I drove back to Virginia Beach to be present for the squadron fly-in at NAS Oceana. I was never so happy to see the rest of the guys back. They were home–safe. Our

aircraft had been repainted with Oriental lettering on the tail and the Skipper's plane had a broom attached to the nose probe, signifying a clean sweep–job well done.

The board in our Ready Room in the hangar had what crews were in which planes. Also posted were other squadron members: Lieutenant Lerseth, Captain Denton and LCDR Tschudy *arrived Philippines 0330 local on a C141.* Captain Jeremiah Denton was skipper of VA-75 during its first deployment and was shot down on his seventeenth mission. He was repatriated on the day the squadron returned for the last time from combat. He spent almost eight years in prison, many of those in solitary confinement while enduring inhumane torture. When he stepped off the plane in the Philippines on 12 Feb., he stated most eloquently: *"We are honored to have had the opportunity to serve our country under difficult circumstances. We are grateful to our Commander-in-Chief and our nation for this day. God Bless America."*

We watched Roger and other POWs deplane on TV. But where were Don Lindland and Harley Hall? They had both been seen running on the ground. How about Mike McCormick and Alan Clark? In the Pentagon there was someone who had kept track of the shootdowns. Next to many names he had written "MB," which stood for *Moscow Bound.* This was all swept under the rug. Roger later told me that he had heard that some POWs were sent to Russia through Czechoslovakia. In 1992 Boris Yelsin, President of the Russian Federation, told NBC news in an interview that some Americans captured during the Vietnam war may have been transferred from Hanoi to the Soviet Union. He stated, "Our archives have shown that it is true some of them were transferred to the territory of the former Soviet Union and were kept in labor camps. We didn't have complete data and can only surmise that some may still be alive." Where were the 250 POWs who were supposed to be released in Laos and never showed up? I definitely believe we left guys behind and that still hurts terribly. At the same time I marveled at the amazing attitude of the returning POWs.

A week later I called Roger in the hospital in San Francisco to welcome him home. He said, "Do you know when I was really scared?"

I said, "Yeah, when you were shot down and captured."

"Nope–that time we lost all the instruments on our Med cruise. You saved us at Crete."

This was the greatest compliment I could ever receive.

LT Jack "Fingers" Ench had been one of Roger's roommates in prison. He got the call sign from the damaged thumb that was "surgically" amputated by the gooks. They put his hand on a wooden block and chopped off his injured thumb with a meat cleaver. His original pilot was LCDR Ron "Mugs" McKeown with whom he had shot down two MiGs. Mugs got orders back to the States and told Jack, "You know you aren't going to survive, you'll be flying with a green pilot." Two days later Jack was shot down and captured. Mugs said he thought about that conversation every day.

During the heavy Christmas bombing, the POWs took slats from their beds and leaned them up against the wall. They got underneath for protection from shrapnel from both bombs and anti-aircraft shells. The bombing was intense, continuous and loud. Over in the corner Roger, who had a bad case of dysentery, was

Navy Lt. Roger G. Lerseth of Spokane embraced his wife, Jean, left, and his mother, Mrs. Lillian Lerseth, as he arrived at Alameda Naval Air Station yesterday.—A.P. wirephoto.

Complete Joy!

doing his thing in a honey bucket, also correctly referred to as the "Jane Fonda." At one point there was a break in action and the silence seemed heavenly. However, Roger was still having at it. Jack yelled out, "Hey, Rog, could you keep it down over there. We're trying to sleep?"

When Roger was being released, a guard asked him if a "friend" of the North Vietnamese could visit him in the U.S. Rog said, "Sure, just send him over!" Roger also told him that, "I get to go home, but you have to stay here!"

Billboards along the roads leading to NAS Oceana read: *"When the going got tough the tough got going. Welcome home VA*

75 from Vietnam." Another sign said: *"Sunday Punchers in WestPac were Monday punchers Tuesday punchers Wednesday punchers Thursday punchers...."* Virginia Beach showed its pride and appreciation and respect. The rest of the country just ignored the war and could have cared less. Most people were just indifferent and many scorned the returning troops.

The euphoria was short-lived since a few days after our return the E-2 squadron from our ship lost a plane with 6 crewmembers. It had a "run-away" prop causing it to crash into Chesapeake Bay.

Paul Wagner's '68 Plymouth Barracuda had been left outside for almost a whole year. Consequently, it was covered with a fair amount of dirt. Someone had written on the rear window in the thick dust: *"Vinny in the trunk"* with an arrow pointing down toward the back of the car.

CDR Greene asked me, "How was leave?"

"Great! I got hired by American Airlines but I need to get out of the Navy."

"Are they going to let you out?"

"Don't know I need a letter from you."

"OK, write it up and I'll sign it."

He did just that, so I called Bupers and read the letter to them. They told me it had to be in there that he "doesn't need a replacement until August." The Skipper had signed it and had already left on leave. Since there was a space between the last sentence and his signature, I asked Yeoman Young if he could type in there, "Doesn't need a replacement until August."

"Sure, Mr. Fischer."

I went to D.C. with the letter and spent three days at the Bureau of Personnel. When I first got to Washington, they asked me if I knew that there was high priority traffic coming in on me. I didn't know what that meant. Unbeknownst to me, Dad and our friend Mr. Adrian Foley had made some calls to high-powered associates. Going from person to person, I would look over their shoulders at the paperwork. Each one said the same. "Not approved, disapproved, unapproved, etc." The last Commander said, "No one wants you, no one needs you and there's nothing for you to do, but you're going to be a victim of circumstances. We need the numbers and you have to stay until August."

I wasn't going to make waves because I was just so happy over being back and being alive. I called Pop and gave him the news. He said, "Don't worry something will pop." That was one of his favorite sayings along with, "Remember, someone dumber than you is doing the job you want."

Before I left D.C., they said the boss would be back on Friday and to give him a call. I called on Friday and was all ready to say, "Who's your boss?" He said, "It's been approved; you can leave the Navy on Wednesday. Thank you for serving your country."

*

400

I was released from the Navy on February 23rd. When I was leaving the squadron, I walked by my plane in the hangar. I thought about climbing up and sitting in it one last time. I couldn't do it, I just couldn't do it – I was physically and emotionally drained, totally burned out. It took me about six months to actually feel myself again.

I drove home and reported to the American Airlines Flight Academy in Arlington, Texas on March 2nd. Pop arranged to have his recurrent training on the DC-10 at the same time–it was like taking your son to kindergarten for the first time. Being the son of a well-respected Captain put some added pressure on me. I certainly didn't have to apologize for being his son so I definitely didn't want to embarrass him. I would say, "you could fire me just don't tell my Dad!"

I found it tough to watch the POWs returning home on TV. I would've liked to have been there. I also was receiving Medals in the mail. I had always wanted to receive a medal while in ranks with the rest of the troops. Captain Denton actually pinned the DFC on Paul Wagner, a medal he truly deserved.

Later that year, VA-75 was presented with the Admiral C. Wade McClusky Award, a hero at the Battle of Midway, for being *"The Outstanding Attack Squadron of the United States Navy. Of particular noteworthiness was the squadron's outstanding performances during Linebacker II operations in December 1972, which brought the Vietnam War to a close."* That really felt good.

In addition, the Seventh Fleet and the Seventh Air Force received the Collier trophy for *the greatest contribution to aviation in 1972.*

*

Our Cruise book had a picture of Jim Lloyd by his plane with a quote from Shakespeare, *"Give me another horse! Bind up my wounds!"* Years later, there was a reunion in San Diego of HC-7, the helicopter squadron that rescued Jim. He stayed at our house

Jim Lloyd and good times

and invited me to the party. As it turned out, I ended up being one of the guest speakers. Amidst jeers of "oxygen sucker, starch wing pilot," I gave my talk. It was a good thing they didn't have any rolls to throw. To their amazement my presentation included a great amount of praise for their work. After the dinner, one of the pilots came up to me and asked if I knew an A-6 pilot name George Hyduck.

I said, "Yes, he was in our squadron, but he died a few years back."

"That's funny, I saw him in Detroit last week!"

"What! The Duck is alive?"

"Yup."

I sent an e-mail to my squadron, telling them that Duck was still alive. Dave "Poppin' Fresh" Warren wrote back: "The most amazing thing about this is that the Fish acknowledged that he hung around a bunch of rotorheads–have you no shame?"

Nothing about *"HALLELUIA!* George has come back from the dead after 15 years!"

CHAPTER SIXTY-ONE

FORESAKEN

When I was overseas, I remember thinking, *if I make it back from this; I'm never going to let anything bother me again.* That didn't last too long as I got caught up with family dynamics, jobs, etc. The welcome home lasted as long as a Hawaiian tan. Adjusting to it was a real challenge. Quickly and deeply I understood the saying about; *"God and soldiers loved in war. God and soldiers forsaken in peace."*

Believe it or not, the hardest thing about coming home was, in fact, coming home. It was almost impossible to reconcile the past year with the homefront. Not even family members understood that we were not the same boys who had left to go to war. No one wondered or even wanted to know or even asked me what it was like. They not only didn't care but also were totally uninterested. It also seemed that they weren't all that appreciative of the fact that I returned safely. I figured if I had a son or brother who went through what I had just gone through that I would be ecstatic the rest of my life. I just didn't see that, as some were just muddling through life. I had a lot of pent up emotion that I had to just keep inside me. It was bad enough being ignored, but I really felt sad because of all the good friends we left behind. I wondered how their families felt. I would've thought that my college brother would be at least a little bit curious, but the closest he got to it was calling me "a so-called hero and a shit hot jet jock" in a most derogatory way. He had started a heated discussion over whether trout could see colors on lures! Then when South Vietnam fell he mentioned "boy that was a waste!" I just walked away. I think Pop just wanted me to get on with my life. But I couldn't unsee, unlive or unremember what I had gone through. You just can't undo such things.

Sometimes Vietnam crowded out all my thoughts. In combat you always had one foot in the present and one foot in the likelihood of another dimension. Now one foot remained in the past. I realized that basically nobody was even willing to ask what we had gone through. It was like being very sick and no one even asking how you felt. This created a wound that was as devastating as any physical wound we may have suffered. One evening I was dropping off a date whom I had gone out with often. I asked her if she was proud of me or thought I was a dumb shit for going. Her silence spoke volumes. Someone said, "Well you weren't in the front lines." I said "no—we were far beyond the front lines, deep in enemy territory or try and tell that to Roger and the other POWs!"

There was no decompression time for me. I was being pulled in two directions—still in a war mode war and trying to understand what was taking place at home. Emotionally it was very debilitating which was stifling me; there was so much of a disconnect and it was so enervating that after a few years I up and moved from New Jersey to California even though I had to leave dear friends behind. I needed to become my own man again. I just had to get away and begin a new life.

I had to laugh at all the *professional* peaceniks. Their peace signs, aka the footprint of the great American chicken, only cheapened the word peace. Many of the flower power kids totally misrepresented the true concept of love. The people who are the most sincere about peace and want it more than anything else are those of us who fought in a war. Although some protestors may have been well-meaning, the majority were just on the bandwagons repeating mindless slogans. I understood better those who had gone before me in service to our country. Those who have experienced it can only appreciate this whole thing. To this day I find it sad that people don't love our country as much as I do.

Then in 1973-74, there was the oil embargo due to the Arab-Israeli war, which of course I had nothing to do with but got hammered by it nevertheless. I couldn't believe that American oil companies were ripping off fellow Americans. I was laid off from the airlines for two years because of this. "Welcome home G.I. you're furloughed!" The first year I was laid off, I earned a whopping $3,700 working in a machine shop putting widgets together. On weekends I would caddie at golf clubs I used to play at. Many nights, pork and beans in a can was the dinner of necessity. It was really hard to convince a date that hot dogs were "tube steaks!" When I returned to American I still had to "ride" as a Flight Engineer for nine years before checking out as copilot and then after reaching a high seniority had to retire two years early in order to receive my pension.

Years later, my wife mentioned that I talked about Vietnam more than Pop did about WWII. I told her that when Pop came back, they had parades. For us there was nothing but scorn. No one even wanted to listen. It was like hitting a home run in Yankee stadium with 80,000 people there, you didn't have to tell anyone– they saw it. But when we hit one, there was no one there. How is anyone to know if you don't tell them? When we came back we practically had to sneak into the country. Many people blamed the warrior and not the politicians for the war. Young soldiers were called warmongers and baby killers. If they wore their uniforms in public they were spit on. It was deplorable the way returning soldiers were degraded. Some poor enlisted guy from the inner city who didn't want to be in the service in the first place let alone fight in Vietnam was drafted at 18. Some were in combat when only six months earlier they were in High School! A kid who had just spent a year slogging through the jungle battered by rain, fighting the enemy, bugs, and disease, and seeing his buddies killed or wounded really got pounded mentally.

It appeared like only a bunch of my friends and I fought the war and were captured, killed, or suffered torment. Not everyone was involved in this. There was no shared sacrifice. Someone asked me how long I was in the Navy for? When I told him five years he said, "That's a lot of time out of your life." I told him I wasn't dead you know! It really hit me when I went to the shore the first summer I was back. I ran into some guys I had known from other high schools and colleges who were lounging on the beach with their wives and girlfriends after sitting out the whole war as if nothing had ever gone on. They had finagled their way out of the draft by conniving to get a deferment by working as a

"Ronny Dean" Lankford, Ken "Knapper" Knapp in center with "The Fish."

teacher or for just being married (referred to as marrying out) or stubbing a toe. It was as if their life was worth more than mine. When I told them I had been in Vietnam, all they said was "Oh." Talking to them, I realized that they didn't have a clue as to what went on and really didn't seem to care. To them, the Vietnam War was a spectator sport on TV while living comfortably at home, enjoying life and moving along professionally. For someone who had gone to war it was hard to abide those who had stayed behind. At least I knew of the camaraderie that only brothers-in-arms would know. We were more like brothers than friends. When we signed on the dotted line to serve our country we said we were willing to die for our country. We took an Oath and were faithful to it. We did our duty.

CHAPTER SIXTY-TWO

MEN, PLUS

In addition to those who had lost their lives, the other real heroes were the POWs. We had a party for former POW George Coker, our schoolmate from St. Benedicts, after his release from over six and a half years as a prisoner. The party was late in starting because another classmate, who was mayor of a North Jersey town, was being indicted. He went on to have the record for the most indictments, the least convictions, and the most time in public office.

George told us that things we take for granted (i.e. filling out a check, figuring what shaving cream to use, etc.) take a lot of effort on his part. The anti-war groups really hurt them because the other side was waiting for us to weaken and give up. The captors only told him of the bad news. George almost lost his leg along with his life until they finally put him in a hospital for 45 minutes, and then it took six months to heal instead of ten days. One time he almost went over the wall with Captain Denton, but later found out that on the other side of the wall was where the guards lived. A few years into their imprisonment George and his cellmate George McNight, figuring they were going to be kept forever, actually escaped with the idea of going down the Red River, stealing a fishing boat, and rowing out into the Gulf of Tonkin to a Navy ship. They got half way down the river and were hiding in the mud when they were literally stepped on by a fisherman who called the local militia. Because of that, he was placed in solitary confinement for three years after being tortured for two months straight. George was forced to hold up a wall with his arms outstretched above his head from 0530 to 2200 everyday. If he dropped his arms, he was severely beaten. He said the only way he made it through was to say, *"I've got to make another 60 seconds."* So he'd count to 60, and then when he wanted to give up, he would remember coaches Sam Cavalarro or Johnny Allen pushing him all over the football field saying, "Get up, you bum." So he'd go on, and when he couldn't take it anymore, he'd see the gray-painted letters on the black wall at St. Benedict's. *Benedict's hates a quitter.* And he'd count to 60 or 30 again. About four to five in the afternoon was the worse time for him. There were other tortures. They would tie him up in a ball or cross his biceps behind his back and pull his legs up over his head as well and hang him from a hook in the ceiling dislocating his shoulders. They would beat him with straps–or make him sit on a stool for two weeks; when he fell off he was viciously beaten. After that the gooks kept him hanging by his thumbs up in a camp by the Chinese border. It was plain and simple, gruesome brutality.

He said whatever he believed in, his convictions were stronger, and he couldn't explain it (religion) but it worked. He said that if they had returned in 1969, they would have been a bunch of lunatics and that he spent the last three years in prison rehabilitating himself. He would repeat another Benedict's motto, *"a winner never quits and a quitter never wins,"* a thousand times over to himself. George said the gooks were like kids who were told not to do something ("don't take over South Vietnam") but would do it anyway 'till they got smacked.

George was classified as "the baddest of the baddest" for the ferocity with which he resisted his captors. This eventually led to a backing off of the harsh treatment toward all the POWs. George is a living testimony to the St Benedict's Coach Kasberger-Allen philosophy of sports–give 100% all the time. George is alive because of it.

*

My friend and former POW, Read Mecleary, had broken both legs punching out of his A-4. In spite of that, he was continually tortured. Like so many other POWs his family didn't know for three years that he was alive. He told me that after he was finally "broken" by months of torture, his only thought was, *what country could I go back to?* He felt he had let down America by not staying true to the Military Code of Conduct, which in part stated, "If I am captured, I will continue to resist by all means available and will give no information vital to the enemy." Some 45 years later, he received in the mail a picture of him on the ground when he was captured. A Chinese gunner of the SAM site that had bagged him had taken the photo!

Bob Jones was an Air Force pilot when he was captured. He told me that at one point they put him up against a dike to be executed. He got so scared, his mind did a complete flip-flop and he wasn't scared anymore. Bob said he stepped outside himself and was watching the whole thing. They fired their guns and missed on purpose. This brought to mind the story of another POW, CDR Gordie Nakagawa. As XO of VA-196 off Enterprise, he was shot down and captured right before Christmas of '72. Thirty years earlier, as a seven year old, he had spent Christmas in a Japanese American internment camp in California. In 2002 he checked himself into the jail in Sonoma on Christmas Eve, feeling that he should spend every thirty years in jail at Christmas. The police accommodated him and locked him up. Gordie expressed the feelings of all the POWS when he said: "I feel indebted to all the wonderful people who, through their thoughts, deeds and prayers, have made a return possible and our homecoming so meaningful. I am particularly grateful to our Commander-in-Chief President Richard M. Nixon, who possessed the wisdom for making those difficult decisions last December and who, despite so much criticism, had the courage to stand firmly by his convictions." Of course, the wives and families who waited amplified this dignity. There were even a few local school teachers who had only been dating the guys when they were shot down yet still waited years for them.

POW LT Robert Flynn was a B/N in VA-196. He carried a trumpet and would blow *Charge* over the radio just before entering North Vietnam on their mission. He was shot down after being jumped by eight MiGs, and captured on August 21, 1967 deep in

North Vietnam. On that mission, three of the four A-6s were shot down. He was captured by North Vietnam soldiers but then kidnapped by Chinese troops who brought him to Peking. He was held prisoner for 2032 days; all except two days were in solitary confinement. No one in our nation's history has ever endured a longer period of solitary confinement. At times he was handcuffed for up to 60 days, had to eat like a dog and live in his own excrement. Although continually tortured, he was never broken, saying that he had only God and his loyalty to his country and his shipmates to sustain him.

Red McDaniel, who spent six brutal years as a POW said it best; *"Courage is not the absence of fear; courage is simply the presence of faith."* Their faith remained intact. I was in awe of their strength. If there was anything noble about the war it was the way the POWs endured their time in hell. I think the fact that they always ended their covert communications to each other with the letters "GBU" meaning *God Bless You* exemplified their love for each other as well as the spiritual presence in their struggle. One of the POWs said that the Cuban interrogators were especially brutal and sadistic. When they finally left, he was happier than if the war had ended.

A "hero," said the poet Rupert Hughes, "is a man, plus." These POWs were "men, plus!"

*

Someone gave a backhanded compliment to my friends when she said in a most arrogant way, "You think more of your friends who were in the military than of those who weren't."

"Well, yeah–I know what they went through."

No epilogue, I pray you; for your play needs no excuse.

(Shakespeare)

Unfortunately, there were times I was completely bored and actually had to fight melancholy. I really felt needed in the service and in the war and that there was something actually worth fighting for in Vietnam. I also felt I was able to be my own person-totally responsible for myself. To me this was a great feeling. However life was a bit dull and I still felt exhausted.

An AOCS classmate and renowned psychologist, Doctor Will "Butch" Parsons told me that I was now a member of "The Club of the Should be Dead."

The way Ray Sandelli said, "Welcome home, I'm very proud of you" was one of the warmest, most sincere welcomes I received upon returning home.

Another meaningful welcome was during the summer of 1973. Mr. Tom Gallucci, manager of the Cedar Grove Pool, told me I could come over anytime I wanted to. One day I was eating lunch with his family and he looked at me and said, "This is really great, it's just like old times. It's really good to have you back!" I could hear it in his voice and see it in his eyes that he was most sincere. It came from his heart with deep tenderness. Later on in a

Christmas card Tom and his wife Catherine wrote "Memories of you at the pool will go on forever."

Rescue Diver John Wilson

CHAPTER SIXTY-THREE

BLACK APRIL

I spoke with friends who were flying off the USS Ranger in March and April 1973. They said they were flying around the clock waiting and preparing to go back into North Vietnam because the Communists had broken the peace agreement and then "Watergate" broke which prevented President Nixon from doing anything. The North Vietnamese then used the next two years to rebuild their military. Even though President Nixon had promised President Thieu of South Vietnam that if the Accords were violated, the U.S. would respond with attacks as well as provide aid to South Vietnam, nothing happened. President Ford and Congress abandoned the war and the allies. We didn't live up to our word.

Between the middle of January and April of 1975, the North Vietnamese had virtually walked over all of South Vietnam. As hard as the ARVN fought, they could not survive without the help of American air power. Henry Kissinger had completely betrayed South Vietnam. The Peace Agreement he came up with let the North Vietnamese keep 145,000 troops in South Vietnam, while we had to pull out. In 2010, Christopher Hitchens wrote that Henry Kissinger is "that rare and foul beast, a man whose record shows sympathy for communism and fascism." Now the whole

North Vietnamese Army was in South Vietnam! They broke every bit of the Paris Agreement of April 1973. I just couldn't believe that we sat idly by as they did so.

29 April 1975–The evacuation signal for loyal South Vietnamese went out over the radio. "The temperature in Saigon is 105 degrees and rising." This was followed by the playing of *I'm dreaming of a White Christmas* by Tennessee Ernie Ford. It was supposed to have been the rendition by Bing Crosby, but the Disc Jockey couldn't find it. The very last Americans were evacuated from South Vietnam. Many Vietnamese were on a Communist hit list of "shoot on sight" for having served their country. To this day, the Vietnamese refer to that time as Black April. Congress had legislated the fall of South Vietnam by restricting the President from acting, forcing an abrupt end to freedom in the South. It was a political sellout. Jim Guirard wrote a great article entitled "U.S. didn't lose the war in Vietnam." In it he explained how the final victory of the North came on April 30, 1975–not over U.S. Forces, which had departed more than two years earlier, but over South Vietnam whose military assistance and political support had been decimated by Congress." The Communists had never planned to abide by the peace accords and everyone knew it. It was a phony document, merely one of appeasement. Gen. Giap, the military head of North Vietnam, in his memoirs said, "It was no civil war, we invaded the South and we won! I knew the United States would not do anything because once Watergate broke, the United States was impotent." This was reported in an article in U.S. News &

418

World Report in the summer of 1976. In it, Gen. Giap said that President Nixon was helpless. This was one time the good guys didn't win!

Over 139,000 refugees escaped to ships off shore during Operation Frequent Wind. Another two million tried to escape in boats. Many of these same families were the ones who had fled to Vietnam from China when Mao Zedong and the Communists took over in 1949. Over a million fled again to the south when the Ho Chi Minh and the Communists took over North Vietnam in 1954 only to flee all over again when South Vietnam fell. They believed that the terrible hardships of trying to escape were preferable over living in a world under Communist rule. People had to flee the lands their ancestors had inhabited–land that they held so dear, leaving the past behind. The UN said upwards of 400,000 Boat people perished, killed by pirates, by drowning or starving to death. In South Vietnam over a million were placed in brutal re-education camps–modern day concentration camps where even more died. Others spent upwards of 18 years under hellish conditions in these camps. Atrocities were unending with tens of thousands of executions.

*

One such person was Long Hoang who spent over three years in a prison camp. He escaped and took his family on a very hazardous sea journey to freedom. He and all his children became very successful U.S. citizens. When Brian Dempsey first met Long Hoang, he asked him what his nationality was. When Long told

Brian he was Vietnamese, Brian said that he had been there. Long said, "Oh yes, how?" Brian told him that he flew there in combat with the Navy. Long replied, "All pilots are good men. All I want to say is thank you."

"What!? We sold you out," said Brian.

"Well we knew how hard it was for you to fight with so little backing from home. We also knew how bad the Communist regime in the North was so we appreciated what you did for us. Brian said that meant more to him than anything.

There is a Slavic saying by Saint Stephan, *"Absolute freedom does not exist, only the choice of freedom. We always have a choice."*

South Vietnam had chosen to be free but was unable to maintain it without our help. After all the suffering and blood spilt you think we could have at least sent dollars to help them survive!

I met Sien Wa, an owner of a sandwich shop in San Clemente, Ca, originally from Bien Hoa. All he said was, "Why did you stop bombing?" A young Vietnamese nurse whose beautiful name means "Heaven Sent," told me her father said the exact same thing. In 1975, her father, a judge, stayed behind, never believing that the North Vietnamese could take over the South. He was locked up in a "re-education" camp from 1975 to 1987. Even though he lives in America now, he still screams during the night. Anytime he sees someone in a uniform, be it a soldier or a cop, he bows. Although these people were beaten down, those who made it to the United States rose up and became a very important, productive part of American society.

In keeping with the Communist dictum that God is a farce and must be removed by force, they even imprisoned Cardinal Francis Haxier Nguyen Van Thuan for 13 years, including nine years in solitary confinement. He would still try and pass messages of hope through his prison bars. In 2007, just like Father Capodanno, Cardinal Thuan was declared a Servant of God, the first of four major steps on the path to canonization as a Saint.

CHAPTER SIXTY-FOUR

RETURNED REMAINS

So many offered so much but a sacrifice's worth is not measured by the outcome. At least we tried to keep them free, fighting for someone else's freedom. I continue to believe it was worth it. We stood against evil and hatred. This doesn't mean the loss doesn't hurt–it always will. But the fact that we stood for something good gives me a great sense of pride. I never felt any animosity toward the Vietnamese people, but still do toward the Communist leadership. They were animalistic in their barbaric treatment of our POWs and they broke the peace agreement, pure and simple. Once again another country is in chains. What else could one expect from a Communist government? In 1968, North Vietnamese generals told POW John McCain that they were going to liberate all of Southeast Asia, country after country. They wanted to overthrow free, capitalist countries.

Between 1975 and 1979, the Communist regime of Pol Pot in Cambodia murdered over two million people through starvation, disease, overwork, and execution. It was written that the goal of the Khmer Rouge was to weaken family bonds, preserving only individuals' relationship to the state. I couldn't believe that the world turned a blind eye to this misery and suffering. Where were all the peaceniks now? There was no outrage from former activist and war protestors who just kept silent.

*

In January 1977, a mere three days after assuming office, President Carter granted amnesty to all the draft dodgers who left the country and beat the draft! Where was the justice? What were the priorities? He didn't say he would help the families of those still missing in action. He didn't visit a VA hospital - he granted amnesty instead. He declared all those missing as "killed in action," basically stopping all paychecks to the families. He was going to have a difficult time getting anyone to participate in the next war. One might as well sit it out in Canada and return with all his limbs. I wasn't looking for anything extra, but they knew what they were doing when they left! He insulted those of us who did what we were asked to do. We had not been allowed to win the war in Vietnam but while we were there we kept from losing it.

As I had done every day for six years, I put the silver metal bracelet on my right wrist. The bracelets were a way of remembering those who were still listed as MIA. Although it had his name and date of when he was lost on a mission over North Vietnam, I didn't need anything extra for me to remember Larry Kilpatrick. This time, as I carefully closed it in on my wrist, the bracelet broke in two. *Oh man, Larry, I'm sorry.* It was Jan 3, 1979. That very day the government declared him Killed in Action. Larry gave so much and asked so little. He was a man with a firm heart and he will always be deep within me. Now he was relegated to "Killed in Action BNR" (Body not recovered). Merely three letters to define a life.

*

13 November 1982–after much controversy over the design of the Vietnam Memorial, a dedication ceremony was held in Washington D.C. Bit by bit the Vietnam vets were coming out of the woodwork and letting their proud feelings be known. People were starting to realize we weren't misfits. We won the war, but politicians lost it. President Reagan had definitely helped us and was proud of us. The President mentioned that the war was a failure not of our making and that he saw us as men of dedication and proven courage. I have so many friends whose names are on the Memorial–dear, brave wonderful men. I thank God for my having survived, yet in the same thought I wonder why I was spared. I know I have the privilege of being alive. Then over the years it became an "in thing" to be a Vietnam Vet. In fact, some people running for public office trying to get the vote said they were Vietnam Vets, when in fact they weren't.

3 June 1983–The Vietnamese communists returned the remains of Don Lindland. A CIA agent told Roger that he wouldn't have wanted to go through what Don did. It turned out that his body had been boiled. The remains of Bob Graustein and Bart Wade were returned on 4 December 1985. Where were their remains kept all those years, and how long were the men alive after capture? These are questions that will never be answered. In the 1980s, former POW Red McDaniel kept up a campaign to obtain a

424

full accounting of the servicemen left behind. He was shunned by our government even though there were reports of sightings. He was told by some members of the Special Forces that they had trained to go back into Vietnam to rescue POWs. They knew who the guys were and where they were at–only to be cancelled twice. I learned that a certain businessman had outfitted a DC-10 with 200 litters with the idea of flying to Hong Kong under the auspices of "route checking." After resupplying in Hong Kong they were to take off and make a right turn instead of a left turn and fly into Laos to pick up former POWs. At the last minute it fell through.

*

In 1988, we were part of a ceremony honoring the POWs in the Rose Garden with President Reagan. Afterwards there was a formal dinner attended mostly by Air Force guys. Diminutive Rat stood up on our table and challenged "all the Air Force Weenies" to a fight! We grabbed him real fast.

In 1991, during Operation Desert Storm, VA-75 was in the midst of the air war flying the same planes we had flown in Vietnam. The young pilots complained that the planes were limited to 3G's. That was because of the harsh workout we had given them by overstressing them while pulling off target or evading missiles.

In 1993, three front teeth were returned and said to have belonged to Harley Hall. His dentist from the ship ascertained that they had been knocked out and that they had been "alive" for at least seven years after his shoot down. He had examined Harley a few days before he was lost. It was common knowledge that the Russians had interrogated him.

I made a bucket list of things to do when I got back from overseas. There was a visit to Vermont, the Christmas show at Radio City in New York, and a West Point football game. I did travel to Woodstock, Vermont, and as it turned out my niece, Helen Conklin, became a Rockette at Radio City so I was able to see my share of Christmas shows in a most personal way. Dear friend and West Point graduate Jim McCall invited us to the Point for his 25th class reunion and game. Prior to the game we were in Washington Hall, the huge cadet dining room having lunch. I of course was the token Navy guy. I got to talking to one of his classmates and asked him when he was in Vietnam, etc. We compared notes and all he said was "you flew close air support for me! I owe you a beer." All through the game cups of beer were handed down to me, which I passed along to those around me. Of course I cheered for Army!

CHAPTER SIXTY-FIVE

UNDER THE SPAN OF HEAVEN

28 May 1996, Colorado Springs–Air Force Academy. Tad Clark, a tall, young, good-looking man with an easy smile and an air of confidence walked with his mother to the front of the chapel. His mother, Tonya Clark, beamed with delight as she pinned on his Second Lieutenant bars.

Tonya told the Air Force News print service that she was not surprised when at an early age her son Tad began expressing the desire to fly. From the days when his dreams were nothing more than crayon sketches of planes to the moment he entered pilot training, flying was his ultimate goal. "Tad always wanted to be a fighter pilot, as soon as he understood what being a pilot was. I have always supported him in this. I couldn't think of too many other things in life that a mother could be prouder of than having her son willing to put his life on the line for others and for the cause of freedom, no matter where it is in the world," she added. Tonya understands that sacrifice.

That sentiment has been instilled in Tad throughout his life, and though there was sadness growing up without a father, he feels grateful for all that his father's spirit has given him. "In some ways I have missed out" he once said. But I am blessed to have had a father who has affected my life in such a meaningful way. He stood up and did something honorable with his life. Many kids grow up with fathers who are there every day, but don't have that kind of impact." Tad looked forward to passing the same patriotic values his parents gave him on to his children. "I think this has all given me a unique perspective on having a family," he said. "It's important to make every second count and wake up every day thanking God for what you do have." Tad said, "I have always been very touched and impressed with Pop's commitment because

he made the ultimate sacrifice during an unpopular war." Afterwards, a small party was held at the home of the Major who was Tad's mentor while at the Academy. Tonya gave Tad a kiss as he opened her gift. It was an alabaster Falcon on a metal base, the academy symbol and mascot. Inscribed are these words:

With Jack Keegan and Major Tad Clark

"No mother under the span of heaven could be

more proud of you. I love you and your father loves you."

*

28 February 1997–After 54 years in existence, VA-75 was disestablished to the call of "haul down the squadron colors." Although there was a new A-6F on the drawing boards A-6s were mothballed after 34 years due to budget constraints and politics. It would have continued to be a great plane since no other aircraft could carry such a big bomb load and fly a great range. Once again artist Hank Caruso honored us with another caricature, "First In, Last Out," commemorating the disestablishment of VA-75 following 54 years of outstanding service to the fleet. The Sunday Punchers were the first and then the last squadron to fly the venerable A-6 Intruder in Operational service. The Sunday Punchers was the first A-6 Squadron to fly in combat and survived to be the last A-6 squadron. Sadly, just like that, the Squadron was no

Rog and me with Mike Schuster and the picture of us that Roger always kept in his wallet

more. Rat bet everyone that he would be the last man standing at the O'Club that night. He was found the next morning hanging in the cloakroom on a coat hanger. He won all bets.

CHAPTER SIXTY–SIX

A SOUL THAT WAS NEVER BROKEN

14 June 1997–Together with her mother Jane, I had the wonderful honor of giving away Larry Kilpatrick's daughter Wendi at her wedding. At the rehearsal dinner I gave a little speech where I wished for Wendi and Keith the same courage that her father had and told them that although he knew he wasn't going to make it back, he went anyway. He was for me, in Cellini's words, the definition of happiness–*a soul that was never broken*. He stood firm. Wendi and Keith have lived up to the challenge in raising their first daughter who was born with special needs.

Wendi Kilpatrick's wedding

I also told Keith, "You're going to take good care of my Wendi, aren't you?" "Yes, otherwise I'm going to die, huh?" "Yup. I'd have all of Air Wing Three roll in on you!" Wendi so graciously honored me in the program with these remarks: "A special thanks to Alan Fischer. A loving friend who has always been there to guide me and holding true to being an honorable friend of my father who is with us in spirit on this special day."

*

From time to time, I would have terrible nightmares of trying to get away from gunfire. But all the other dreams about the war were of Larry Kilpatrick and the fact that he was still alive. In my first dream, there was a mirror with the center missing, forming a jagged edged frame around Larry's face. "Larry, if I could just pull you through…"

It was another five years before I saw him again in a dream. I said, "Larry, I told everyone you were still alive!"

A full ten years passed before another "visit" in a dream. I was in Hawaii on vacation. He didn't have his moustache anymore. "Larry, it's good to see you–you actually look younger without the "stache." Then as fast as he came, he was gone and I woke up.

Another dream was that he had been sent through Czechoslovakia to a camp in Russia. Then on 27 Dec 1997, I dreamt of a large room of POWs.

"Where's Larry Kilpatrick?"

"He's over there," someone said.

"Larry, how are you?'

"How's my family?"

"They're fine–Jane hasn't dated much and I gave Wendi away this summer."

432

"Thanks, Alan I really love you."

A few years later, on Christmas morning, I had the last of those dreams. "So, Larry, where in Russia are you?"

"Kiev."

Odd that it should take place on Christmas. Even stranger that it should happen at all. The war was so long ago. Indians believe that ancestors communicate through dreams. I know Larry was trying to tell me something and feel that he is still alive somewhere and was probably told that his family would be harmed if he tried to return to America. He was just one of the many our government left behind. I tried and tried to get an accounting of him from a government agency–the DPMO (Defense POW-Missing Personnel Office) but to no avail. At one point a young fellow told me "I think they are blowing smoke, telling you they don't know anything about him!"

"Everything in war is simple, but the simplest thing is difficult"
(Carl von Clausewitz)

CHAPTER SIXTY-SEVEN

SHORT ONE FEET WET

25 February 1998–Tonya pinned Silver Pilot wings on Air Force 2nd LT Tad Clark at Sheppard AFB Texas. Although he finished at the top of his class, he was held back as an instructor. He had wanted to fly F-15s.

Tad flies with a piece of paper with Psalm 91, part of which reads:

> *Whoever dwells in the shelter of the Most High*
> *will rest in the shadow of the Almighty.*
> *I will say of the Lord, "He is my refuge and my fortress,*
> *My God, in whom I trust."*

Tad went on to fly with the Thunderbirds and later command a Base while flying very successful combat missions in Afghanistan in the F-16.

On the cold and snowy morning of January 9, 2004, the remains of LT Robert Alan "Arlo" Clark were laid to rest at Arlington National Cemetery with full military honors. This was exactly 31 years to the day he and Mike McCormick were shot down. During a reunion dinner the night before, many of his former shipmates had shared their memories of "Arlo" in an attempt to honor his memory, as well as to help Tad fill in the picture of who his dad had been as a friend, a squadronmate and a warrior.

Tad read a poem he had written in honor of his dad, whom he had never met.

"Short One Feet Wet...
Which included:
In the dark of the night,
After calling "Feet Dry"
They were declared "MIA"
We may never know why.

He did what he loved,
When he strapped on that jet,
He was committed to the end,
As he was short one "Feet Wet."

Tad is a worthy son of a grateful father and mother.

Former squadron mate and roommate Bob "Woody" Wood wrote that Arlo's remains spent over three decades away from American soil, but now they were finally home. We finally said the goodbyes that we never got to say 31 years earlier. It is said that those who are remembered live on forever. Al Clark's memory is still very much alive.

Afterwards, we had a get together at the O'Club at Fort Myers to celebrate Alan. I ran into Joe Kernan who had been shot down and captured in the Fall of 1972. I said, "So, Joe, what are you doing now?"

"I'm Governor of Indiana."

"No, really Joe, what are you doing?"

"I'm Governor of Indiana."

"Come on, Joe–it's the Fish–tell me!" Out of the corner of the room from behind a fake palm tree came an Indiana State trooper wearing a Smokey the Bear hat.

"He is, sir, and I'm his bodyguard."

It was like asking a Priest, "So what are you doing now?"

"I'm Pope."

"No really, Father, what are you doing?"

Seemed Joe was the Lieutenant Governor and the Governor died.

"I've got this big mansion; you ought to visit."

"You went from being a convict (POW) to Governor? What a great country!"

CHAPTER SIXTY–EIGHT

A FINAL FLYBY

In 2005, after five years in the making, Professor Carol Reardon, of Penn State, finished her book, *Launch the Intruders,* which chronicled our service in Vietnam. Cartoonist Hank Caruso honored us with a caricature entitled, "Feet Dry, Palms Wet" for the book signing ceremony. There was even talk of a movie. Everyone was picking out whom they wanted to play their part. I picked actor Danny DeVito, a little guy from Jersey. All my boys said, "Dad, you can't do that."

During this time, I was doing volunteer work helping to restore the A-6 Ready Room of VA-115 on the USS Midway, which was being transformed into a museum in San Diego. Ray

More laughter with Rog, Doug "DWA" Ahrens, and Bob "Chis" Chisholm

Donnelly, Alan Clark and Mike McCormick died flying out of that Ready Room. I was sitting on the floor working on some chairs while a few guys were behind me talking in a muffled voice. I turned and mentioned I needed a different size wrench–but there was no one there! This actually happened twice.

In 2004, B/N Roger Lerseth died at a young age, as did many other POWs from the injuries and the vicious torture they endured. I spoke to him a few days before he passed on. We talked

Laughter with Jay Swigart and Rog

about how much we loved and respected each other. The last thing he said was "Fish I'm a dead man walking." A kindlier man I have never met. He lived with joy in his heart. His wife told me that Roger always kept a picture of the two of us in his wallet. That touched my soul. I'll always miss him. What a man!

We buried Roger with full Military honors at Arlington National Cemetery. The day after I returned home from Roger's funeral, I was reading a newspaper spread out on the kitchen counter by an open window and thinking of Roger. It was a beautiful, clear, calm day and the flowers on the hillside in the back were all in bloom. All of a sudden there was a great torrent of air that seemed to drop straight down out of the sky from the heavens like a waterfall onto the right side of the hill. This strong driving wind that came out of nowhere raced through the backyard from right to left on the hill in one big swirling dimension, blowing the trees and flowers. The whirlwind swung around and down coming in through the open window rustling the newspaper and engulfing me as well. I had the sensation that I was not alone. This amazing tempest of wind that rushed through the backyard was teeming with familiarity. It had the sound of eternity–a moan of truth. There was an all-engulfing reality–Roger's spirit, Roger's farewell. Although I couldn't see the wind it embodied Roger. As fast as it came, it disappeared. The Mayans said that the appearance of a land breeze that showed no visible weather carried spirits instead, and that ancestors spoke to them in the wind. That was confirmed with Roger doing a "flyby" to say goodbye to me. So odd yet wonderful that something as invisible as air could fill my soul and speak to my heart.

When all the laughter died in tears

439

CHAPTER SIXTY–NINE

STEADFAST FIDELITY

The Saratoga was put in the mothball fleet at the Navy Shipyard in Philadelphia. As it so happened, it was right beneath the final approach into Philadelphia International Airport and as an airline pilot I would fly right over it while landing in Philly. Paul Wagner strongly encouraged that I do a 'touch and go' on it before landing at the airport. He said, "The guys would love it and your wife will understand." It was eventually sold to a salvage company for one cent. Doug Ahrens was in the bidding until the price went too high. When I retired from American my wonderful wife wrote the following poem:

> *An Aviator you were born to be*
> *The heavens called you, wings set free.*
>
> *The finest Naval Aviator around*
> *Your proudest time on earth was found.*
>
>
> *Following in your Dad's footsteps*
> *To American Airlines you proudly went.*
> *For 32 years you flew the skies*
> *Contentment and happiness at your side.*

But to us, your family, your most valuable gift
Is Dad and Husband, we love you for this!

Happy Retirement!!!

Love, Nance, Tim, Kevin, Mary and Brian

April 2010 marked the Thirty-Fifth anniversary of the fall of Saigon. There was a remembrance on the USS Midway–now a fantastic museum in San Diego. Many Vietnamese from all over the U.S. converged on the ship for what they'll always refer to as "Black April." I was wearing my flight jacket and one by one they came up and thanked me. But I thought, *we sold them out.* I asked one young man why he was thankful. He held out his arms wide and said, "I'm free!" This gave me some closure, but I'll always feel bad about how our government let the communists take over. Actually a good result of the war was that we helped the Berlin Wall fall because we basically bankrupted the Russians. We, the military, won the first Vietnam War while we were there, but the politicians forfeited the second. North Vietnam's military commander, General Vo Nguyen in his memoirs in the Vietnam War Memorial in Hanoi stated: *"What we still don't understand is why you Americans stopped the bombing of Hanoi (in Dec '72). If you had pressed us a little harder, just for another day or two, we were ready to surrender! It was the same at the battle of TET in '68. You defeated us! We knew it, and thought you knew it. But we were elated that the media was helping us. They were causing more disruption in America than we could on the battlefields. We were ready to surrender. You had won!"*

Victoria Vu a young Vietnamese nurse in our local hospital told me her father said, "We should have kept bombing the North to really finish them off."

We had joined other Americans before us who had fought for another's freedom. Although the final outcome hurts, we can take pride in the fact that at least we tried. We did our best to keep another country from being suppressed by Communist tyranny.

"It is a worthy thing to fight for one's freedom.
It is another sight finer to fight for another man's."
Mark Twain

In March of 2018, I was able to get in contact with someone from the Defense POW/MIA Accounting Agency (DPAA), which conducted field activities in search of those missing in action in Vietnam. I asked him the status of Larry Kilpatrick and was told they had been to the crash site five times over the years and had found no remains. I didn't get an answer when I asked if they had found the ejection seat. Then–Memorial Day 2018 was like all the others–a time for reflection and thought. Larry's daughter Wendi was watching the local news in Georgia. They were doing a spot on the Marietta National Cemetery. The cameraman panned the entire cemetery and for some unexplained reason stopped and focused for the longest time on Larry's memorial gravestone while the announcer was explaining

Memorial Day. Wendi's uncle called it a "God Moment." Larry's wife Jane told me that the whole weekend she felt very sad and was crying for no reason. The very next day they were notified that they had found Larry's remains. Wendi had never given DNA and Larry had left his dog tags in his room on that particular mission. So how would they know it was his remains unless he had been held all along? The official report was misleading and more of a guess than actual facts. It seemed they started with the findings they wanted and worked backwards to substantiate it. It was not convincing at all especially when it stated; "The laboratory analysis and the totality of the circumstantial evidence available establish the remains are those of LCDR Larry Ronald Kilpatrick." Also "the dental remains of one tooth are possibly that of LCDR Larry Kilpatrick." "Circumstantial evidence" and "possibly" just doesn't hack it for his family or me. Something real fishy here. Either "accidently on purpose" they got it wrong, or they were trying to cover it up that Larry was in fact captured and was, or is, still alive!

To add to the mystery, there was a website "U.S. Accounted-For from the Vietnam War, Returnees and Remains recovered." In the column "Country of Return" most had Vietnam or Laos but Larry's was left blank leading me to believe that perhaps it should read Russia. Also it stated BR for Body Returned instead of RR (Remains Returned) that in the official report tells of only one tooth. The really baffling thing is the Returned Date of 12/12/2015! No one was ever notified of this. It doesn't end.

Bittersweet for all of us–I had always held out hope that somehow, somewhere he would show up alive. Personally I felt that I had let Larry down by not following through on my initial investigations years earlier. AOCS classmate Tim Truett said, "It has weighed heavy on my heart for 46 years while classmate and dear friend Navy Captain Jack Anderson said it best; "One of the lost is found… May his soul, his character and his sacrifice be strong in our hearts. Bless his memory."

Sweet memories abound
Of valor and friendship
Sad memories, tender memories
Of our fallen brothers
Grand memories of heroic virtue
Sublime by grief.

(Extracted from a speech by Massachusetts Gov. John Andrew Dec 22, 1865)

Having served my country, especially in time of war, is the thing I am most proud of. It was a privilege and an honor to do so. It was tough and I wouldn't want to do it again, but I am glad I did it. I took an Oath and stood up to it. There is nothing glamorous about war but there should be tribute paid to those who devoted so much. The real story has to be preserved. I felt blessed to have been born in America and thankful that I love this country so much –so very much. My father used to say, "with all its faults it's still the best country on earth."

Paul "Boot" Wagner said that whole era of '72 was spent with a great bunch of guys. *"I think back and ask, 'did I really go through that stuff?'"* He recalled us landing with sunlight reflecting off the flight deck, making it look like it could be off asphalt of a New York city street–we couldn't even see the water!" It is all an engaging memory he keeps in a neatly wrapped mental package.

Looking back, it amazed me that the very first real job I had was with an actual group of heroes. Great guys that I was blessed to serve with. This whole thing was a real eye and heart opener. So many magnificent virtues were not just sentiments or abstractions but were made visible and put into practical action thanks to these men. I remember them all with cordial reverence. Cordial is "of the heart" and reverence is "deep respect mingled with love and awe."

I would also add the indelible fact:

STEADFAST FIDELITY THAT ENDURES TO THIS DAY

EPILOGUE

In 1982, our dear friend who also had become an accomplished wildlife artist, Gayla Wiedenheft, wrote the following poem in response to a letter I had written her about my experiences. It truly embodies the heart and soul of what took place and I thank her.

Combat Pilot

The story is now over, the chapter's closed and yet . . .
written in my memory is a place I can't forget.
Where all my boyhood dreams met the light of day
And long forgotten values refused to fade away.

This place of men and heroes, the finest I would meet
Whose actions spoke of virtue and whose courage stood concrete.
Where love took on new meaning, where friendship did too,
while the serious side of life shouted 'attention' at you.

A time for nerves of steel, when shaking to the core,
knowing all my limits–I learned to push for more,
'cause beneath my trembling hand that mighty bird could shine,
but it was living, not power that was always on my mind.

Every call a close one, any time of day-
And every flight out was another time to pray.
Another mission over and I'd be worn to the bone
adding hope to weary hope that I might make it home.

I never dreamed back then standing face to face with fears
Someday they'd be behind me; all those worn-torn years.
And the medals still remind me every birthday is a friend
'cause I lived to read that story,
from its beginning to its end.

Made in the USA
Middletown, DE
20 August 2019